Greg Tate

Flyboy
in the
Buttermilk

ESSAYS ON CONTEMPORARY
AMERICA

Simon & Schuster

New York   London   Toronto

Sydney   Tokyo   Singapore

FIRESIDE
Simon & Schuster Building
Rockefeller Center
1230 Avenue of the Americas
New York, New York 10020

FIRESIDE and colophon are registered trademarks
of Simon & Schuster Inc.

Designed by Chris Welch
Manufactured in the United States of America

10 9 8 7 6 5 4 3 2

Library of Congress Cataloging in Publication Data
Tate, Greg.
    Flyboy in the buttermilk / Greg Tate.
        p.   cm.
      1. Afro-Americans—Music—History and crit-
icism.   2. Popular music—United States—
History and criticism.   I. Title.   II. Title:
Flyboy in the buttermilk.
NL3479.T35   1992
781.64′089′96073—dc20   91-41561
                                               CIP
                                               MN

ISBN: 0-671-72965-9

Grateful acknowledgment is made for permission to
reprint copyrighted material. Every reasonable effort
has been made to trace the ownership of all copyrighted material included in this volume. Any errors
that may have occurred are inadvertent and will be
corrected in subsequent editions, provided notifi-
cation is sent to the publisher.

"Beat Bop," Copyright © 1983 by Protoons, Inc.
    All rights reserved. Used by permission.
"Armed, Sophisticated, and Violent, Two Drug
    Gangs Blanket Nation" Copyright © 1988 by The
    New York Times Company. All rights reserved.
    Reprinted by permission.

(Continued on page 286)

TO THULANI DAVIS AND ROBERT CHRISTGAU FOR
GITTIN' THIS PARTY STARTED RIGHT; STANLEY
CROUCH, WHO CLUED ME THAT MY REAL SUB-
JECT WAS MYTH; GREIL MARCUS, WHO QUES-
TIONED MY HUNGER FOR HEROES; LISA JONES,
FOR MAKING ME REALIZE HAIR IS EVERYTHING.

Acknowledgments

All praises to JAH, Grandmothers Queen and Callie, Mom & Dad, Brian & Geri, Konda Mason, Faith Childs, Malaika Adero, Linda Bryant, Joan Thornell, E. Ethelbert Miller, Sharon Farmer, Suzanne Miles, Bill Quinn, Vernard Grey, A. J. Fielder, Flip Barnes, Vernon Reid, Ronnie Drayton, Living Colour, Eye & I, Women in Love, Faith, PBR Streetgang, JJ Jumpers, Michael Veal's Afro-Physics Research Ensemble, Jamiylah Samuel, Julie Dash, Mark Montgomery, Bob Wisdom, Danny Dawson, Renee Raymond, Scott Poulson-Bryant, M-Base Collective, Black Rock Coalition, Black Filmmaker Foundation, 40 Acres and a Mule Filmworks, Geechee Girls Productions, Hudlin Bros., JAM Inc., M. Mark, Kit Rachlis, Scott Malcolmson, Geri Allen, Craig Street, Barry Michael Cooper, Harry Allen, Jennifer Jazz, Danny Hamilton, Co Valli, Nelson George, Trey Ellis, Ben Mapp, Lisa Kennedy, Hilton Als, Lorna Simpson, bell hooks, Michelle Wallace, Laura Mulvey, Skip Gates, Cornel West, William Gibson, Ramm-El-Zee, AND to all the Black British posse blase blase, Lina Ghopal, Isaac Julien, John Akomfrah, Kobena Mercer, Paul Gilroy, Maureen Blackwood.

The author humbly acknowledges the selfless dedication of Katrina Karkazis, for permissions research at the risk of life, liberty, and the pursuit of happiness.

Contents

Foreword by Henry Louis Gates, Jr.   13

Section One

Knee Deep in Blood Ulmer   17

Hardcore of Darkness: Bad Brains   20

Cecil Taylor's Monster Movie   24

The Atomic Dog: George Clinton Interview by Greg Tate and
Bob Wisdom   29

Beyond the Zone of the Zero Funkativity   41

Baby Miles and Baby Wayne: Wynton Marsalis   45

Stagolee Versus the Proper Negro: The Treacherous Three
Cross Over—Prince, Wynton Marsalis, and Eddie Murphy   48

Are You Ready for Juju?: King Sunny Adé   56

The Electric Miles   68

Silence, Exile, and Cunning: Miles Davis in Memoriam   85

Call Me Abraxas: Santana   90

Beat the Message Too: Ramm-El-Zee vs. K-Rob   93

Contents

I'm White!: What's Wrong with Michael Jackson   95

The GOP Throws a Mammy-Jammy: Black Stars Bowl Over Bush
at Blues Summit   99

Clitoral Madness: A R Kane   108

'Tain't Nobody's Business: Adeva   112

Change of the Century: Ornette Coleman   113

Invisible Man Overboard: Marc Anthony Thompson   118

Homeys on the Range: Public Enemy   120

The Devil Made 'Em Do It: Public Enemy   123

Diary of a Bug   128

Posses in Effect: Ice-T   132

Yabba Dabba Doo-Wop: De La Soul   137

Section Two

Yo! Hermeneutics!: Henry Louis Gates,
Houston Baker, and David Toop   145

Ghetto in the Sky: Samuel Delany's Black Whole   159

Growing Up in Public: Amiri Baraka Changes His Mind   168

Guerrilla Scholar on the Loose: Robert Farris Thompson
Gets Down   178

Harlem When It Sizzled   184

Cult-Nats Meet Freaky-Deke   198

Signs and Cymbals: Nathaniel Mackey's Postmod Pop   210

You Look Fabulist: Steve Erickson's Wild Kingdom   214

White Magic: Don DeLillo's Intelligence Networks   220

Dread or Alive: William Gibson   228

Nobody Loves a Genius Child: Jean Michel Basquiat, Flyboy in
the Buttermilk   231

Fear of a Mutt Palette: Art and Ancestry in the Colored
Museum   244

Contents

Cinematic Sisterhood   252

Section Three

Leadership Follies   265
New York 8 + , Feds 0   268
Now We Come by Thousands   278
Love and the Enemy   281

Foreword

The first task of the cultural critic is to create a voice: and through the voice, a persona. It hardly matters who's behind it. Greg Tate could be a balding, middle-aged white guy with a potbelly and an unlit briar clenched between yellowed teeth, occasionally spilling crumbs of a cherry-flavored Cavendish mixture into his Underwood manual. He isn't, but he could be for all it mattered.

That's because Greg Tate has a voice—more than one, actually. Like writers as varied as Hunter S. Thompson, T. R. Witomski, Tom Robbins, or Richard Fariña, Tate has a deceptively loose-limbed style. It's an illusion, of course: Tate manipulates the tonalities of an urban vernacular, true enough, but his writing is also informed by (for example) contemporary cultural theory. And the result of Tate's experiments in recombinant syntax—a sort of teen-age mutant b-boy cadence—is something all his own.

Part of what's so valuable about Tate's role as a cultural critic is the way he negotiates the contradictions that underlie black American culture. The traditional failing in black criticism has been to accept a dichotomy between a bland universalism and a parochial black nationalism, and then to side with one or the other. What Tate understands is that culture, Afro-American culture in particular, is never a matter of either-or. He can both celebrate the energizing pull of cultural nationalism *and* register its limitations, moral and intellectual.

Tate thus reflects the maturity of what he and the novelist Trey Ellis have taken to calling a New Black Aesthetic, a body of creativity unfettered by the constraints of a nationalist party line. "There is now such a strong and vast body of great black work," Ellis notes, "that the corny or mediocre doesn't need to be coddled." Black critics have passed beyond the time when their only critical implements were the pom-pom and twirled baton.

And critical honesty is also part of what makes Tate required reading. While he's a leading intellectual exponent of the hiphop generation, Tate (unlike some white liberal critics) isn't afraid to call the rap group Public Enemy on "the whack retarded philosophy they espouse." He demands better from them: insists they ought to know that "dehumanizing gays, women, and Jews isn't going to set black people free." Tate feels but resists the temptation to romanticize black culture. Like Ishmael Reed, he can parody black nationalism because he has a real measure of sympathy for it. At the same time, he's learned too much from feminism to let black misogyny go unremarked, and he has too much respect for black culture to want to apologize for it. But what makes his critiques so effective is the fact that they're often aimed at himself as much as anyone else.

Tate's analytic prowess serves him well in threshing out the wheat from the chaff in critical theory. (I admit this even though I take well-earned knocks myself.) He also has an unerring eye for what's vital in contemporary literature, having served up some of the most intriguing and complex views on Samuel R. Delany, Amiri Baraka, William Gibson, and Don DeLillo I've encountered. Take on board, too, Tate's sensitive treatment of Isaac Julien's cinema of desire, the faux-naïve art of Jean-Michel Basquiat. . . . and, most abundantly, his reflections on the realm of Afro-America's greatest legacy, music. It was Walter Pater who ventured that all art aspires to the condition of music: a condition, that is, of pure aesthesis, unsullied by the function of representation. But for Tate music doesn't exist in a space apart from the other expressive arts; on the contrary, it opens a window on black culture, and it's a privileged view.

I often disagree with Tate, but I seldom fail to learn something. That's why I read him, in the end. The truth is, we have enough cheerleaders and we have plenty of hanging judges, too. Both have their uses. What Tate represents is a much rarer combination of caring and critique. So, gentlefolk, read him, argue with him . . . and, most important of all: keep this nigger boy writing.

Henry Louis Gates, Jr.

14

The Iron Man Cometh

Knee Deep in Blood Ulmer

hen George Clinton uppercased The Funk out of the gutter and into capital gain, he also made it community property, signifying like Muhammad Ali that Black and bad were once again synonymous: say it loud I'm funky and I'm proud. A generation before the Brown Bomber and bebop also proclaimed "up you mighty race." So goes the axis. But since the rise and fall of the Maggot Overlord The Funk has gotten uppity and gone "universal" on the everyday brothers and sisters, contaminating realms long defunked, namely black and white bohemia. Always eclectic, now it's "funk-wave"; always hip, now it's "avant-funk"; always a ho', now funk's crossed over with a brand new pimp (introducing Dick Dames and the Prophylactic Band). Funk used to be a bad word, now everybody's trying to get knee deep. These days there's a lot of funkploitation going down. But don't read me wrong, 'cause pimping The Funk ain't bad per se—truth is, pimping it's always been half the gameplan. Besides giving Funk mass ass appeal and liquid assets, Uncle Jam also gave it a metaphysic, proposing that the bottom of the human soul, its bass elements one might say, are what makes life a song worth singing. So contrary to the funky-come-latelies, it's always been possible to have your funk low in the saddle and eat-it-cum-intellectualize-it too. I mean, conceptualizing the funk as mind, body, and soul music ain't no new type thang—just listen to your "Loose Booty." Or for that matter, *Agharta*, side two, by Miles Dewey Davis. Say what? The art of Jazz meets the art of Funk? Well, Funk's been there before too. Or so we thought. All of which brings us to the much-acclaimed James Blood Ulmer.

Although Blood's Ornette-mentored free jazz-funk gets better press than Miles's, that's only 'cause it conforms to your average aging young jazz critic's '60s-retentive notions of what's "avant-garde." But Miles's funk circa 1970-1976 is inarguably more advanced. And even though Blood's been tagged "the most innovative guitarist since Hendrix," there ain't no such animal, except for maybe Pete Cosey. And besides, who'll accept hype like that from a dude who wrote a book on the blues that doesn't index its *one* mention of Hendrix while Eric Clapton gets four. C'mon now, fella, let's be for real.

Truth is, Blood's funk deserves the attention. But the misinformation preceding it deserves debunking. Which is a shame because Blood's hustle can roll joints without the critical overreach. Sure, Blood is pimping the funk, but like Miles he's pimping it on his own terms.

Three albums of Blood-funk are currently available. *Free Lancing* (Columbia) is the latest, *No Wave* (Moers Music import) is the free-est, and *Are You Glad to Be in America?* (Rough Trade import) is not only the most frenzied but, despite the muddy mixdown, the most Ital. (Blood's 1978 Artists House debut, *Tales of Captain Black*, has bass but not much bottom.) Pre-release hype touted the latest as the greatest—and *Free Lancing* is good—but *Are You Glad* cuts it (though it's a close call). *Are You Glad* also features Blood's only decent mumble-mouthed vocal performance on the record, "Jazz Is the Teacher, Funk Is the Preacher." That cut's also Blood's only tight vocal tune. Otherwise he don't take the singing shtick too seriously. Not because he ain't got no voice (these days, who does?) but because Blood sings like a rambling, clodhopper takeoff on Taj Mahal. Some find this cute but it infects the music: when Blood goes vocal the bottom drops out like a stumblebum and the bridges take it to the hokey-pokey. Blood does write some catchy little tunes though. Like Ornette's they're nerve-wracking, asymmetrical exercises in urbane primitivism: witty, wham-bam ditty-length city-life narratives full of sarcasm, discord, and frivolity. Polyrhythmically these nutty metropolitcan nursery rhymes either stalk or they rumble. The ones that stalk are sardonic modal menaces while the rumblers rollerskate on Amin Ali's hyperkinetic bass and Calvin Weston's omnidirectional upbeat-is-the-downbeat-downbeat-is-the-offbeat drumming, which continually drops bombs in rotary fashion from left and right angles. In tandem on the rumblers, these two give up the syncopated jungle boogie pogostick style, kinda like a harmolodic Bow Wow Wow of the funk, alternating savage tom-tom beats with rapid return-fire ostinato riffs and Blood's goofball changes. Imagine Andrew Hill refiltered through Mississippi Fred McDowell and you've got a handle on how Blood's eccentric guitar fits in with the many ridims.

See, Blood doesn't play sensuous, explosive space-blues lines like Hendrix or architectonic distortions of the antimatter universe like Pete Cosey or warpspeed sheets of exotic scales like McLaughlin. What he does play is shrill, disjointed fragments, nervous bits and rickety pieces tied together by a staggered but wryly swinging thematic sensibility. No flash-in-the-pan runs or simulated heavy-metal orgasms here. Instead, Blood's into slapstick. His idea of a rave-up is smacking spiky chrome-metal crash chords upside the groove. In between he strings oodles of cryptic licks that noodle towards unorthodox and unsettling pattern shifts. Essentially, Blood's lead lines are almost incidental; his rhythm chops are what kick in the accelerator.

Though both *Free Lancing* and *Are You Glad* show off Blood-funk at its best, any bias towards the latter is reinforced by David Murray's bullyish presence. Throughout *Are You Glad* Murray swaggers in strutting plenty bric-a-brac, fusing Albert Ayler and rhythm and bebop more assuredly than anybody since 1968's Archie Shepp. Unfortunately, Murray—along with Oliver Lake and Olu Dara, who also appear on both LPs—only turns up on three of *Free Lancing*'s 11 tracks. Though horns give Blood's flip, sinewy numbers a wackier punch, of late he, Ali, and Weston been taking it to the stage as a threesome. At their Peppermint Lounge gig a few weeks back, as on a number of *Free Lancing*'s trio tracks, Blood, Weston, and Ali shattered stompdown funk into skronking shards, which is cool I guess. But when Murray fleshes out Blood's cackling skeletal riffs they roar like bull elephants. Murray, by the way, also appears on *No Wave*, which I'm told Blood doesn't much care for. Relatively speaking that's understandable, because *No Wave* is a raggedy-assed free-funk date with scant funk and mucho aimless energy.

Blood's funk has George Clinton and Junie Morrison for fans and where it goes from here is anybody's guess, maybe even Blood's. But the real question is whether Blood will ever funk in Peoria. Or for that matter, down here in Chocolate City. Because one thing he does have in common with Hendrix is a whiter shade

19

•

of patronage. And no matter how you hyphenate it, funk without funkateers has got to be missing one beat too many.

—1981

Hardcore of Darkness: Bad Brains

ardcore? I can't use it. Not even if we talking Sex Pistols. 'Cause inner city blues make me wanna holler open up the window it's too funky in here. And shit like that. Or rhythms to that effect. But listening to the Sex Pistols is like listening to a threat against your child, your wife, your whole way of life: You either take it very seriously or you don't take it at all. Depends on whether or not you're truly black or white I guess. Or so I thought. Because never mind the Sex Pistols, here come something for the ass. Namely, the Bad Brains. Baddest hardcore band in the land, living or dead. So bad bro that even if you ain't got no use for hardcore on the blackhand side, you'll admit the Brains kick too much ass to be denied for the form. Whether you dig it or you don't. Besides which, sis, sooner or later you got to deal with this: The Brains are bloods. That's right, I'm talking a *black* punk band, can y'all get to that? Because in the beginning, the kid couldn't hang—I mean when I was coming up, you could get your ass kicked for calling another brother a *punk*. Besides which, very few black people I know mourned the fact that Sid Vicious fulfilled his early promise. But, then, being of black radical-professional parentage, the kid has always had the luxury of cultural ambivalence coupled with black

20
•

nationalist consciousness. That's why my party affiliation reads: Greg Tate, Black Bohemian Nationalist. Give me art or give me blood. Preferably on the One, but everything I do ain't got to be funky. So, a black *punk* band? Okay, I'm game.

Dig: Formed in District Heights, Maryland (a black low-moderate-income D.C. suburb) around 1977, the Brains turned to hardcore from fusionoid-funk after getting sick of the AM/FM band and hearing a Dead Boys LP. Or so the story goes. Less apocryphally, virtually anybody who cares will tell you that Chocolate City's hardcore scene begins with the Brains. Which means that to this day defunct punkateers like Minor Threat, Teen Idles, S.O.A., and the Untouchables still owe the Brains some play for being the first to say, "Let's take it to the stage, sucker!" Or however one punks out to that effect.

Now when spike-headed hordes of mild-mannered caucasoids came back from the Brains' first gigs raving that these brothers were ferocious, I took the brouhaha for okey-doke. Easily intimidated, easily titillated white primitivism is how I interpreted that mess. Just some freak-whiteys tripping behind seeing some wild youngbloods tear up white boy's turf. No more, no less. But when my own damn brother—Tinman we call him—came back raving the same shit, I had to stop and say, well, goddamn, these furthermuckers must not be bullshitting. And now that the Brains got this 14-song cassette out on ROIR, it's for the world to know they ain't never been about no bullshitting. *Hardcore?* They take it very seriously. *You say you want hardcore?* I say the Brains'll give you hardcore coming straight up the ass, buddy. I'm talking about like lobotomy by jackhammer, like a whirlpool bath in a cement mixer, like orthodontic surgery by Black & Decker, like making love to a buzzsaw, baby. Meaning that coming from a black perspective, jazz it ain't, funk it ain't hardly, and they'll probably never open for Dick Dames or Primps. Even though three white acts they did open for, Butch Tarantulas, Hang All Four, and the Cash, is all knee-deeper into black street ridims than the Brains ever been and ain't that a bitch? Especially considering that sound unseen some y'all could easily mistake these brothers for soulless white devils. Because unlike Hendrix or Funkadelic, the Brains don't transmute their white rock shit into a ridimically sensuous black rock idiom:

When I say they play hardcore, I mean they play it just like the white boy—only harder. Which is just what I'd expect some brothers to do, only maybe a little more *soulfully*. Complicating this process in the Brains' case is that while 95 per cent of their audience is white, they're also Jah-praising Rastafari who perform hardcore *and* reggae (albeit discretely). Making them two steps removed from the Funk, say, and a half-step forward to Mother Africa by way of Jah thanx to the Dead Boys. Or more specifically the British Rasta/punk connexion.

While only three tunes on the Brains' cassette are Ital—if mediocre—roots musics, Rasta permeates their hardcore via a catchphrase they use liberally: P.M.A., or Positive Mental Attitude. In practice, this means that unlike many of their hardcore contemporaries the Brains don't shit on their audience—which last time they played D.C. was two or three dreads, a whole lotta skinheads, lunatic funkateers, heavy-metal rejects, and some black fashion models—but instead *reason* with them in hardcore dialect, a messianic message of youthful unity, rebellion, and optimistic nihilism. Which is somewhere not even a "progressive" punk anarchist like Bellow Appalachia of the Daft Kindergarteners has gotten to yet. In *The Meaning of Style*, Dick Hebdige says that the critical difference between Rasta and punk rebellion—one life-embracing, the other death-defying—derives from Rastas holding to the dream of an African utopia and punks seeing themselves as locked into a culture without a future. The Brains' extraordinary synthesis of the two is of course made possible by the fact that they're black. Nobody seems to know how or why they arrived at this synthesis— apparently not even them. But the contradictions such a fusion reconciles are not only profound but very handy: How to be black (not Oreo) punks and how to be punks and look forward to waking up every morning.

And while that may just sound like some seriously schizzy shit to you, sis, I don't think the Brains' mutation into triple-identity Afro-American/Rasta/punk was brought on solely by an identity crisis. It was also encouraged by their convictions. Because when the Brains adopted British punk's formal conventions and "classic" thematic antipathies—toward mindless consumerism, fascistic authority, moral hypocrisy, social rejection—they took to them as if they were religious sacraments. And when the Brains play hardcore it is with a sense of mission and possession more intense than that of any of the sadomasochistic Anglo poseurs who were their models. And yet, though locked into the form by faith and rebellion, the Brains inject it with as much virtuosic ingenuity as manic devotion. Their hardcore juxtaposes ergs of sonic violence against a surprisingly inventive slew of fusion-fast sledge hammer riffs, hysterical stop-time breaks, shrieking declensions, and comic asides (like the surf harmonies and soul arpeggios in "Sailing On" or bassman Darryl's gonzo Segovian intro to "Banned in DC"). And onstage, the band's Scot-screeching frontman H.R. throws down like James Brown gone berserk, with a hyperkinetic repertoire of spins, dives, backflips, splits, and skanks.

Ironically, the Brains' genuine feeling for this music isn't unlike what British rock's first generation felt for the blues. Ironic because the Brains are black; hardcore is white (and no matter how much Hendrix and Berry they ripped, it still ain't nothing but some whiteboy *sounding* shit now) and who would've ever thought that one day some bloods would go to the white boy looking for the spirit? Not to mention the revolution! I mean, if the Brains wasn't so serious I'd think they were trying to revive minstrelsy. Because while they play hardcore as good as any white man ha ha, like it was in fact second nature, their reggae ain't shit. Not only does it have less bottom than their punk, it also sounds half-assed and forced; more an outgrowth, like Dylan's nascent gospel, of sanctimonious intent than of innate religious fervor. Signifying, if nothing else, how far down river the Brains' missionary work has taken them from the wellspring of most black music's spirituality— namely, the black community. Because where punk's obnoxious energy is an attack on the parent-community, Rasta-influenced reggae draws strength from the ideal of a black community working in harmony. An ethic which isn't foreign to black music not from Yard either: The Funk Mob identified it as one nation under a groove, James Brown called it soul power, and I call it doowop tribalism. The need for which makes even such outre individualists as Jarman-Moye-Favors-Mitchell-Bowie bind into "Great Black Music" ensembles; makes Cecil Taylor work himself into a "Black Code Methodology/Unit Structure"; makes Ornette Coleman im-

23

•

provise a funk-based, democratic system of notation. The need, in other words, for a unified black community respectful of both holy tradition and individual expression. An ideal which leaves me respecting the Brains for their principled punk evangelism and worried for their souls.

—1982

Cecil Taylor's Monster Movie

I like to think of Cecil Taylor as someone whose art pushes the question of Afro-American identity beyond mortal ken. In this respect he resembles Jimi Hendrix and the Bad Brains. And of course, I'm not alone. Betty Carter, for instance, once told me that Cecil's music wasn't black because whatever *thang* it was black music was supposed to have, Cecil's didn't have one. Now, for a substantial portion of Cecil's audience the blackness or non-blackness of his thang is probably, perhaps even properly, irrelevant. Only what keeps the subject at hand such a prickly matter is Cecil's own demands that his black thang be given its propers. Not only through iconic identifications with Horace Silver, Bud Powell, Monk, and Ellington, but through speech, dress, and mannerisms which at times seem inherited from one of Miles Davis's former incarnations. Further confusing the issue for some is Cecil's apparently strange love for soul music and black social dancing—why just the other day someone I know saw him dancing to "Nasty Girl" on Channel 31, and freaked. Adding to the confusion is the maestro's "Black Code Methodology," a cosmology with Cecil at its infernal core.

Now, truth to tell, I find none of this odd at all. Recently a brother told me he thought Cecil's identifications with black pop were nothing more than a pretentious apology for his music. To which my response was like, hey man, Cecil knows what's hip— I mean, who is he supposed to identify with, Leonard Bernstein? (Later I realized the prejudices I'd betrayed pairing Cecil off, even ironically, with Bernstein. The *noive!*) And intellectually, Cecil seems to have resolved the question for himself 25 years ago: as far back as 1958, he would tell Nat Hentoff, "Everything I've lived I am. I am not afraid of European influences. The point is to use them—as Ellington did—as part of my life as an American Negro." Now go on with your bad self Cecil.

Someone once said that while Coleman Hawkins gave the jazz saxophone a voice, Lester Young taught it how to tell a story. That is, the art of personal confession is one jazz musicians must master before they can do justice by their tradition. I couldn't relate to Cecil's music until I learned to hear the story he was shaping out of both black tradition and his complex "life as an American Negro." The chapter on Cecil in A. B. Spellman's *Black Music: Four Lives* attests to the maze of ambiguities. *Solo*, a record Cecil made May 29, 1973, in Tokyo at 2:30 A.M., makes of this labyrinth lucid, lyrical poetry. And poetry isn't a word I drop in here simply because I like the sound of it. Because to make sense of Cecil's music you have to consider the ways he masks allusion in rhetoric. One reason I'm writing about a record 10 years old rather than reviewing Cecil's new *Garden*—as I'd originally intended—is that while I've heard *Solo*'s story so many times I could recite chapter and verse, I realized *Garden*'s four sides would require years of digging before I could hum a few bars. *Solo* is where I learned that Cecil's music does not speak only for itself.

In Cecil's music as in poetry, the game of allusion is played to give spiritual and historical resonance to a language of self-invention. Whether this is done consciously or instinctively doesn't matter in the end. What does matter is how game playing nourishes

25
•

both the poet's iconoclasm and his faith in holy tradition—two character traits essential to any people whose artists must invoke release, revolt, and remembrance to survive a culture dedicated to the disposable—and dangerous, therefore, to those who love holding on to their own.

Only here is where the responsibility of the black artist to tradition becomes trickiest. Because for any black person to get over in this country the way Mahalia Jackson sang about getting over, they have to learn to play the game without fouling out. And then even learn the handy trick of going *out of bounds* to bring the ball back into homecourt. To my mind this is what black avant-garde music is all about—and in this league Cecil Taylor's got my vote for MVP any season. What I learned from the performances on *Solo* may help to explain why.

The basic building blocks to many a Cecil Taylor solo performance or improvisation (improvised composition) are two types of motifs I'll label Figure A and Figure B. Figure A consists of randomly hammered discords which come off like beginner's luck. Or maybe at best like 1930s monster movie music. Figure B is a variable-speed tone spiral usually shadowed by melodic variants. This figure I believe Cecil finds kind of romantic; I know I do. Initially, Cecil sounds these two figures out for their opposing emotional values. He also plays coy with them, like a child who's discovered he can tease the cat with the goldfish bowl—reminding me more, in fact, of those manipulative scenes in monster movies where the thing grabs the girl. If Cecil's music were in fact a monster movie I'd characterize Figure A as the Doctor Makes the Monster scene and Figure B as the Doctor Macks On the Girl scene. What Cecil does besides dress up these two figurines and set them on collision course is go off and speak in tongues. This scene is of course known as the Monster Speaks (on *Garden*, the monster literally even *sings*). What this monster be saying can be as frightening or as fascinating as that scene in *Blade Runner* where the replicant tells his manufacturer, "I want *Life*, fucker!" before smashing his brains in like they ain't got nothing in 'em.

To what degree you find this scene black humor or horrorshow depends on whether your heart is with the runaway slave or the slayed master. Or in the case of Cecil's music whether you find the technique he's using to wreak havoc on Western classical form blasphemous or some beautiful black magic. Perversely, it's possible to do both, like the andro-erotic replicantist—prior to *Blade Runner* this scene was made into an entire movie, *I Loved a Monster*. In a way this recurring drama helps explain why certain of Those People build Our Blacks up only to shoot them back down when they figure winning is too good for that No-Good Nigger. Which brings us to the heretofore unmentionable Figure C, a bluesy kind of gospel refrain Cecil likes to throw out every now and then (on *Garden*'s "Stepping on Stars" he throws down on it). His way of saying even though he's *gone clear* when he's out there whipping all that mumbo-jumbo on those black and white keys to the castle, he knows he's still got to come back and taste those maggots in the mind of the universe, just like the rest of us—because ain't no rising above it all if you're black and knee deep in this shit here. Moreover, this being the case, you best keep the blues as near and dear to your heart as your prayerbook. Which brings us, strangely enough, to the D and E sides of Cecil's thang. Now, the D side is best exemplified by *Air Above Mountains, Buildings Within,* a marathon (52-minute) architectonic solo where Cecil designs a cathedral with one hand and hammers that sucker together with the other. *Garden,* by the way, offers three sides worth of these jackhammered monoliths, and Carlos Fuentes's El Senor Presidente never had it so mad. E side Cecil takes place anytime he works in his ensemble context, Unit Structures, a calling together of the flock to chase the money lenders out of the temple. Or the L7s as the case might be.

I tend to favor Triagonal Cecil to Cecil Taylor: the Pentagon—with the exception of course of side two of *Three Phasis* where Shannon Jackson's backbeat gave us C.T. Goes Barrelhouse and sides E and F of *One Too Many Salty Swift and Not Goodbye* with its bloodspurting Jimmy Lyons exorcism and tender violin/piano duet and *Dark to Themselves* which unleashed David Ware upon us and *Akisikilah* where Andrew Cyrille banishes Cecil to the nether depths and "Morgan's Motion" where Tony Williams puts the clutch on Cecil's motor and "Pots" which prefigured Miles's *Nefertiti* in

27

•

its use of pulse and percussion and "Communication #11" where Cecil engulfs the entire Jazz Composer's Orchestra with a tidal wave of his hands and well, what I'm saying is that if I enjoy Cecil's *Solo* stuff more than some of his other sides it's because *Solo* has such Debussyan decorum and Chopinesque restraint going for it, such Ellingtonian sweep and Monkish symmetry, such Worrellian grace noting and Theraconian movement. Not to mention a quality of calm-in-motion akin to Aikido that may say much about being black and by yourself in Japan at 2:30 in the morning making music that does not speak for itself alone. Music that in its transmutation of virtuoso technique into articulate syllables and jabberwocky in the same breath reminds me more of Spoonie Gee and the Treacherous Three's strafing and swooping rap-off "The New Rap Language" than any other music I can compare it to. If you think you'd like a more Germanic version of the same rush, check out "Introduction to Z" on *Garden*. Or for that matter Soul Sonic Force. (Same difference.)

—1983

The Atomic Dog: George Clinton Interview by Greg Tate and Bob Wisdom

W here it all began is a barbershop in Plainfield, New Jersey, back in the early '60s. Before he was cutting vinyl, George Clinton was cutting hair; before he got involved with the recording process, my man was chemically processing hair—mixing down wave, curl, and conk jobs for all the slick splib hustlers that ran the streets of Plainfield. We know now that this cat had a lot more on his mind than snipping naps and knotting up doo-rags for the rest of his natural born life.

Along with a couple other barbers and a few high school chums, Clinton organized a doo-wop group named the Parliaments. Modeling themselves after groups like the Temptations and the Four Tops, they gigged around until Clinton one day got the bold idea to head for Detroit and try to bogart his way into a Motown recording deal. So Clinton and crew wind up in '67 with a minor hit, "(I Wanna) Testify," on Motown subsidiary Revilot. For whatever reason, Berry Gordy decided he had enough male vocal combos in his stable, and the Parliaments languished on the label until Clinton decided to strike out on his own. Problem was, Motown owned the name the Parliaments, and so Funkadelic was born—out of desperation, the Parliaments' back-up band, and Clinton's warped notion of fusing the hippie counterculture with parodies of black pop, pimp, and prayer culture.

Between 1968 and 1975, you opened up a Funkadelic record and you couldn't guess what was coming next—a straight-faced take on the Fifth Dimension, like "Can You Get to That," or a heavy-metal hydrogen bomb test like "Superstupid." And go figure *Cosmic Slop*, where the title track, about a welfare mother who pimps for the devil, is followed by a country-swing ditty, "No Compute (Spit Don't Make Babies)," about a hard dick on the prowl who raps like a poolhall version of Jimi Hendrix and waxes philosophic the morning after about being turned out by a transvestite. If that's not enough there's "March to the Witch's Castle." A fairyland goof? Nope, a holy-roller preacher's benediction for soldiers returning from Vietnam—and maybe the only song of the period that embraced the Vets as wounded mortals rather than as babykillers.

Get the picture? If so, you're doing better than the mass recordbuying public of the period, black and white. Funkadelic was too wacky for the souled-out splibs and too black for the spazz whiteys who believed hard rock only came in caucasoid and got nothing to do with bloods getting happy feet besides.

Then Clinton struck the mama lode with 1975's *Mothership Connection*. This one was the turning point, all right. Not only did it give Clinton his first gold album and launch P-Funk as damn near a musical genre in its own right, but most important, it provided the impetus for the Mothership tour, which in turn begat the Flash Light tour, which begat the Clones of Dr. Funkenstein tour, which gave rise to the One Nation Under a Groove antitour—all barnstorming black guerilla theater extravaganzas that between roughly 1977 and 1980 made P-Funk seem a cross between the old Apollo and the circus.

Having written off Clinton as a has-been in 1981, few expected the success he found upon the release of 1983's "Atomic Dog." Those few who weren't surprised weren't just diehards, they were folk who knew that if nothing else, George Clinton was a longtime survivor of the vicissitudes of the American music business. George Clinton is as cagey a ringmaster and self-promoter as P. T. Barnum, as charming a stage ham as Fats Waller, as charismatic a bandleader as Duke Ellington, as hardworking a showman as anybody else this side of James Brown.

Listen to Clinton's lyrics and you find him playing plenty roles: hustler, preacher, poet, pimp, professor, psychoanalyst, student of politics and sexual manners, carny barker, soulman, swing-meister, bebopper, doo-wopper, druggy, subliminal seducer, free spirit. And the band he leads is the best rock band in America.

Like some folk live for Sunday morning prayer meeting, I live for the gestalt achieved by these virtuosi. And for the image of Clinton—his living deathhead's grin spreading across his Nubian mug like the stitchings on the Frankenstein monster's neck, teeth strung cadaverously from jawbone to jawbone, his limbs and torso madly whipping the crowd's emotions until they're all feeling the funk as much to the fullness as he is. Ain't nobody got fans that know as much about pure musical possession as funkateers, unless we talking disciples of vodun, juju, or hoodoo. We are a tribe unto ourselves, y'all, with our own language, lore, rites of passage, and articles of faith. One nation under a groove.

If George's rap is the positive side of P-Funk, the down side is what you'll find in the margins from the mouths of the men who've propped up Clinton's thang for lo these many years and are now crying the blues of unpaid-for dues, misspent youths, and sacrificed creative muses. You're gonna ask yourself why, if this cat seems so righteous, has he treated these bloods so badly, and why, even more outrageously, they keep hanging in for more abuse. Ahh, but I told you we're talking church here, family even, as well as cold-blooded business. And as much as George took from these guys he gave back. And dem's da facts. Now, here's the funkies.

Why are you into such a heavy Thomas Dolby trip these days?
He's a motherfucking genius, man. He is so baaad. The only thing about his show is that it's too slick. It was so slick that when he got to "Hyperactive"—which shoulda been the one to tear it on down—it was only three minutes long. That chick who sings and plays the keyboards is baad. Not only can she play her ass off, but she has style. When she opened up, it was Patti LaBelle all up and down. White chick, too. She burned that mother down, and soon as she did it they ended the song. People got

mad, too. You gotta know what to do with an audience, man. I don't care how slick you are: if you get their dicks hard, you better make 'em come. Know what I'm saying? That's why we don't do encores. If there's even a possibility of an encore we don't waste no time leaving the stage and coming back. We just stay up there and do it. Like one night when the crowd thought it was all over, we let Maceo and them go off into that heavy jazz shit they do. See, Dennis and Skeets, the drummer and bass player, are seriously into that. They were about to go with Weather Report when we first got 'em, but their dream had always been to play funk. And man, that tickled the shit out of me to find that musicians of that calibre wanted to play some funk. I went to school with Wayne Shorter [of Weather Report] and we used to laugh when he played that crazy shit in school. I went to school with Larry Young, the organist, too. Matter of fact, he used to sing bass with the Parliaments before he got seriously off into the other thing. I used to cut his hair.

The first time I heard "Maggot Brain" back in '71, I said, "This is the only shit out here that picks up where Jimi left off." It was acid funk, taking all the hip R&B of that period and then throwing psychedelia on top of it. Eddie told me y'all did it in just one take!

32
• Yeah. I knew we needed one of those serious sad songs, so I told Eddie, "Imagine your mother died"—and me and his mother Grace are real close—"and then you find out she ain't really dead." And he said, "Man, that's fucked up." But I knew the idea had been planted. Matter of fact, the whole band played on the record, but they weren't as intense as he was so I had to take them off. And that's been the classic ever since.

After listening to "Free Your Mind and Your Ass Will Follow" the first time, I thought that record had one fucked-up mix, but now, in the light of Jamaican dub, it was really ahead of its time.
I've always said I really didn't know what the fuck I was doing. That was the first time I was really turned loose in the studio. So I found out like, wow, I can *pan*. Well, shit, lemme pan the foot over *here* [laughs]. We did the whole album in one day,

mixed it and all, on three or four tabs of yellow sunshine. Both the first and second albums we did in one day, tripping out of our minds like a motherfucker. When I heard 'em six months later, I said, damn, this is sloppy. I could never let myself do that again—and after that, engineers wouldn't allow it. They'd say naw, man, there *has* to be a better way. Sly told me there was an easier way to do a tape loop, which is to do it on two-track and then bounce it back.

How is Sly doing?

He was in the hospital, but he's doing fine now. First time he's ever wanted to be alone, and he's working now. I got him one of them Linn drums, because he don't know nothing about all this new shit! He's *never* played synthesizer.

Did you know that the Mothership Connection *album, which became a gold record, and the tour, with all those flying saucers and funky extraterrestrials, a kind of black sci-fi extravaganza, would launch funk as a musical movement?*

Oh, shit yeah! This business is run by association and money. When you can say you've spent $350,000 on something, and Jules Fisher did the spaceships, and Larry Gatsby did the costumes, you've just associated yourself with the Rolling Stones, the Who, Patti LaBelle, *The Wiz.* The magazines know those names, so we made *People* the first week out and *Newsweek* the second. We're gonna have to bring the spaceship out again, because there's a whole bunch of new kids who never saw it.

Kinda like the black Woodstock?

Or like Barnum and Bailey. We took it to Japan last year. They got a big club over there called Bootsy.

Yeah, I've been there. It's out. Everybody walks around with big sunglasses on and their hair dooed up. It's deep. Man, they got Japanese Rastas over there with Japanese dreadlocks.

They say they got all black music covered over there. I saw a Japanese chick singing, sounded just like Sarah Vaughan. This girl couldn't speak English too tough, but when she sang she had Sarah Vaughan *down.*

33
·

*Where did that Zulu coat and headgear you wore on your last tour
come from? That's a powerful thing. It's a totem boy.*

Ain't that a baaad motherfucker, with all them feathers on there
and that spear and that shield. Larry Gatsby made that one. He
does David Bowie's costumes, too.

You done much study of the Egyptians and Nubians?

Just after I did the record "Nubian Nut," a Chinese guy called me
that, a Nubian nut. I didn't know what the fuck that meant.
Thought it meant a naked motherfucker. I went to look it up in
the dictionary because I liked the rhythm of it. It said African,
so I said cool. Then I went out and got some books by this
German chick, Leni Riefenstahl, *Last of the Nuba* and *The People
of Kay*. There's one motherfucker in one picture looks just like
me. I decided to make that the lead tune, since rapping was
happening and it needed another elevation. In New York, the
only allies to the funk are the rappers and the breakdancers,
and rap is a good thang. It needed to go somewhere else, because
it's like hopscotch music. After you do that for a few years you
gotta take it somewhere else or it'll get stale. So when we did
"Nubian Nut" we said, "Let's do a song and rap to that."

34
•
*You took it back to the church on that one, because a preacher ain't
nothing but a rapper.*

Preachers, pimps, and politicians.

*Isaac Hayes did 25 minutes of rap, remember? "By the Time I Get
to Phoenix She'll Be Gorgeous." Mug went through three divorces
before he got there, too.*

*Seems like now, for the first time, the press is finally giving
you all the serious push.*

Ain't that something? And in Europe, "Pumping Me Up" was the
No. 1 record. You know, CBS acted like they didn't even know
we were there. The record was selling like a motherfucker—
busting out in Dallas, Houston, Chicago, L.A.—and CBS acted
like it wasn't even theirs. Dude over there told me that I was
embarrassing him with that news, because over there, it's such

a big machine they only know records by numbers. The record came out before Christmas, and usually they like to get rid of records that come out before Christmas. We forced the record to stay around. I went out on a promotional tour for Capitol, and while I was out I promoted both records, and that kept it alive. I had to send a bunch of clippings over to Walter Yetnikoff [CBS president].

Well, you know all his eyes could see then was Michael Jackson.
Well, shit, he had to. I can't blame him. I understand—Michael sold 35 million records. Shit, that's like having 35 smash acts selling a million albums apiece. I just hope that now they got all that money they'll spend some of it on the rest of us.

P-Funk is an institution now, though, like James Brown. Maceo Parker once said that James Brown doesn't need a hit record to get the people out.
The boy has got energy up the asshole. I mean, he don't just stand there, he don't just make it, he *mashes*. I was talking to him and said, "Hey James, give me 17 splits." The boy gave me 18 faster than a motherfucker. And *hard*, too, like bam, bam, bam! My nuts go crazy just thinking about a mug doing that many. But, oh yeah, P-Funk is beyond commercialism now.

We got off in Minnesota and there was nothing but white people at the gig. See, that's what's weird now—a lot of white people come to the shows. And all they want to hear is *Let's Take It to the Stage, Maggot Brain, Standing on the Verge*. One girl came in one night with 51 albums. I didn't know I'd been on that many records. And she came in there talking about, would you please sign these for me. I said, baby, I really appreciate you got all these records, but I tell you what I'm gonna do: since all the members of the group are pretty much stars, I'm going to give each one two records to sign. Well, she was elated. Little bitty white girl couldn't be no more than 19. And that's been the trip all around the country with white people lately. Their thang is to come up to me and say, "I got all the records P-Funk ever put out."

Which is cool, but man, I saw you all at Howard University back in 1969 when you came out with nothing on but your jockstrap. Nobody knew how to handle it then.

And we cleaned up considerably for those shows, because back then we used to come out naked for real. I did that again five years ago when we were out with the Mothership and Sly was with us.

I was there, man. That was in D.C.

Sly came out cool as a motherfucker and people was screaming because I came out behind him with no clothes on whatsoever. Sly said, "Man, I thought they was loving me because I was back, only to turn around and find you with your motherfucking dick hanging out."

I tell you, though, y'all were rag-ged-y as a mug on that tour.

Well, what it was about then was that the record company was treating us so bad, trying to destroy us. So my thang was like, well, since this was a farewell tour and wasn't nothing going right anyway, I said fuck it. And then Sly, his whole thang was just to get on stage and face people. He wasn't really trying to play or nothing, just psyching himself up to get out there again. I told him, "Man, don't worry about doing the show. If you can make it through the whole tour and just don't quit you'll be all right." And he did. Sometimes he played good, sometimes he played excellent. The band didn't even think he could play, because most of them were too young to even know him. They didn't pay him too much attention, but every once in a while he'd get off and they'd say, wow, he is a baaad motherfucker. And right after that he started playing a lot. But on that tour he was just in the band and was getting paid like $20 a day. Everybody left the tour with $20 and a bus ticket to get home from Detroit. That's how bad the industry was dogging us on that tour.

I remember that when you got to Madison Square Garden, everything had gotten lost.

Yeah, motherfuckers sent our shit to *Milwaukee,* on purpose. They were really trying to fuck us up, but we did the show anyway.

So they were messing over you because you were getting your own business thing together?
Oh, yeah. Because we fired all the managers and lawyers who were fucking us up. I knew they were doing it, but I wasn't going to fire them until I got the Mothership tour off the ground. No way we were going to get that motherfucker up in the air if we fired them motherfuckers before the tour. But once it got out of the reach of gravity I said fuck 'em. And once I did that, everybody was, like, hands off. But we weren't going to quit the tour. That was the main thang: nobody quit. But when it came time for the Atomic Dog tour [in 1983], even I had to wonder who was going to show up. Because I knew that the '79 tour had been rough. See, we don't do a whole bunch of communicating, we just *know,* and it's cool. And when I got to Miami for rehearsal and saw everybody was there, I cried. Because they had gone home with 20 motherfucking dollars. I mean, me and Sly didn't get nothing. We was like, give us a gram a night, you know, that was the joke. Sly said we ain't no one-gram niggers now, man. But I said, man, ain't no money for us to do it no other way. I mean, I was retiring and he was *definitely* retired, so we was just out there hanging out. So, if we got a gram and a room, we were cool. Did the whole tour and didn't get shit but something to eat every day, and usually didn't get the gram [laughs]. But everybody went through the whole motherfucking tour. And when it came time for that Dog tour, everybody had the vibe, and they played with a vengeance. First show was the Red Parrot in New York, and we tried to kill, because everybody knew everybody could play, but our show had never been about any seriously articulate playing. We had a vibe. But this time out we said, "Let's do it articulate and let's give 'em the vibe."

The tapes from that concert you all did for the Budweiser festival out in Beverly Hills are awesome. It's like funk on the Ellingtonian or symphonic level. You have to release that commercially for all the funkateers.

37
•

Oh, did you hear that? Ain't that baaad? That is our baaadest shit, man.

What's up next?

Next Funkadelic album, *By Way of the Drum*, has got an island vibe to it. Not reggae, but more like junkanoo and calypso. Done that one with the band and some drummers down there in Nassau. Then Parliament has a real interesting one coming out called *Upsouth*. It's about—like, are you hip to lobotomy? They tried to legalize it about four or five years ago as a treatment for so-called violent criminals. There's a place out in California called Vacaville Medical Correctional Facility. You dig, that's where they're gonna *correct* you *medically*. And now they can do it with a laser beam. They don't even have to open up your head any more.

People like Hinckley and all the political prisoners from the '60s went there: Leary, Cleaver, Huey Newton. And if you notice, every one of them is acting very strangely now. Walking around with dick suits, beating chicks and getting busted, doing stand-up comedy, hanging out with the Moonies and 700 Club and shit. They couldn't get followings of a radical nature again or be leaders of revolutions again, I don't think. So the album is about upsouth, where a dude dies of a headache because he vows never to pick another lick of cotton out of a pill bottle. See, it's about funny farming, hoeing in concrete, and the Vacaville Thrill, where they drill into your will, cut into your consciousness, and dissect your dreams. Because that's what they're all about now. The Hinckleys and all those that go out and shoot people—they're not just nuts. They are the product of somebody pushing buttons.

Like, you ever see *The Manchurian Candidate* with Frank Sinatra? Well, now they can push buttons and set two or three folk off at once without even making contact with them.

There's a brain research scientist up at Columbia University who says just having a normal conversation with someone can run strange changes on your brain cells and metabolism.

Oh, yeah, because chemicals start moving the minute you hear certain words.

What do you think about what happened to Bob Marley?
I know they wanted him dead two or three years before he died. It was inevitable that something was going to happen to him, because there were too many different attempts being made on him. He was putting out too much vibe that they had no control over. So I knew something had to happen to him. Because even if they didn't literally do it, they can, like, put a vibe around you so deep until, like with John Lennon, they can make somebody come up in the name of love and kill you. I mean, they can do that now.

Commercials made people dislike Michael Jackson. Like, they had a contest where they asked are you getting sick of Michael Jackson, but what they really meant was are you getting sick of his *face*. Michael needs to change his face again. Because they've shown so many pictures of him now that it'll be beneficial for him to come up with a whole 'nother anti-Michael Jackson look. And he has got to do it for himself. Because if he waits for them to do it, it's gonna be negative. He had to be going through one helluva head trip when the machine started trying to come between him and his family. I have no doubt that they'll maintain, because they're close and basically too funky and rough. They might look cute and have been through Motown, but they ain't that vulnerable. Don King was a good thing for them because he could do nowhere near the damage of the sophisticated corporate machine.

When you think about that one cat being bigger than the Beatles and not even having three other cats in there to take the weight, it's frightening.
You know, when him and Paul got together he was like the fifth Beatle to me. I liked that concept when they hooked up. The Beatles are my all-time favorites. They were at the right place at the right time, and they made the best out of it. Sly was my next favorite, but there was just one of him, and there was nobody

to bounce shit off of. Jimi was the same way. But the Beatles had the right opportunity and that vibe that comes through all of us to make us write that shit. That shit just comes through your ass, and if you can take advantage of it, you're doing pretty good. And the Beatles were able to take advantage of it, four at one time. Each of them had a different drummer, and they was on the one. Michael right now has that chance. I hope he knows more than the politics of the music and his own energy, because he has that. But, see, his manager is somebody from the motherfucking record company, and that ain't no accident.

That's about charisma control, man.
You know what I'm saying, that's all it is. And it's good, because it's given him access to 30 million records. I'm not saying that's wrong, but he should be aware that that is what it's about and that he ain't got to be grateful to the motherfucker. He should still be the one to direct his own image. At a certain point you have to change before you reach the point of saturation.

That's why when we finished the Mothership tour we said, now let's go on the antitour immediately. Soon as we had finished four years of all that glitter we said let's go to all these little bitty places and play three hours for *us*. No limousines, get to the gig the best way you can, and just get your ass out there and jam. Or else you'll start believing that star shit. And when a motherfucker says you ain't shit, you will die of a heart attack. Especially after you have psyched yourself up to believe you are the equal of 30 million albums. Right now I say fuck a limousine. I'll take a cab in a minute. I *walked* to see Thomas Dolby. And that gives you strength. Because people ask, man, ain't you tired, and I say I don't feel like I've done shit. I rehearsed for this for 17 years of my life. When I was younger I used to walk down side streets in Newark on Sunday when the stores were closed, screaming, "Parliament, Parliament!"—just so I could hear what it was going to be like when I made it to where I wanted to be. So if I'm crazy now, I was crazy then.

—1985

Beyond the Zone of the Zero Funkativity

A true god must be an organizer and a destroyer.
—*Thomas Pynchon*

Unless you want to get on your knees, throw down.
—*George Clinton*

George Clinton's *Computer Games* is a work of genius and a piece of shit. A masterpiece of mindless pleasure made for both mass-ass and Maggot consumption, showing once again how intelligent life can devolve from do-do into some *terrible* Afro-pop. Fusing the dance-floor funk-intellechy of Parliament and the hardcore jollies of Funkadelic, *Computer Games* is Clinton's response to the deadliest dookey shtick of our times: information overload. *Computer Games* got more signifiers than half a Thomas Pynchon novel, likewise it begs decoding only to figure you an idiot for deciphering instead of just getting off. The intent is obvious: to make folk dig themselves becoming more like dysfunktional machine parts every day, whether at work, play, or meditation. (Though as always, y'all suckers will dance now.)

The reason *Computer Games* is a Clinton and not a Parliament or Funkadelic LP is probably still tied up in court, but it makes sense content-wise too. Because *Computer Games* programs in both bands' primary splanks: dance with your mind (P) and freak-out and be free (F). Like I said upfront, however, *Computer Games* is also one signifying furthermucker 20 times over. What it's about in part is having the brains of a dog and liking it ("Man's Best Friend," "Atomic Dog") and how much guilt-free, nasty fun you had when you were a baby ("Pot Sharing Tots") and the discipline it takes to be monogamous ("One Fun at a Time") and how much better the world would be if we treated each other like we treat our clothes ("Free Alterations") but mainly, about kids whose brains been damaged from playing too many computer games ("Loopzilla," "Computer Games").

Computer Games also got some serious reconnections going for it. Back to play are Bernie, Eddie, Junie, Bootsy, Freddie, and Maceo. Gone are the liner notes à la weltanfunkenschauung of Sir Lleb and the whiz kid gee-tar of Michael Hampton. What's new is some humility. Now way I figure it, this is George's way of saying P-Funk is dead but rising from the grave as of *Computer Games*. Of course he could also be making apocalyptic allusions on the order of the first funk is the last. Especially since the slippery body slam of a rhythm track sounds like some Bootsy's Rubber Band seven years in the can—which is also of course about how long it's been since the Funk Mob was anybody's opening act. Now way I figure it, this old funk for new with a side dish of humble pie is George's way of begging his maker for reincarnation into mass-ass appeal; especially so as not to forfeit any more games to the likes of Dick Dames, the Tame, Primps, Vanity Sucks, Knave, or the Slackback Band (though the LP's backcover does generously give thanx to "Grandmaster Five"—Clinton's sic, not me—for "The Message.")

42
•
   "Loopzilla," the current single out from *Computer Games*, struck me as more dysfunktional than the competition first time I heard it. Basically because being as how I'm no "Planet Rock" junkie, even given the social relevance of Mr. Bambaataa himself, I had no use for the way my main Maggot Overlord was pimping that Monochrome Drone Brainwash Syndrome beat and doing free pro-mos for 'KTU and 'BLS on the side, just to get some fairplay. Only way I now figure it, in light of further listening, is that "Loopzilla" has to be understood within the conceptual continuity of *Computer Games* to be dug for the sweet scam it truly is.

   See, there's a set-up going on. While the title track has a readymade P-Funk groove routine going against it from jump-street, the lyrics be signifying how computer games are fast replacing even cartoon reality for kids as in "I can out-woody a pecker I can out-porky a pig, I'm your computer game and of course I'm insane." Course, if that ain't clear enough, the vocoder processing at the tune's tag end is definitely meant to give the impression of some kid who done flipped out behind thinking life is more an Atari than a material thang. George however ain't just worried about the kids. Dig the line where the computer game say "I can out-drummer a beat," and ask yourself if that wouldn't shake you up if the next dance was your next dollar. But we got to hold that thought for later. Because moving right along, the next song in our tautology, "Man's Best Friend," is musically speaking a "(not just) Knee Deep" retread sporting one snazzy Eddie Hazel jazzbreak. The gist of it is that a well-stroked dog is a fool of a friend forever. Though its throwaway line, "a dog is a woman's best friend," surely alludes to other forms of hound. A left-handed way of saying perhaps how with them kind of dogs the love you get won't be shit no matter how much love you put out. But even a good dog can be loyal to a fault, which is to say *too good* for its own good, eh brothers? Leading us of course to the Parliamentary notion of a dog led by its primal urges toward behavior modification or the Nose Zone whereupon the following maxim applies: the dog who *chases* [its] *tail* will be dizzy. This comes from "Atomic Dog," a synthfunk throwdown replete with Pavlovian slobbers, woofing and *bark* beat in paw-paw meter. By which I mean this song definitely sounds like a dirty dog at bay besides being the ravefave of everybody I've played it for (hint, hint, Capitol Records). Content-wise "Atomic Dog" asks the perennial male question "Why must I feel like that, why must I chase the cat," then suggests bloods do a dance called the "Dogcatcher." Which means, cool that hound out before he gets hurt running around untrained in this here atomic society.

Now how all this ranking database figures into the "Loopzilla" hustle is as you might imagine pretty deep, so sit back while I try to break it all the way on down for ya'. See, George Clinton has always been like a radio to me. A cat who could tune in on everybody else's signals and fit 'em in on his wavelength band. Namely that of W-EFUNK or deeper still THE ONE, an orgiastic concept of democracy modeled after the dance floor where folks can both groove en masse and freak to their own beat. Though for this booty politic to work as ART, you do need somebody like Clinton or Bootsy (or Sun Ra, Miles, Ornette) to fine-tune the many freak-when-sees into one mass-ter stroke. The problem however is that if you jam too many signals on one channel you might get not deep dub but static, distortion, entropy, and finally the Zone of Zero Funkativity. So that the more impulses the P-Funk sent out in the form of offshoots and spinoffs, the less radio-active the Mob actually became, as radio itself grew more and more formulaic, more about pimping that one beat up and down, which Clinton said just wouldn't do on *Uncle Jam Wants You*.

Likewise, on the streets of New York, another contrary motion was occurring. The dances were getting more complicated as the music to them became more a simple matter of breaks, mixes, and beat instead of tunes (thanks to DJ's like Bambaataa). Hence came the street appeal of a goosestepping unit by the name of Kraftwerk (see Barry Michael Cooper for more detail on this than can be provided here), which of course begat "Planet Rock" which in turn has made the new sound of New York urban-con radio great if you're a breaking member of the boogie box brigade and tired as shit if you ain't. "Loopzilla" is a work of genius because it ambivalently cracks on and applauds this invasion of the system from the streets while warning of the madness in store for folk if they submit to that Monochrome Drone Brainwash Syndrome beat and turn, like Pavlov's dog, from charismatic funkateers into routinized robotic electric boogaloos. Course "Loopzilla" is still a piece of shit because it tries to cash in on that beat by being just as danceably unlistenable. Though on another level the snippets of old Motown and P-Funk Clinton has spliced in as double-talk ("calling out, around the world/are you ready for a brand new beat") tell us how that monochrome drone will either carry us forward or bury us if we get out of step ("unless you want to get on your knees, throw down"). The trick lies in who calls the tune. Therefore the only way to keep your ass from being up for grabs is to do like the brothers and sisters on the streets and outmaneuver that beat by breaking, smurfing, and murdering it to death. Or by doing what Doctor Funkenstein has done on *Computer Games:* pimp that sucker for all it's worth to get over on the system and then make an album that blows up in the system's face with the atomizing diversity of P-Funk, uncut funk, THE BOMB!

—*1982*

Baby Miles and Baby Wayne: Wynton Marsalis

B ecause jazz was once a music defined as much by brinksmanship—social and aesthetic—as by virtuosic refinement, the music's current hidebound swing toward bop and post-bop revivalism has to be seen as not only regenerative but reactionary: not just re-evolutionary but atavistic. But necessary. Because where the music's foremost experimentalists of the '60s—Taylor, Coleman, Coltrane, Shepp, Ayler, Ra, and later the Art Ensemble—produced music exemplary of a disciplined, genre-expansive personalism, the period's significant mainstream modernists—Miles Davis, Wayne Shorter, Andrew Hill, Herbie Hancock, Bobby Hutcherson, McCoy Tyner, and Sam Rivers—made music which paid academic heed to bebop's harmonic, rhythmic, and formal strictures while surreptitiously incorporating avant-garde ideas.

Yet while the '70s has seen the experimentalists' heirs apparent retain revolutionary status—at least in the jazz press—the latter's bandwagon fell by the wayside when Herbie Hancock disbanded his Sextant band to turn golddigger, and Wayne Shorter, tenor saxophonist and composer, retired for a vacation in Weather Report. Thereby depriving the music's succeeding generation of adventurous formalists of their leadership. (Though the question of whether or not jazz's fragile economy could have weathered the '70s without fusion is far from moot.)

In this context, the arrival of the prodigal Marsalis brothers—

trumpeter Wynton and saxophonist Branford—becomes heraldic for reasons other than just their fast, young chops. The first bona fide "new stars" the jazz mainstream has had since the '60s Blue Note crew, their hip, youthful elan can't hurt a music that long ago lost much in the way of glamour for young black people. More substantively, they represent the first new generation of black musicians to take impetus from Miles Davis's seminal quintet of the '60s, a band whose nonpareil innovations—notably its liberated yet synaptic group interplay, postmodernistic lyricism, and seeming infinity of compositional directions—were overshadowed for years by the justifiable stature and emotional impact of their less oblique revolutionary counterpart, John Coltrane.

Neither freemen fuzhacks, nor funkateers, the Marsalis brothers, on evidence of the trumpeter's CBS debut, declare themselves adroit student archivists of acoustic jazz's last band of "inside" futurists. And while the music on *Wynton Marsalis* hardly measures up to, say, *ESP* or *Miles Smiles*, it does successfully articulate the brothers' ideas about standards. Especially in terms of composition. The trumpeter's "Father Time," for example, reminds me of both Shorter's "All Seeing Eye" and Hancock's "Eye of the Hurricane" in its flighty meter shifts and percussive piano comping, while "Hesitation" deploys an abrupt, jagged head as festive and neurotic as any handful of Shorter originals from the Miles days ("Dolores," "Pinocchio," "Schizophrenia"—take your pick).

The upshot is that the motivic and historical demands of such material make the leader appear much less the cocky wunderkind he seemed with Art Blakey—where his spunky, spontaneous replications of Freddie Hubbard and especially Lee Morgan evoked welcome nostalgia as much as awe—than an intelligent but unfocused young improviser substituting technical braggadocio for his lack of Miles's incisive, shaping omniscience. That Davis's implosive charisma and invention overshadow Wynton's inexperience and bluster doesn't detract from the younger man's chiming tone and unerringly fleet articulation. But to date I've found him a more relaxed and personable player in less demanding contexts—particularly on Chico Freeman's recent *Destiny's Dance*, where he puckishly recalls the verve and intervallic daring of Booker Little, *Amarcord Nino Rota*, which finds him given over to a brief but funny, funneled takeoff on Lester Bowie, and especially *Fathers and Sons*, the recent CBS doubleheader reuniting *peres* Von Freeman and Ellis Marsalis with *fils* Chico, Wynton, and Branford. The Marsalis side of the reunion is a sumptuous, modern hard-bop date, with Daddy Marsalis's easygoing, labyrinthine modulations, infectious heads, and warm, architectonic right hand ably enhanced by Charles Fambrough's sturdy bottom and the thoughtful, strident navigations of his budding boy wonders.

I think Branford is a more mature improviser than his brother. The real difference between them is that the saxophonist worships not so much the history of his horn as the more concise history of Wayne Shorter—from Blakey through Miles to Weather Report and *Native Dancer* (with tangential references to one-time Shorter sidekick James Spaulding's exaggerated scalar effusions thrown in for good measure). For this reason reedman Marsalis's improvs have a more resolved and readymade logic and mystique about them than do trumpeter Marsalis's probing yet overanxious grapple for identity, especially on his debut's ersatz plunge into M.D.'s space/time. It's not even so much that Branford sounds like Shorter as that he constructs the same kind of tough musical syllogisms— and uses space and pure sound with the same kind of affecting lyricism.

When Wynton's band played D.C. May 14, 1983, the saxophonist sculpted a taut, levitating break on Monk's "Thelonious" that was presciently interpretive of the piece's tricky rhythmic and spatial angularity. No mean feat, given how much felt cerebration Monk's tunes demand of players of whatever experience. His brother, though, splattered brass everywhere, recklessly running through a surfeit of devices, riffs, and scales. What remains to be seen, regardless of each sibling's ability now, is whether it's harder to find your own way out of Shorter as a discipline or forge a style out of every ba-ad trumpeter the music has produced. But as it's been a while since I've heard any young saxophonist swing with the abstracted intelligence of Branford Marsalis my bets are on him to get there first.

—1982

47

•

Stagolee Versus the Proper Negro: The Treacherous Three Cross Over—Prince, Wynton Marsalis, and Eddie Murphy

Okay, so like a few years back the brother here is sitting in on one of those conferences on the state of the race muh peebles likes to convene—the topic at hand is *Black Images in the Media*. Now you got one platoon of splibs advocating that we lobby, picket, and boycott Hollywood until the cows come home for positive black images. On the other side, the more revolutionary brothers and sisters are proclaiming the need for an independent black film industry. In the midst of this charged dialogue one of my more apocalyptic walkpartners jumps up and pronounces that any people who don't exist in the mass media in the 20th century will soon cease to exist and that given our current media coverage we're close to the edge of extinction.

Certainly it seemed a few years ago that the millennium was at hand. When this brouhaha took place such sterling ethnic role models as Jimmie Walker's "J.J.," Antonio Fargas's "Huggy Bear," and Garrett Morris's closet full of drag queens were weekly uplifting the people's spirits and making D. W. Griffith chortle in his grave. Lately, though, it's come to seem that salvation, rather than the judgment day, is at hand. Because right now black America's got more crossover acts happening than it's had since the '60s, and the funny thing is they're all taking Babylon by storm in an era noticeably absent of agitation from the streets. I'm talking about the Jacksons (Michael and Jesse), Ray Parker Jr., Vanessa Williams, Grace Jones, Louis Farrakhan, Toni Morrison, Tina Turner, Edwin Moses, Alice Walker, Jennifer Beals, Carl Lewis, Eddie Murphy, Wynton Marsalis, Prince.

Now this phenomenon begs the question whether good old redneck racist America has gone so color-blind that we people who are darker than blue (well, the spectrum begins at off-white) are now judged solely by the content of our character and not the color of our skin. I mean, glory be, has Massa granted us equality without us eben knowing it? That, lo and behold, we're now fully assimilated citizens of the republic—given so many starlit woogies showboating all over the Grammies, the Democratic National Convention, MTV, *Penthouse*, *Nightline*, and the Hollyweird screen? Well, let's not get too full of ourselves here—much as we love our symbolic victories y'all. Because what puts the lie to such emancipation proclamations is that all the aforementioned are yer super-blacks, Biggers so baad thay can't help but outshine (no pun intended much) the honkie competition. Which is to say, we really ain't come much further than those days when a black man had to have a PhD to get a job in the Post Office. (Leading me to say that equality will arrive the day brothers and sisters can get over by being as mediocre as their white counterparts.)

Nevertheless, what is fascinating to contemplate about three of these Negro leaders—Eddie Murphy, Wynton Marsalis, and Prince—is their Stagolee (read: "Bad Nigguh") dimension, the degree to which they seem to be in manly control of their respective images. (Yes, Virginia, Grace Jones probably does deserve an invite to this black macho weenie-roast, but let's stand firm here for the much abused African-American male.) First fascinating

49

thang to note about this triumvirate is their immediate antecedents—respectively Richard Pryor, Miles Davis, and Jimi Hendrix.
Second is how they've managed, unlike their forefathers, to make
it in the mainstream without compromising their edge.

What this means is that we probably won't ever have to suffer
through Eddie playing second fiddle to Gene Wilder's Al Jolson
or kowtowing before that ultimate white man, Christopher Reeve;
nor hear Wynton fake the funk with a band that's just hunky-dory;
nor find Prince facing a life-and-death decision to appeal to either
mixed or exclusively white audiences. This isn't to suggest the
three are the artistic equals of their progenitors but to point up
how little their heirs to the throne have had to play politics, unless
we're talking the politics of Negro subversion. Because in a way
the success of the treacherous three derives from how they've
managed to merge their Stagolee sides with their Proper Negro
profiles.

Shee, in Eddie's case, there's even Stepin Fetchit aspects. If I
recall correctly, he did his first bit on *SNL* as a bedpan orderly
and from there diversified with a gamut of African-American ar-
chetypes ranging from Buckwheat to his black Muslim film critic
who enjoyed splatter films because they depicted the wholesale
slaughter of white people. Sometimes the boy ran numbers so slick
couldn't *nobody*, black or white, figure whose side he was on—
there was his Marley takeoff, "Kill the White People (but Buy My
Records First)," and his even deadlier lampoon of Jesse performing
a doowop version of "Good Old Hymietown."

Equally befuddling have been some of Wynton's interviews,
where in one breath he'll assail black people being denied their
culture and in the next breath crack that black musicians who wear
African garb don't know nothing about Africa ($800 Eye-tal-yun
suits being a more ethnically correct cut of cloth, I guess). Then
there was the time the boy called Miles Davis, fer chrissakes, an
Uncle Tom for saying in *Ebony* that he liked Journey and Styx
more than contemporary jazz—like can't this hothead show any
more respect than that for those getting on in their years? And
while you have to applaud the balls behind his acceptance speech
at this year's Grammies and his band's performance on that freak-

show, you know it's his ability to play that classical shit which gives him so-called legitimacy.

And then there's Prince, who includes on the same album one song made-to-order for Apartheid-Oriented Radio ("Little Red Corvette") and another that snidely instructs all the white people how to clap on the beat ("D.M.S.R.")—schooling by the way which puts the lie to the opinion that Prince doesn't know on what side of the color line he's down by law. Stagolee as the Proper Negro, see?

How slick a hustle these brothers have pulled in mainstreaming their models for middle-American consumption can be seen in Eddie's having made Richard's crazy nigguh telegenic, Wynton's having gotten over reprising the Miles of *Nefertiti*, and Prince taking over like the Hendrix of Woodstock (and not the Hendrix forced to disband Band of Gypsies and hook the Experience up to an artificial respirator).

All of which is cool until you realize what's won America's heart isn't the designer original but the reasonable facsimile—not crazed black genius but black subterfuge. Let's face it, Eddie's James Brown may make your sides split, but Richard's Wino and the Junkie throw your ass into some convulsions that ain't even about jest fer fun. And while Prince leaves you blinking trying to figure out how he got so much style, music, and sexuality together in Minnefunkin'sota, Jimi's visceral and visionary embrace made you wonder what quasar he was picking his signals up from. As for Wynton and Miles—well, not to backhand the brother, but that comparison ain't even a conversation, let alone a quip.

On the other hand, you can say depths of soul and innovation be damned, man, Eddie, Wynton, and Prince is what's happening now. And you'll get no argument from me on that score: Eddie is the funniest muthafunka on the scene; Wynton the best news in jazz trumpet since Eddie Henderson; Prince the killer act in rock and roll right now (matter of fact, those of y'all going gaga behind *Purple Rain* and never seen the boy live ain't seen shit).

To the younguns' credit, you can also say that none of them seem likely to fall prey to their models' flair for substance abuse or self-destruction. And maybe this is because they're all careerists rather than demigods. The degree to which you can say Jimi's, Richard's, and Miles's arts were fueled by exorcising personal demons is the degree to which you can say their work was always being renewed by unavoidable self-confrontation. Like the blues men of old, Jimi, Richard, and Miles have all spoken of their muses as demanding dominatrixes. But what our young turks lead you to wonder is not whether mere talent can stand up to driven genius, but whether their talent lies in making sociocultural break-throughs equal to the aesthetic ones of their mentors.

Murphy, whose gifts for cutting mimicry are matched by his impish charm, has already proven himself capable of parodying white psyches in a less threatening way than Pryor. And, as a result, he's more race-leveling. Simply because he's a member of the suburban television generation he's come to assimilate so much more Americana than any other black comic. Witness his Hon-eymooner or Gumby bits or his takeoff on Mr. Rogers. All of which make you realize that unlike black film actors of the past, Eddie has the opportunity to mold roles that don't deny his African-American complexity in favor of the bleached black Everyman gliberal directors would have you believe accords blacks equality. (Man, talk about yer condescending attitudes.)

Likewise Marsalis. For all the cracks his tres-piece dress code will draw from a bohemian slob like me, he's still the hippest PR man jazz has had since Miles (who took up the Louis and Dizzy tradition of trumpeters being the music's ambassadors). Through his erudite presence, he's already begun to make jazz and jazzfolk intellectually stirring and glamorous to young black people again, especially the sisters. You also have to applaud Marsalis for basing his musical conception around Miles Davis's and Wayne Shorter's composing, arranging, and bandleading of the '60s. And though I don't share the blood's disdain for either fusion or the black avant-garde, I respond positively to his daring in picking up from where Shorter and Davis left off.

On the flipside, what you worry about with Murphy is whether he'll continue to choose or accept vehicles that only scrape the Stagolee surface of his comedic abilities, a la *48 Hours* and *Trading Places*. With Marsalis, you fret that after trading off a spate of classical and quartet dates, Columbia will make the same mistake

with him that Prestige made with McCoy Tyner and try to maintain
sales with a dozen or so quixotic superstar sessions or concept
albums. (There's already talk of a ballad date and a Gil Evans
collaboration, and you can bet a trumpet summit is going to be
convened.) But what in the long run would probably prove a
more challenging and progressive tack would be for Marsalis to
pick up on David Murray's lead and explore the small orchestra
format. Here, he could merge his Waynish sensibilities with the orchestral techniques of Morton, Ellington, Monk, Fuller, Dameron,
Mingus, Russell, Dolphy, and Hancock. This kind of setting could
give him a forum for bringing other young mainstream players to
the fore and also widen the range of colors his trumpet could play
off.

As far as Prince goes, any concern you had about his survival
in the marketplace has become moot now. With *Purple Rain* (the
movie and the album), he's established himself as the most cunning
black producer since Berry Gordy in plotting a course of conquest
over American pop apartheid. Let me eat some crow here: heretofore I'd always considered him nothing but a bodysnatcher, fash-
ioning himself a monster from the brain of the dead (Jimi) and the
bones of the defunkt (Sly, J.B., and Dr. Funkenstein). But *Purple
Rain* won me over by making good on my prophecy after "Beat It"
that black rock was coming back with a vengeance. Although
Michael may have kicked the door in, Prince done stormed the
white castle and come back handing the brothers and sisters the
keys to the rock-and-roll kingdom (or, to paraphrase Bill Murray
in *Ghostbusters*, he came, he saw, he kicked ass).

And don't be fooled by the scandal sheets out to turn Michael
and Prince into the Romulus and Remus of American pop. Because
naw, buddy, what's happening with these two is akin to, say, Jesse
and Farrakhan. You got one playing the Proper Negro to the other's
Stagolee, one making off with the kids like Peter Pan, with elfin
charm and fairy dust, and the other sucking 'em up into his trip,
like the Pied Piper when he blew into his magic flute. The question
is whether the industry will provide equal opportunity to all the
other black rockers rising en masse to the battle cries of *Thriller*
and of *Purple Rain*—thereby ensuring that MTV will soon look
like *New York Hot Tracks*. Or whether it'll merely update Daddy

53
•

Jim Rice and Colonel Tom Parker and attempt once again to clone the funk. (I for one wish them luck, because if they can brew up a caucasoid replicant who can write, sing, dance, style, profile, and rock the microphone as viscerally as Sensitive Mike and His Royal Badness, won't nobody be able to say white man just got a God *complex*.)

Although you can already hear the influence of *1999* on this year's records, from Cheryl Lynn, Shalamar, and the Pointer Sisters to Billy Idol and Van Halen, that spectrum will widen behind the success of *Purple Rain*. No album since Funkadelic's *Let's Take It to the Stage* has so amorously bedded down black and white pop. As much as that record is a coup d'etat, it's also Prince's homage to his roots in black and white rock of the '50s, '60s, and '70s. It's the record Prince has been wanting to make all along, since the music sounds like the kind of mulatto variation he probably was piecing together and performing in Minnesota before he got his deal. The record's diversity proves that Prince is a consummate pop chameleon capable of composing a song in any pop idiom you'd care to name. Visually of course he's already proven himself a quick change artist on par with Malcolm McLaren and David Bowie. (Up at the Warners publicity offices there's a series of stills taken from 1979 to the present, and the kid sports a new bouffant in each one.) But until this album, I didn't know how wide his sources were: ranging from Hendrix to Run-D.M.C. ("When Doves Cry"), Marvin Gaye to Joni Mitchell ("The Beautiful Ones"), Bee Gees to Weather Report ("Take Me with U"), Funkadelic to Mahavishnu ("Computer Blue"), Henry Miller to Led Zeppelin ("Darling Nikki"), James Cleveland to Sly Stone ("Baby I'm a Star"), Willie Nelson to Pink Floyd to Keith Jarrett ("Purple Rain"), Reverend Ike to the Yardbirds ("Let's Go Crazy"). Granted it's hit or miss all the way, but the hip thang is that the LP's airplay on urban contemporary and AOR playlists will give black popsters more legroom to stretch out in. At least in my naive expectations, we're at the dawning of the age of Radio Utopia.

Like the album, *Purple Rain* the movie rises above, rather than drowns in, its own pretensions. Take the scene in which Prince finds his father at the piano, which evokes something tragic about the frightful gaps in communication that can go on for years between black father and son. Or take the scene in which Prince whimpers when Apollonia mocks his body; there you get the Napoleonic vulnerability behind his kinky stud moves. Also to the film's credit are Morris Day and Jerome Benton's black vaudeville routines on and off stage, which make you wonder how so much cold-blooded coon bidness could be going on out in the snowy white heartland. For all this, though *Purple Rain* ain't hardly the millennium when it comes to black images on the Hollywood screen; it is certainly truer to the humanity and milieu of its black principals, looney-tunish as they may seem, than I've come to expect outside of independent black cinema. And for giving us that much and for securing the black rock revival—hell, for possibly clearing the way for black crossover acts in the future—I for one am willing to forgive Reverend Roger Nelson for wanting to have his apocalypse now and eat it too. Noblesse oblige that puts me in mind of some 17-year-old Hendrix lines: "Sing on, brother/Play on, drummer."

—*1984*

55

Are You Ready for Juju?: King Sunny Adé

*T*wo days before I go out on the road with King Sunny Adé and His African Beats I am certain that no known theories of pop apply to juju music. After three shows I become convinced juju music can unite the world. By the fourth I realize Sunny Adé is on his way to becoming the first truly international star in the history of pop.

Sunny Adé and the 21 other Nigerians performing in the U.S. for the first time are not the only ones who go through some changes behind this trip; within a week of traveling with this band of Yoruba I experience a spiritual awakening. I finally know why, if you are Afro-American the blues is your Rasta, your Yoruba, your way of knowing life to the fullness as me bredren like to put it. Somewhere along this journey I lose the African Beats and find myself back in love with John Lee Hooker and the World Saxophone Quartet. Believe me, juju music can take you all the way back home again and then some. So that while the kid may have begun with no theories, right now he got more theories than the King has Beats. Along the way to figuring them out I got beset by hallucinations, visions, prophecies, revelations even.

The first of these occurs when Sunny's French producer tells me he invited Stevie Wonder to Sunny's show in L.A. I get a chill thinking of Bob Marley, because I know that the tour Bob was supposed to do with Stevie would have gained him a substantial black American audience. My chill quickens as I get to speculating on a shall-we-say comic scale that Bob may have been forwarded so that Sunny could save the West with juju music—there really being no room for two kings of third world music in this Babylon star system we got going down the road to damnation here. There's an irony in that Sunny was supposed to meet Bob in Zimbabwe for Independence Day but had to cancel due to illness. At different points along the road the differences and connections between juju music and reggae, Rasta and Yoruba, rear up in my head and the heads of others.

In New York at the Savoy a white woman asks me don't I think Sunny is just like Bob Marley. I'm feeling Irie so I am cool.

"This is different music from a different world."

"Yes, but don't you think he could get on MTV with this stuff? Do you watch MTV?"

"Try not to."

"Why is that?"

"Why? Because it's racist. There's never any black acts on it. Shit, Michael Jackson can't even get on MTV."

"Yes, but this is *so different* from mainstream black pop. I think young white suburban kids could really get into it. I mean, don't you think he could be like Marley?"

"I don't think we know yet what Sunny's impact is going to be."

"*Oh, but I think I do!* I think young *white* kids are really going to get into this stuff. You know, you should really try to be more visionary in your thinking."

I want to tell her I don't give a fuck if young white kids get into Sunny Adé but she whirls around and is gone. And so there, once again, stands one more black man stewing over what some white person thinks. Later I actually concede her point about vision, with the exception that seeing Sunny Adé on MTV isn't exactly my idea of prophecy made manifest.

The first show on the tour is in D.C., and there I run up on one of my ace homeboys feeling very Irie and him-a-rapping very dread, Episcopalian School and Columbia University notwithstanding. "Wha'hap'n Rasta?! You know me meet the man Sunny Adé today and him *wicked* star. This man, him *cool* Rasta. They call this man the Chairman and the Chairman him cool-star-Rasta, him *wicked!*"

"So he's really about a bad motherfucker, huh?"

57
·

"Him *cool* mon. This man him *wicked!*"

Okay, Rasta, gotcha.

Here for the American premiere of so much cool, of so much wickedness, are four times as many black folk as I see during my weeks with the tour. We don't call D.C. Chocolate City for nothing, you know. We got Nigerians decked to the nines in exquisite Cultural Attire. We got Afro-American cultural nationalists in equally beautiful traditional garb. Afro-American bohemian nationalists looking street regular, Dread Lions and Jah Daughters on the side and dressed to cool. And even still, plenty white people.

In D.C. the band's two sets combined run almost four hours. Besides being the hardest rocking of the tour, the concert also features Michael Olatunji leading off the money-pasting ritual, a Nigerian custom of coming onstage to reward performers with bills stuck to the head, face, and shoulders. Because people are allowed easy access to the stage, the band makes nearly $400 off the crowd alone that night.

For sound and spectacle, my first African Beats performance is one I'll always remember as a marathon celebration—life and music as two forms of the same joy. Seeing all these brothers from back home dance, sing, and play exhilarating party music dressed in a flashy confusion of styles from Psychedelic Cowboy to Neo-Cultural is what we on this side of the color line call the joint, the bomb. The joy in the music is evident in the band's sincere big grins, in the ringing shingaling of the four rhythm guitars; the scatting, heartpopping gallops of the talking drums; the sly, swooping iridescent slides of the steel guitar; the smooth moves and choral mantras of the band's lead singers. But most of all, it's right there for the world to see in the sanguine, smiling, sweet, traffic-directing face of Sunny Adé, the man they call King because he earned the title, whom they call the Chairman because he's got investments in some 10 businesses back home, the man whose charm, charisma, guitar, and terpsichore are bringing to life D.C.'s Wax Museum. The energy and enthusiasm is so infectious and so on the One that everywhere you look people is getting happy feet, giving it up to the funk, getting down, getting off, moving, grooving, working up a sweat and being swayed, soothed, and cooled out in a single motion. This juju music is wicked, mon, and it's so cool too. And for the next three weeks I hear this band twice nightly in seven cities and in some of them the shows aren't half as kicking as D.C., but the response everywhere is the same—nuts! Even when these cats ain't but half-cooking, there is no way you can see them for the first time and not be rocked to your knees 'cause they begin where we peak.

My homeboy in fact gets so keyed into this music's magnetic claim on all living things that he proclaims juju music to be every man's music and I laugh, 'cause when did this cracker-baiting negro turn integrationist? A smile given a mud rub of reality when this half-drunk white boy spots me and homeboy's natty dreads on the way out the door and declares himself our Rasta brother, like that's the funniest thing he can imagine. At this moment I've regained a healthy dose of good old American racial territoriality and dig that while Sunny might not have no problem with the boy being all up in his thang, I don't even want this motherfucker in my face. And that's simply because that's just the way shit is here. And gonna be, for a long time to come. This black woman said on her J.O.B. the next day: "Yeah, them white people loved Sunny and them last night all right, but that ain't gonna stop them from coming back in here and treating *us* like shit again every day." And so it goes in Babylon. Where juju music can take your black ass all the way back home again and then some.

59
•

God's smiling on you but God's frowning too because only God knows what you'll go through.
—Melle Mel and Duke Bootee

Sammy, who looks like a cross between Albert Ayler and Amiri Baraka in a cowboy hat, is Sunny's ramrod road manager in Nigeria. Martin, the Frenchman, is Sunny's personal manager and record producer outside of Nigeria. In addition to working with Sunny, he works with Manu Dibango. Ian and Malcolm, two Englishmen, are the American tour's road managers and roadies. They worked on the British tour and have also worked for the Selecter, Toots and the Maytals, and Black Uhuru, at home and stateside. Katherine, the French soundwoman, knows the band from as far back as the motherland. Both Sammy and Martin came to work with the

Chairman after leaving Fela. Sammy says he left Fela because the man is getting old, smokes too much, mixes music and politics, and was responsible for Sammy getting arrested 86 times; this is nothing of course compared to Fela's 472 arrests, all with no convictions "because the people love him too much." Fela, Sammy says, is an honest man but a hardhearted man who believes he's always right, and that kind of man you cannot communicate with too well about business. Martin says that of all the artists he's ever worked with, Sunny is by far the most professional, the most receptive to new ideas, and, of course, the coolest.

The only time I sit down with Sunny for a formal interview is in Washington. I find him *the* friendliest stranger I've ever met. Sitting in the band's suite I feel myself immersed in a world where sincere love and mutual respect are the rule. And when Sunny tells me the message in his music is peace and love, I don't wonder if the cat is jiving me because the vibe is everywhere in the room, and it's as infectious as the music and I just start grooving toward a high off it. I hallucinate a toy-size hologram of last night's show right before my eyes. The music these brothers play is less a realization of self than an unbroken extension of it. As in the homeland, private and public are on the One.

When I ask Sunny how do musicians get in the band, he says there are no auditions because it's really a band of brothers and when they need a new musician they simply call on one of their brothers and he shows. Where did he get the idea of using steel guitar? He originally wanted to use an African violin but his violinist was a lush who'd wake up on stage in the wrong key, and he'd heard the steel guitar in some of the country music he likes (like Jim Reeves and Hank Williams). Then, by coincidence, he discovered Demola, the steel guitarist, playing in a country band in Lagos. And despite all the "correct" journalistic stuff we get into, I hear things like how a nice guitar riff on the next LP is based on a head sway a Nigerian might do before being moved by the spirit to dance. There's this moment when we're not talking and he gets this gaze in his eyes and slowly says to himself, "I love to sing . . . and dance . . . and play music for people . . ."

Sunny's cool isn't like any of the cools I've ever known. It's not the hipper-than-thou cool of the jazz set or the aggressively aloof cool of dreads or the yeah-fuck-with-me cool of the B-boys. Sunny's cool is a congenial cool, a secure, calm cool. The kind of cool I imagine Jonathan Jackson had when he walked into that Marin County courtroom and said, "I'm taking over now, gentlemen." The kind of cool that could walk into battle respecting an enemy as a man and still go heads up. And though the principal theme in Sunny's lyrics is said to be love, the words in his catchiest tune, the mesmerizing "Ja Funmi," mean, "my head shall fight for me." Onstage in "Synchro System" the Chairman tells folk if they want to dance to juju music keep everything from the waist up still and everything from the waist down in a slow grind. Like the P-Funk, juju music is about keeping a cool head and a hot body in motion.

In Boston I am two seconds off this white boy's ass because he starts slam dancing to Sunny's music—with no respect, obviously, for anybody including me and my big feet. But before I go off, an African brother in flowing Cultural Attire gets to swaying in front of this punk and slows his slam down to a spastic grind. Then with a mischievous grin the African snaps his fingers like a genie and disappears into the crowd mobbing the floor.

I never thought I'd see skinheads and Africans partying to the same groove, in Boston of all places. Only that doesn't surprise me as much as learning from Milo Miles and Doug Sommers of the *Boston Phoenix* that a 90 per cent white crowd is the most integrated it gets in this city. Boston is very weird. The people least willing to let juju take their minds here are the dreads and the Afro-Americans. In this instance, fear of music seems to mean fear of life, liberty, and the pursuit of happiness. Probably because I came up in that deceptive bastion of blackness, D.C., it never really hits me until Boston how free white people are to just be themselves in this country. And how much repressive psychic armor Afro-Americans wear to protect white people from their wrath and to preserve their own lives.

In the lobby of the band's hotel in New Haven I meet this slim, dark young brother named Brian who works there as a luggage carrier. Brian's cool on the gig is about becoming a cipher, a blur, a peripheral vision that melts into the surroundings—the cool of a man whose optic nerves constantly remind him you best watch your ass up in here buddy. Shaped by common blood but different histories, Sunny and Brian share a presence. The difference is that where Sunny's cool comes from being a Yoruba prince, Brian's is all about trying to survive in white America.

Great Black Music: Ancient and to the Future
—credo of the Art Ensemble of Chicago

In New Haven, an old friend from Howard U., Rick Powell, introduces me to Robert Farris Thompson, who proceeds to pour a libation of beer on the floor of the club. This old white guy is all right, I say to myself. Author of *Black Gods and Kings* and *African Art in Motion*, Thompson is responsible for two extraordinary works of scholarship on the cultural systems governing African aesthetics. Before racing back to the bus I hang outside his classroom at Yale catching wild snatches of sermon the day after the New Haven gig. "A lot of people there last night thought they were seeing entertainment, only you can tell by the patrilineal scars on this man's face that he is no mere entertainer, but the progeny of kings. . . . because if you are Yoruba just like if you are Anglo-Saxon, or if you are Jewish, you know who you are and you know where you're coming from. . . ."

Re: knowing who you are and knowing where you're coming from department. Gerald, our bus driver, is a five-year veteran of the rock and roll road, a Newark blood, and has seen plenty action driving for the Commodores, Bob Marley, Gil Scott-Heron, the Kinks, and the Rolling Stones. Not that I get much out of him on these subjects, the driver-rocker relationship having doctor-patient overtones. In any event, Gerald says he's just tied down the upcoming Michael Jackson and Marvin Gaye tours; those, my man tells me, are your Real Deal tours. What have been his favorite tours? "Kleeer, Manhattans, Change. My kind of bands. *My* music." And I relate to that, figuring that explains as well as anything why Gerald will not be moved by the magic of juju.

On the way out of New Haven we make a half-hour pit stop. I drop dub poet Mutabaruka's tape on the bus sound system. Jacob, one of the singers, comes forward to listen. On one number Muta gets into this rhetorical thing about how the black man in the West doesn't know where he comes from. Like "West, yes, but me no Indian. . . ." After he's disassociated himself from half the hemisphere Jacob wants to know where Muta came from. When Muta finally identifies himself with Africa Jacob tells me, "I really like this man's lyrics. Not the sound and not the rhythms. You know when we get back to New York I want you to take me where I can get the latest dance records, the stuff that's really happening." Taking us all the way back home again and then some.

D.C., New York, Boston, Sunderland, New Haven, Rochester, Buffalo, Ottawa, Toronto, New Orleans. There were things that happened in D.C. that I couldn't make heads or tails of until Rochester. Things in D.C. helped me figure out Boston. But I'm wondering, if this band played for a real black American throwdown party crowd, would the people accept or reject them? Despite what I learn on this tour, that's really all that matters to me. Would the same folk whose lifeforce is responsible for Trouble Funk, Grandmaster Flash, Slave, Cameo, and even Michael Jackson check the righteous connection between juju music and the funk and go with it?

For a number of reasons I don't expect the show in Sunderland, Massachusetts, to be shit. Things seem on the verge of falling apart. The band pulled into this dozing suburb of the University of Massachusetts, hungry, tired, and in one case very sick. It's Sunday and there are no groceries or doctors to be found. And barely after we pull into this dump of a roadside motel, everyone is off to soundcheck at the Rusty Nail. Sammy pressures Gerald to find a doctor and a grocery store, and after nearly a week with these Yoruba Gerald is beginning to feel like they need somebody to translate their English into English. On the way to soundcheck Katherine and Tajudeen, the Nigerian soundman, curse each other out over something that went down in Boston. When Ian tries to intervene, Tajudeen fires on him for assuming that he, Tajudeen, does not have an education, something Ian says Tajudeen is assuming he is saying when he, Ian, is not saying that at all. As for me, I think I'm just beginning to space out. When Gerald points out Sunderland's version of your typical, high-steepled white New

63
•

England church, I have a vision: I say to him that the church's steeple looks like a Klansman's hood and then begin seeing KKK filing out of the church with burning crosses. Home again, home again.

During soundcheck a brother named Fred introduces himself. Tells me he's interested in talking to the band about their religious concepts. We go on for some time.

From there Fred and I get to talking about a whole lotta shit. Like freedom of the soul. I tell him about seeing bloods resist the magic of juju music in Boston for fear of what it might make them do. After which he tells me an interesting little story about when he was going to SUNY and belonged to a Black Unity house named Shango, after the Yoruba God of Thunder. One night Shango's undergrads went to hear Pharoah Sanders. The music got so intense Fred wanted to get up and scream. But he didn't because he was afraid the other black people would say he wasn't being cool, that he was acting like a white boy. That night the music got so intense that the white boys did get up and start screaming. And when Fred and the folks went back to Shango the brothers got to cracking on these wild-acting whiteys. So Fred told them he felt like screaming too. And they said, "So you wanted to get up and act like a white boy, huh?" Thus spake the sons of Shango.

64
•

But as we talk about black Americans and their self-repression and psychic armor, Fred remembers something he once heard Archie Shepp say in a class: white people, said Shepp, are becoming more like black people and black people more like white people every day. Hearing that makes me go off.

"Man, you tell Shepp next time you see him I said why don't he just speak for himself because the black folk over here closest to what Sunny and them are about are the mass of black folk Sunny and them ain't even gonna see on this tour. What they got in common is spontaneity and a capacity for spontaneous resistance, spontaneous love, spontaneous violence even, and if these black folk out here *talking* about revolution want to connect with the masses then they better plug into the funk because that's where the heart and soul and energy is and the joy, you dig? And if you black in this country you can't let nothing deny you that release because the music is all you got, because that's the only place you can go to be everything you are in this society, you know?" Or something like that.

After the show in Sunderland I meet a brother named Carl who's a DJ at U. Mass. So I ask him how many black students attend the university and he tells me roughly 400. So where, I ask him, are they tonight? "Oh, man," he says, "they don't know nothing about this. Shit, they ain't even heard the blues yet."

A minute or so after Sunny and the band leave the stage, after what turns out to be a great show, someone drops Stevie's *Songs in the Key of Life* on the system. And a few of the African Beats dance around the room to that neo-African beat. Then we pack up and walk out into the worst snowstorm New England has seen all winter.

Clickety-clack, clickety-clack, won't somebody please bring the spirit back

—Rahsaan Roland Kirk

The bus is tobogganing down I-90. We're halfway between New Haven and Rochester. It's dark outside and except for the light over my seat, it's dark inside too. I feel very alien here. I am very alien here. Because as warm as these brothers are to me in English they know each other in a human tongue unknown to my ears. And as I'm hearing soft-shelled pellets of Yoruba go off around me on the bus I feel like I'm in the jungle undergoing tracer fire.

The bonds between us are sometimes imagined, sometimes real, often confused. For example, Mofes, the drummer, looks like Elvin Jones to me. And when we talk he tells me he's played with James Brown and, once, with Louis Armstrong in Lagos. But when I ask him why do so many Nigerians love country music while many black Americans don't care for it at all, he replies, "That's because we're brothers," thinking I said we *do* like country. I don't restate the question though, because to my mind he's answered the only question that really matters.

The cultural differences between Afro-Americans and Africans can make us seem worlds apart to each other. They can also make the connections between us take a strange turn or two. To give an example: one day Garry, the band's press agent, asks me do I have any country music among my many cassettes. So I half-joke with him, like black Americans don't listen to country music because it reminds them of the Klan. Demola walks into the room and tells us he's just seen a program about the Klan on TV, but not enough of it to understand what the Klan is really all about. So I break it down for him. Then Garry asks me a few questions just to make sure he's got this thing straight.

"This Klan, is it a racist organization?"

"Very."

"White?"

"Very."

"You know if I see one of them I will kill him."

Now, we're singing the same song, brother.

On the way to Rochester Mofes puts on some music from back home. Nothing like the balm of Sunny's music, this song comes at me as the most cryptic, discordant, and unnerving sound I've ever heard in my life. The drums seem to be preparing for war, the voices for a party, and the African violin has the mournful bliss of John Coltrane's tone on the LP he did with Johnny Hartman. After a week in serious white man's country like New England with 22 Yoruba, two Brits, two Frenchies, and a Newark homeboy, I can't deal with it. Seeking shelter, I shroud myself in my Walkman. Only the music I use for cover isn't funk, reggae, Van Halen, or Hendrix, but the World Saxophone Quartet's new doo *Revue*.

As much time as I've already spent listening to it, I've never heard things in it like I do now. *Revue* is knee-deep in the blues. This is, excuse my French, some avant-garde shit you could play for your mama. But *Revue* doesn't just resonate with blue notes— it makes reference to a whole spectrum of blues modalities. Especially on the B side where Ray Charles, Ellington, Mingus, and the spirituals haunt the writing. David Murray conjures up visions of cutthroat Chicago saxophonists like Lockjaw and Jug taunting Tin Pan Alley with a switchblade and Hemphill swirls through the urban threat of Bluiett's bottom with the finesse of Kareem, Magic, or the Doctor making ghosts of three-man guards. The mack Bluiett puts on "Ming" beckons Duke's "Come Sunday," while Lake's wailing soprano finds cries hushed in cottonfields, the masks of black people's amazing grace in captivity.

Hearing the reverberations in this music of every style we've ever cut to keep from being beat back I also hear what Robert Farris Thompson said about Yoruba, Jews, and Anglo-Saxons. He was also talking about any Afro-American who knows the meaning of the blues. Bebop. Free jazz. Black rock.

I come from kings and queens too, only mine have patrilineal scars you cannot see, but have to hear. They have names like Howling and Muddy, Bukka and Blind, Leadbelly, Lightning, Big Mama and Bessie, Papa Joe and Mississippi Fred, Callie, Grinner, Queen and Tate, Uncle Will and George, Charles, Florence. Mama listen:

Bird flew Miles to Trane who Jimi'd the Mothership exit/ us exodus movement of Jah people to juju music blues dance raid/ revue don't say the baby isn't yours Michael row the boat ashore/ else the message will get stuck in that little red corvette. Nobody can be you but you urban bushmen of human feelings in the garden again/ this generation shall crawl out from under the junkyard of American pop culture and slip into the darkness/ remembering more than the last commercial shedding Cameosis/style psychosis to become/ the vibration society their world is doomed with our unification/ Chinara spat out the waste and walked upon the new day/ may God receive Ja red's wombman.

When the bus pulls into this Howard Johnson's halfway between here and there I look into the glass darkly separating me from Gerald and my face becomes a nest of dreads. When I step off the bus into the cold whitenight stillness, my sense of time has slowed down to a creeping drift. I feel like I'm walking on water. My sense of vision is cinematic and animistic. My eyes no longer just see but now pan, zoom, cut, and frame. And to everything with color, form, and a function there is a persona and a soul.

When I walk around the front of the Howard Johnson's I find a one-way sign pointing north and it says to me this way is past. A Sunoco pole is making light of the sun 50 feet away and it says this is the way things are now. Looking up, the sky is split as if

a V-2 had come screaming from the heavens to declare a change
is gonna come.

When I walk into the Howard Johnson's and sit down to break
bread with Sammy and Sunny while they speak in Yoruba tongue,
I don't know what the fuck they're talking about but feel very much
at home with myself and then some.

—1983

The Electric Miles

Part 1

68
•
Before we begin, look: exhaustive essays on Miles Davis usually
bore me to no end too. Mainly because like many other Miles
freaks, I've got a few theories of my own—theories so inspired by
devotion as to border on church dogma, theories so anxiously air-
tight they favor choking off dissension from within the ranks, theories so conceived in arrogance all some other critical bozo will
receive for repeating them is my Olympian nod of approval. Like
religious passion, musical hero worship has often been known to
induce such high hysteria—and on the subject of especially Miles's
electric music, I won't deny raising the spectre of Cain over a few
of my brother critics' heads. Not that I'm alone in this: ask some
of the M.F.'s I know (*Miles Freaks*, okay?) what they think of the
three bios out on my man, and they'll tell you, dem's fighting words
jack!

Given the gauntlet before me, I'll explain upfront why I'm throwing my two cents into this ring. The first reason is *down beat* asked

me to put my head on the chopping block. The second is that I've got a few axes to grind. Because to my mind the music Miles made between 1969 and now demands revisionist history, and no writer in my reading has made sense out of its revolutionary aesthetics or adequately appreciated its visionary beauty. Nor have many, if any, of Miles's critics shown enough background in black pop to place his electric music within the cultural context which spawned it. Moreover, when it comes to his last mid-'70s band, I don't think many of my, uh, esteemed colleagues could make heads or tails of *Agharta* or dig it in reference to Funkadelic and a punk revolution that was just around the corner. And don't let me get started on how none of them realized Miles's lead axe of the period, Pete Cosey, is the Cecil Taylor of the guitar (just hold on to that catchy bit of hype for later), or how they slept through the fact that Miles presaged current directions in modern pop and "classical" forms, or how deviously he revamped his own past and black music's avant-garde through the use of electronics.

Besides feeding all that grist through the critical mill, what we're about to do here is explain the continuity between electric and acoustic Miles, and then beyond that, make a case for his much-disparaged *Agharta* as the work of a genius not in decline, but in ferocious forward motion, on fertile ground.

In his 1967 essay "The Changing Same (R&B and New Black Music)" Amiri Baraka (LeRoi Jones) prophesied a black music unity which would be "Jazz and blues, religious and secular . . . New Thing and rhythm and blues." Seven years after its release, Miles's *Agharta* remains the closest anyone has yet come to seeing Baraka's prophecy of black populist modernism made manifesto. And the evolutionary process through which Miles will come to deliver this Unity Music sermon from the mount begins not with *Bitches Brew*, but with the 1966 release of *Miles Smiles*. On that LP Ron Carter and Tony Williams so radically transform—indeed, so radically *subvert*—the role of bass and drums in improvised music as to make the solo skeins of Miles, Wayne Shorter, and Herbie Hancock come off like a tightwire act run through a rain forest: adventuresome perhaps, but given the setting more a quixotic excursion than one undertaken by musicians in full command of their senses.

Operating in telepathic and telekinetic union, Carter and Williams mutate the LP's uptempo song forms into mazes where the bassist's line, pulse, and meter shifts and Tony's symphonic drum rituals impose syllogisms which dictate rather than follow the soloist's logic. Confronted by these puzzling equations, Miles, Wayne, and Herbie respond with linear, if contorted, harmonic suspensions—superbly balanced ones which don't play off the Carter/Williams axis so much as they cut across and through it. In a way, their brainy bypass surgery reminds you of the two-dimensional floorplans astrophysicists make up to map three-dimensional space. Because when there's no fixed center of gravity, space warps and curves like crazy, and when there's no set groove, what Carter and Williams lay down can't really be navigated, but at best only graphed, like space-time.

The impact of Carter and Williams's relativity theorems on Miles's music was instantly felt in the band's next two releases, *Sorcerer* and *Nefertiti*. These LPs, however, bear the stamp of not only the Einstein and Heisenberg of bass and drums, but Ornette Coleman as well. Jumping ahead a bit and taking the physics metaphor a quantum leap further, we can say that these two poles of attraction made Miles's polite chamber jazz world collapse, implode, then expand towards infinity from the inside (or as Wayne Shorter once put it, ". . . from the soul on out to the universe"). To be more musically specific about these transformations is to say this: the difference between the music on *Miles Smiles* and the two subsequent dates is that on the latter the melodies function more like elliptical motifs than like heads made to kick off a string of solos. On *Sorcerer* and *Nefertiti* melodic interpretation as much as harmonic improvisation is the rule—with the melodies continually being recycled into the improvs as structural devices. These lend symmetry and shape to the moody mise-en-scene which unfolds on both records, phrase by eerily lyrical phrase. Once again Carter and Williams play a game of disorderly conduct by design. Only wise to their antics now, the soloists don't compete. Instead they open up expansive passages which possess the thematic resolve of the melodies at every turn. And inasmuch as this music makes freedom, composition, chaos, and lyricism coexist in a collective improvisational organism—well, given all that, it refers us back to Ornette, whose music not only influenced Miles's direction in this regard but also, I believe, inspired the odd-man-out lines in Wayne Shorter's writing and playing. Coleman and Lester Young have been overlooked as influences on Shorter, though all three's strange phrasing is alike in seeming alienated, innocent, and knowing at the same time. Miles's is too, but then I've always had this other theory that the two musicians most responsible for Miles's style were Prez and Lady Day, especially on ballads.

As amazing as the level of playing and writing in the quintet was, equally so was the way in which each member's conception gave itself over to the fabric of the music. Ron Carter, for example, brought a rhythmic feeling which throbbed like the human pulse rather than just grooved you to death. And by working it into his extraordinary harmonic technique, made free improvisation sound as cyclical as eight-to-the-bar. Shorter's writing gave the band an intellectual persona equal parts rational, mystical, and romantic, while his playing provided crazed models of mathematic concision. Whether comping or improvising, Hancock gave the music orchestral breadth, and Tony's drumming, a force of nature unto itself, came across like a cross between a hurricane, a forest fire, and a cast of thousands conducted by somebody like Ellington, Disney, De Mille, Rostropovich, or hey, Tony Williams himself.

As an arranger and leader, what Miles did in making this cabal of artful astrophysicists cohere is create a context where the sublime funk of *Kind of Blue* and the firepower of *Milestones* could be fused, accelerated, and then fissioned across four years and now nine albums—records whose breadth of texture, mood, and composition remain unparalleled in small band jazz. As a trumpeter, Miles made the band focus on how much emotional energy could be compressed, expressed, and released through pure tonality and imaginative phrasing. Like Lester Young's, Miles's solos have come to possess a quality of the inevitable, almost as if their beginnings contained their middles and ends. And as Miles's playing has assumed this capacity, so too has his way of organizing a band into a cellular organism. In all of Miles's bands since the one Trane fell into, the parts have come to sum up the whole, as the players became the tunes and the tunes then became absorbed into the ensemble's communal sound. As Ellington achieved with orches-

71

tras, Miles has done with smaller units: turned them into palettes which somehow work for him more like the democratic process than like pigments did for Picasso. Though for all of that, his charisma has also made each band seem like the product of his genius alone.

This enigmatic quality isn't of course Miles's and Duke's alone, since all the great jazz leaders have had it, as have the *baad*est urban bluesmen—like Howlin' Wolf, Muddy Waters, and Chuck Berry—and the major black pop innovators as well: Berry Gordy, James Brown, Sly Stone, Jimi Hendrix, Stevie Wonder, Marvin Gaye, George Clinton, Maurice White, and Bob Marley. Now, speculation as to why Miles stepped out of a black musical universe where Ellington to the nth degree was the directive into a parallel one where funk was its own reward has assumed motives on Miles's part that are racial, social, sexual, psychological, economic, and even musical. I think all probably apply, though only when understood as integral to the music rather than as proof of the music's supposed lack of integrity. Because to a brilliant hustler like Miles, all games are the same, everything is related, nothing is really left to chance, and like a good offensive runner, he knows how to cover his ass and when to take orders from the sidelines, if not, in fact, from his accountant.

72 • On the purely musical side however, I think Miles left post-bop modernism for the funk because he was bored fiddling with quantum mechanics and just wanted to play the blues again. The blues impulse is charismatic because of its sexual energies, but as a ritual process, as a rite of passage, the blues are alluring because they make the act of confession a means of publicly redeeming your soul, as Mass does for Catholics and as speaking in tongues does for those in the holy-roller church. As an art form the blues are seductive because they give soulfulness and simplicity the same constructivist value harmonic complexity has in European symphonic music and bebop. This is what makes the blues the most difficult black music to perform convincingly, because not only do you have to convert its cliches into your own style, but you've also got to mean every note since the only thing more tired than some tired blues is some fake funk—and that's because when you come looking for the Holy Ghost and find nothing but some lame hyp-

ocrites thumping on a back-beat in the name of The One, well, your soul it do get weary. Leading us to reconsider Bootsy Collins's axiom: "Fake the funk and your nose got to grow" (see "The Pinocchio Theory"). Proof that Miles's funk wasn't fake, wasn't just the fetish work of a clone, is in the fact that all the real funkateers I know dig Miles as much as they do some P-Funk, and that's because the feeling in Miles's funk is just as for real while the schizzy musical fusions are maybe twice as surreal.

What Miles heard in the musics of P-Funk progenitors, James Brown, Jimi Hendrix, and Sly Stone, was the blues impulse transferred, masked, and retooled for the Space Age through a low-down act of *possession*. And in them all he probably recognized pieces of himself. Like James Brown he was a consummate bandleader who knew his way around the boxing ring, like Sly he was a bourgeois boy who opted to become a street fighting man, and like Jimi he was a musician whose physical grace seemed to declare itself in every bent note and sensual slur. Visual evidence of Sly's and Jimi's impact on Miles can be seen in the dress styles he adapted from them: the multiple-hued fabrics and talismanic flow of attire. Now, I could try to be all cool and academic like only music is what matters here, but that would be about some bushwah. Because when you're out to unravel a legend, study of myth *and* material is inescapable, the two having assumed like proportions over time. And what any longtime Miles freak will tell you is that for every Miles Davis album, there's a crapload of Miles Davis anecdotes equally astonishing to the average human mind. And when Miles began exploring Sly's and Jimi's musical frontiers he also, so the stories go, made his way through a few human mine fields they'd cut across before him. So that we don't, however, degenerate into rank gossip here, we'll keep the discussion pretty much musicological—though with the understanding that when myth intervenes, we'll lay that sucker into it too.

With *Bitches Brew* Miles crossed over the threshold of bebop into Sly's and Jimi's stereovision New Jerusalems. While the music on *Miles in the Sky, Filles de Kilimanjaro*, and *In a Silent Way* marks his progressive march to the brink, it also depicts, in retrospect, how cautiously the move was being made. In fact, for my money, the least interesting things about those LPs are their overt pop borrowings. *Miles in the Sky* haunts for how it extends upon the elliptical heads concept; *Kilimanjaro* is provocative for how much *static* tension Miles generates using James Brown riffs, for Tony Williams's ambient drumming, and for how the voicings on "Tout de Suite" spookily predict Herbie Hancock's Mwandishi band. (If you ever want to experience musical deja vu, play "Tout de Suite" back-to-back with "Water Torture" from Hancock's *Crossings*, then hear that against the third and fourth sides of *Agharta*—curiouser and curiouser.) As for *In a Silent Way*, it just may be the epitome of the beautifully designed and recorded artifact, being something like a Taj Mahal of music: that rare, manmade thing of beauty which rivals nature in its fixed and dreamlike universal perfection.

The difference between these records and *Bitches Brew* is the difference between Alex Haley's *Roots* and the novels of Gabriel García Márquez. Where Haley prosaically told a people's hellish collective history and redemption, Márquez through more poetic language uses history as a means into his folk's collective unconscious, that Jungian hideaway where the spooks really sit beside the doors to the kingdoms of heaven and hell. Where J.B. and especially Jimi and Sly took music isn't something that can be summed up in a few quotidian riffs any more than a Márquez novel can be experienced through synopses. It's at once a thought process, a textural language, and a way of reordering tradition and myth unto itself. On evidence of *Bitches Brew* and the music thereafter, Miles seems to have believed that to go as out there as them he would first have to lose some ego and enter their worlds not as a master but as a disciple. And in time as he became a master of their language, he would affirm Jung's observation that in ritual sacrifice, the sacrificer gives of himself to become one with the sacrificee.

On musical terms though, *Bitches Brew* is an orchestral marvel because it fuses James Brown's antiphonal riffing against a metaphoric bass drone with Sly's minimalist polyrhythmic melodies and Jimi's concept of painting pictures with ordered successions of electronic sounds. *Bitches Brew* can also be heard as a devilishly Milesish takeoff on John Coltrane's spiritual energy music and that music's saxophone, percussion, and bass batteries, modal improvs, tone clusters, and cosmic yearnings, thus making the double-set rank as an act of comic blasphemy with Richard Pryor's Preacher routines or with certain African genesis myths in playing prankster with God's tongue by dragging the heavens back into the province of the vernacular—namely the streets—and the language of the streets, the dozens, sermons made scatologies which find their musical parallel in what funk did to gospel. The streets though aren't just a funky run of avenues where mom-and-pop stores front for numbers runners and storefront churches pimp for jackleg preachers. They're also a place of mystery and romance, and given that Miles knows them and their music inside out, it's not surprising that the melodies on *Bitches Brew* croon, sway, and reveal themselves like those of such balladeers as Smokey Robinson, Marvin Gaye, Curtis Mayfield, and Stevie Wonder—all of whose gorgeous melodies and harmonies have yet to overcome the precious corn of Tin Pan Alley in the ears of other improvising composers— excepting Zawinul, Cecil Taylor, and Bennie Maupin, whose overlooked *The Jewel in the Lotus* ranks beside Miles's *Great Expectations*, Weather Report's *Mysterious Traveller*, and Cecil's *Solo* in channeling the charm of exotic musics into forms which are as tightly knit, free-flowing, and fetchsome as Stevie's, Smokey's, Curtis's, and Marvin's vocal arrangements.

In 1970 Miles recorded two live dates, *Black Beauty—Miles Davis at Fillmore West* and *Miles Davis at Fillmore East*. I've never cared for the latter because two bands are fighting for control on it: Miles's and Circle, the collective Chick Corea and Dave Holland formed with Anthony Braxton and Barry Altschul when they left Miles. In this battle of the bicameral bands, Miles's night-trippers dig into blues and ballads like they were victims for slaughter; the Holland/Corea twins meanwhile run away from the murder site to throw temper tantrums which are quite gonzo given the context, but lacking in the anthemic-cathartic qualities of say, Trane.

Black Beauty is another story altogether, debuting a 19-year-old bassist named Michael Henderson, who brings with him lessons learned from Motown's legendary James Jamerson and from maybe a few listenings to Ron Carter and Buster Williams besides. As far as focus and intensity, the performances of Zawinul's "Directions" and Shorter's "Masquelero," which open and close the double-set, get the prize hands down—primarily for the brassy blur of blips Miles phrases in implosive runs akin to Hendrix's experiments with backlooped guitar, and for Corea's explosive solos, which come about as close as anybody ever will to cutting Cecil Taylor and McCoy Tyner on Rhodes electric piano.

On evidence of the music that Miles released following *Bitches Brew*, it's clear he was out to create not only a new trumpet voice, but also a new improvisational process—one which would enable his electric band to make music equal, on its own terms, to the music of the quintet. What he discovered, however, as he progressed further into electronics, was that those terms would first compel him to overturn his prior aesthetic sensibilities, and to enter into a zone of musical creation as topsy-turvy as the world of subatomic physics—which is to say, one governed by laws as seemingly random as those of material reality seem fixed and eternally observable.

Part 2

Discussed in Part 1 of this essay was how Ron Carter and Tony Williams proposed a quantum model of the bebop universe—one wherein freedom and structure became wedlocked to the improvisational/compositional urge underlying all jazz. As in the labyrinthine narratives of Jorge Luis Borges, this seeming chaos of order and precision had a character half-polymath and half-mad, one part whimsical in nature, one part obsessive about functional design. From the resultant music we can deduce Miles gained insights from Carter and Williams into the ways in which jazz could be disintegrated and rearranged without having ever seemed to change face. What funk and black rock brought to Miles's speculations isn't unlike what considerations of gravity bring into speculations about four-dimensional space-time—namely a feeling for how the earthly parts of our being impact upon our perceptions of the cosmos, spacially and temporally. And similarly to modern physicists, Miles found in embarking upon his electric journey the relativity of his quantum experiments to the everyday ebb and flow of Afro-American popular culture.

Though the soundtrack *Jack Johnson* was recorded before either Fillmore date, it stands as the culmination of everything Miles had been reaching for since *Filles de Kilimanjaro*. A masterpiece, a landmark, a signpost, and a synopsis, the record sums up the first leg of Miles's electric reincarnation. What makes it a masterpiece is no less Miles's constructivist trumpet bursts than Michael Henderson's extraordinary bass playing on "Right Off," where Henderson's lines function as both an anchor and a flow chart, giving the music mucho cool, bottom, and movement. This performance can be heard as either 20-or-more minutes of imaginative grooving, or as 20-or-more metamorphic and metalogical minutes of extremely composed bass improvisation. In terms of instrumental prowess, it is rivaled only by mentor James Jamerson's work on Marvin Gaye's *What's Going On*, Boogie Mosson and Bootsy's more condensed rides with P-Funk, and Marcus Miller's throwdown on "Fat Time" from *The Man with the Horn*. Two models besides Jamerson which Henderson might have used were Carter (behind the infinity patterns on "Madness" from *Nefertiti*) and Buster Williams (check the fluid undergirding he gives Hancock's aqua-velvet arrangements on *The Prisoner*).

Jack Johnson is a signpost because it's a prelude to every major act of fusion in the '70s; on "Right Off" we hear where Zawinul learned to weave funk and bop into an organic continuum, hear John McLaughlin wail with Billy Cobham bashing away behind him, and hear Herbie Hancock break down on electric keyboards like solo and rhythm parts were one and the same. On "Yesternow"—whose creepy bass part is ripped right off of James Brown's "Say It Loud, I'm Black and I'm Proud"—we not only get a taste of Miles's direction from here on out, but can catch wind of Return to Forever and the harmolodic funk of Ornette Coleman and James Blood Ulmer (dig the overlays of polytonal thematicism against pulse). Besides all this prophetic stuff however, *Jack Johnson* is a bitch because of Miles's brilliant use of space and swinging single notes, and for the funked-up rhythms and passing chords he provokes McLaughlin into. (Their dialog here goes beyond call-and-response into formulating a communications system as complex as the Yoruba people's talking drums.)

Following *Jack Johnson* came *Live-Evil*, which tracks like a gonzo invasion of the ghetto by technically advanced booty snatchers from a parallel universe. This music finds counterpart only in the mutant funk rites George Clinton was taking to the stage around the same time—though I'll give Frank Zappa and Captain Beefheart their propers for wallowing in similar sties on the other side of the tracks. Listening to this music is like listening to a "History of the Blues" as told by Richard Pryor, George Romero, and Sun Ra. In it wretched excess is the norm, sinister-but-sarcastic sums up the tone, and blues riffs are continually being splattered like blood bags and revived as cartoon zombie figures. The trick about the music is that its textures rather than musicianship make it sound like garbage, like maggot-brained cosmic slop or, if you will, like cosmic debris (to cross-reference a funka-zappic tune or two). Because of this, to truly love the music you have to want in on this filthy mess as a way of life. I favor Clinton's and Miles's worlds over Zappa's and Beefheart's because Don and Frank run romper runs by dictatorship whereas Miles and Uncle Jam are more like groundskeepers at insane asylums for black *and* white radicals. Leading us back to the notion of genius through democracy rather than fascism, Miles took this principle even further than George, however, by nailing "The One" through collective subversion rather than perverse collective arrangements.

In this sense *Live-Evil* is also a riotous avant garde revival of New Orleans polyphony like the Art Ensemble of Chicago, using the blues to speak in tongues ancient and to the future. Besides, what Gary Bartz's sax does with Ornette and Shorter is all-out funk personified; what McLaughlin does to the blues and ragas is mondo pervo; Jack DeJohnette suspends backbeats in a levitation act like Houdini wouldn't believe; Keith Jarrett comps with Worrellian weirdness; Henderson's bass lines are as absurd as the adventures of Plastic Man; and Airto is a hoot. As for Miles, nobody outside of Hendrix and Jeff Beck has ever played a more hilarious wah-wah pedal.

Between bands in 1972, Miles conjured up a session which took its cues from Sly's *There's a Riot Goin' On*, Stockhausen's *Tele-*

musik/Mixtur date, and once again, The Streets (though this time we're talking the streets of the world). In *On the Corner* Sly's *Riot* vocalese turns up in Miles's raspy, guttural trumpet (only as Sly's singing sounds like Miles talks; who's influencing whom I wonder?). Sly's synaptic minimalism figures heavy in the big-band-converts-into-drum choir arrangements (only you get hints of this hookup in "Sivad" on *Live-Evil*, too, and Stockhausen's theories on random, mixed, and reprocessed sounds are a presence in "Gemini/Double Image," where two contrite melodies cross each other for a show-down on a sci-fi set). But from Ian Carr's new bio we learn Miles got excited over the *Telemusik/Mixtur* work because of how distortion converted acoustic sounds into electronic colors. Miles subverted this process to transform African, Indian, and funk rhythms into a One-World Festival. Anybody who thinks Talking Heads came up with anything new in terms of synthcraft and uncanny rhythm mixes on *Remain in Light* better check this one out, not to mention Bernie Worrell, Junie Morrison, Stevie Wonder, Edwin Birdsong, Leon Sylvers, and Greg Phillinganes—to name a few bloods overlooked in the race to crown Byrne and Eno the Kings of electric swing (Paul Whiteman and Benny Goodman, look alive).

Except for Miles's incendiary improvs, 1973's *In Concert* is little more than a sad rehearsal date put out for public consumption. The album which followed—*Get Up with It*—though is notable for three reasons: the protopunk "Rated X" which lays the groundwork for *Agharta*, and two 30-minute-plus works, "He Loved Him Madly," a wake held in honor of Ellington, and "Calypso Frelimo," a "dub fugue" in honor of the freedom fighters who liberated Mozambique from Portuguese oppression. The Ellington funeral is ambient music for the hereafter. Its colors, moods, and textures derive from Tibet, India, Micronesia, and Memphis. The three guitars favor sitars and soul band strokes; Miles's organ smears remind one of Tibetan harmonium voicings, while Henderson's bass sinks to lows as gut-plummeting as those in gamelan music. Across this aural sarcophagus Miles's horn sobs and hobbles like a bereaved widow in a shroud. Beyond mourning Duke, the piece seems to suffer more from wanting to join him in the afterlife.

"Calypso Frelimo" is a fugue because it is orchestrated with antiphonal coordination through its 32-minute thematic evolution.

It is dub because, as in that Jamaican craft, musical ideas are restructured by their echoes, or if you will, by shadows of former selves. The work is also a suite in three movements: allegro, adagio, and allegro non troppo. As in reggae, the tonal center is a single bass drone, though in the adagio section, Henderson's suspenseful line variations and declensions dramatize the polytonal modulations of organist Miles and guitarists Pete Cosey and Reggie Lucas.

Cosey's staccato guitar simultaneously functions like a second set of congas to Mtume's, a second rush of cymbals to Al Foster's, a second steel drum simulacrum to Miles's Gnostic organ, a second rhythm guitar to Lucas's, and as one of three solo voices. In effect, the ensemble music isn't dissimilar to that of Sunny Adé or Steve Reich—especially in terms of its conversion of multiple melodies into polyrhythms and subtly swelling formal metamorphoses. Where Miles's work goes beyond theirs is in having his trumpet and Cosey's guitar *improvise* a swinging infinity of new colors, lines, lyrically percussive phrasings, and needlepoint-by-laser stitchings out of the given melody. The singularly transcendent thing about jazz is that it allows one human being's voice the right to assume universal proportions through self-expression in a collective framework. And because Cosey and Miles can continually solo, and enhance rather than rupture the communal fabric of the calypso, they celebrate jazz as a way of life and as an aesthetic model for the human community.

Where these principles take on their highest form of expression outside of Miles is in the music of Ornette Coleman's Prime Time and the Art Ensemble of Chicago. Where Miles goes beyond them on *Dark Magus*, *Pangaea*, and *Agharta* is in having an entire band of improvising composers onstage creating a pan-ethnic web of avant garde music locked as dead in the pocket as P-Funk. Heard in its 100-minute entirety, 1974's *Dark Magus* tracks as a surrealist collage of the crossroads where African rites and urban Afro-American means converge. In this it resembles the work of black artists Romare Bearden, Bettye Saar, and David Hammons, and poet Jayne Cortez. In the music we hear a patchwork assemblage of guitar and saxophone multiphonics riff over a logjam of percussion until squelched by more Gnostic organ and inaudible hand signals from Miles. What keeps this frenzied jungle boogie in sync are the systolic bass vamps of Henderson, who by this time had assumed as dominant a role in the band as the bass had in black pop, thanks to Larry Graham. Miles's horn work here is the finalized fusion of Stockhausen and Sly, scribbling blurbs of feline, funky sound which under scrutiny take on graphic shapes as wild and willed as New York subway graffiti. On *Dark Magus* Cosey's guitar leads are a cross between Miles, backlooped Hendrix, and Trane's sheets-of-sound. On *Pangaea* and *Agharta* his lines sizzle into exotic scales distorted to run subterranean channels while orderly tracking to thematic resolution.

Like Miles and Cecil Taylor, Cosey is a constructivist whose improvs affirm fellow architectonic-anarchist Taylor's belief that music from a man's innards will systematize that gut-bucket spillage on its own terms. For Cosey those terms derive from years studying the guitar systems of the country bluesmen, and from applying the microtonal intervals of sitars and koras to electric guitar. (In conversation recently, Cosey told me he has "32 systems for tuning the instrument," meaning Glenn Branca can sit down and Robert Fripp has got a lot of scales to go.) Cosey's improvs extend upon the orchestral guitar techniques of Hendrix by likewise moving successive waves of harmonic distortion (that's *noise* to you, mom) which have the logic and density of symphonies and the filth of the blues. Where his vast scalar armament takes him beyond Hendrix is in the elongation of microtonal scales into multidirectional hooks and tentacles of curvaceous, screeching sound. What's even more amazing is that he makes these monstrous creations swing like a Basie band arrangement or a tenor solo by some of his former employers named Sonny Stitt and Gene Ammons. For what it's worth, protopunk axemaniac Robert Quine claims Cosey as an influence, and hearing *Agharta*, *Dark Magus*, and *Pangaea* will make you think Keith Levene, Andy Gill, Adrian Belew, and Robert Fripp oughta own up too. Besides Hendrix, the only music which comes close to his in terms of all-out heavy metal furor and invention is the Sex Pistols' *Never Mind the Bollocks*, hardcore punk's Bad Brains, and what Eddie Hazel roared out of the gate with on Funkadelic's "Super Stupid" in 1971.

While Cosey and promethean firebreather Sonny Fortune dominate *Agharta* and *Pangaea* as soloists, these LPs are also magnificent ensemble works. Because by 1975 Miles, through his decades-old practice of paying cats to practice on the bandstand, had created the world's first fully improvisational acid-funk band— by which I mean one capable of extemporaneously orchestrating motifs from Santana, Funkadelic, Sly, Stockhausen, Africa, India, and the Ohio Players (check how their 1974 hit "Fire" gets revamped on *Agharta*'s first side). The band's cohesion amidst sonic chaos knows no parallel in fusion, funk, rock, or either the black or white avant garde. And while others may have achieved similar ends since, these furthermuckers (sic) were making it up night after night on the road, making new music every time they hit like they'd been possessed by whatever god or demon demands that black musicians push themselves all the way out there and then some. In the final analysis, this is music in the spirit of jazz to me, r&b, New Music, and by way of abstraction, even the gospel truth.

Before we end I'll admit to being unable to take Miles's comeback seriously. Not that I'm alone in this mind you: I don't think Miles does either. And more than anything, what the release of his new LP *Star People* has convinced me of is that The Return of Miles Davis has to be understood as one of the goofiest promotional campaigns in the history of hype, to be understood at all. This isn't to say Miles hasn't occasionally pulled off some miraculous music since we've been graced by his presence again. It is to say, however, that when you take a good look at his new packaging imagery . . . well, you can't say it doesn't do Madison Avenue proud. Figure it as a movie treatment and the scenario would run something like so: alleged to be drug-ridden, debilitated, and dying of cancer, jazz's legendary Prince of Darkness returns from a six-year sabbatical to triumphantly reveal functional chops and heroic recovery from a painful joint operation. His first act is to release an album sporting the title *The Man with the Horn* (just like it was some 1950s film noir flick) and fronting slick cover art that wouldn't be out of place as a *Vogue* cologne advertisement. Next comes marriage to a famous actress, surprisingly cordial and candid interviews in *Ebony* and *People*, followed by pictures in *Jet* that depict the brooding black brujo laughing and shaking hands with fans and tuxedoed-*down* at bourgeois black affairs where Our Hero almost looks like he was born up in there (which he was, remember). Months later comes the concert tour album, *We Want Miles*, a title which in the best Madison Avenue tradition sought to create demand for a commodity by trying to convince the public they were dying to have it in the first place. Now comes *Star People*, an LP of simple blues variations containing cartoon aesthetic artwork by Miles and liner notes wherein the maestro explains his music to Leonard Feather, then defines his contributions to modern art thusly: "All Drawings, Color Concepts and Basic Attitudes by Miles Davis." Is he kidding us or what? Hard to tell with a man who admits, as he did to Cheryl Hall, that he's always been a big ham at heart. Nevertheless, for all the ribbing Miles definitely seems a happier, healthier human being than ever before, and I'm glad. Up to a point. Which is to say that when it comes to Miles's new band and new music, my ambivalence toward the situation tends toward the critical side.

That said I'll in fact force my hand here and say that to these ears, Miles's new band is the first one to ever become progressively *less* interesting to listen to as time marches on. And for my money the most profoundly musical moments I've had with Dewey's new crew are to be found on *The Man with the Horn*, while the most banal are on *Star People*. For sheer structural complexity nothing Miles has done since matches "Fat Time" on *The Man with the Horn*—a lean blues march featuring extraordinary bass from Marcus Miller, whose supple line variations and asymmetrical turnarounds supply enough power and imagination to deserve credit as a solo show of force alongside the killer guitar work of Mike Stern, guitar made all the more stirring in its movements by Miller's telepathic shadowing, shading, and undergirding of them. Nor when you talk about gut-bucket funk has any other of Miles's new music come close to matching "Backseat Betty," where again Miller's rump-rolling funk grinds can be heard to spur Miles to some of the sexiest, tenderest trumpet work of his career as a funkateer. And on "Aida," the bassist's sproingy ricochet shots and declensions provoke Miles to heraldic scalar peaks and daring intervallic

83

leaps, revealing the trumpeter at the top of his form rather than trying to regain it.

Seeing Miles at Avery Fisher for his New York premiere in 1981, I was struck by how restrained Miller seemed while Stern and hornman Bill Evans were given ample noodling space. Stern is a guitarist of sure power but limited imagination, and while by his own admission he's more a bebopper than a rocker, hearing him in behind, say, Cosey, Fripp, Belew, and Eddie Hazel is a somewhat atavistic experience. Evans is a player of gorgeous tonality and rigorous logic, but somehow he just never catches fire. With Miller kept under wraps, the backbone of Miles's new band is, of course, drummer Al Foster, whose driving downbeats and crisscross fills whirl up a polyrhythmic firestorm that at least maintains an illusion of power behind this band. Though, again, after hearing the Cosey/Henderson-fronted unit, this group's funk comes off like so much staid hackwork, while its oblations to 4/4 seem calculated to satisfy Miles's old crowd as the funk pulls in a new one.

Now, what I've come to love about *Star People* is that it doesn't sound like Miles wants this band to become capable of anything but playing a simple blues. And while seeing Miles in concert recently made me think he was trying to reconstruct his mystique out of thin air, *Star People* reveals him capable of delightful self-parody. Like Picasso when he ran out of ideas, Miles has taken to enjoying poking a little fun at himself. So that on *Star People* we hear the innovator of modern music make a big to-do out of playing muted blues cliches over funk vamps that were old in 1970, hear him riotously romp through a cornball Tin Pan Alley variation like he was born yesterday, find him spurting soul band trumpet squeals in and out of a number whose head and rhythm arrangement come across like a cross between Basie, Bird, and James Brown. Moreover, we find Miles enjoying working with musicians not on the cutting edge, but on the backburner of bebop conservatism. (If guitarists Stern and John Scofield play one new lick here, it's news only to maybe, say, T-Bone Walker.) On the other hand, I'm not going to say the record doesn't swing when it wants to, and all in all it just may be the most accessible LP Miles has ever made. (I mean it could've come out on CTI, you know?) Furthermore, when you stop and consider the source of this oldhat comedy routine, it kinda leaves you in stitches. (When genius mocks itself, what other response is there?)

When Miles first came back, I thought it was with a whimper—but I was wrong: Miles Davis has come back to partay y'all. Laugh with him at your own expense.

—1983

Silence, Exile, and Cunning: Miles Davis in Memoriam

85
•

*P*ronouncing the death of Miles Davis seems more sillyass than sad. Something on the order of saying you've clocked the demise of the blues, the theory of relativity, *Ulysses*, or any other definitive creation of this century. Miles is one of those works of art, science, and magic whose absence might have ripped a chunk out of the zeitgeist big enough to sink a dwarf star into. A friend of mine once said that you could not love being black and not love Miles Davis because Miles was the quintessential African American. African American, not as in two halves thrown together, but a recombinant entity born of sperm and egg to produce a third creature more expansive than either.

Quincy Jones has opined, if someone asks what jazz is, play them *Kind of Blue*. For some of us coming from the African-centric tip, Miles Davis *is* the black aesthetic. He doesn't just represent it, he defines it. Music, poetry, philosophy, fashion, sports, architecture, design, painting, scholarship, politics, film, physics, femininity, even if not feminism—it don't matter, Miles is the model and the measure for how *black* your shit really is. Miles rendered black a synonym for the best of everything. To the aristocratic mind of this East St. Louis scion of a pig farmer/dentist, it naturally followed that if you were playing the baadest music on the face of the earth with the baadest musicians living, then of course you were driving the baadest cars, wearing the baadest vines, and intimate with the most regal of women and celebrated of artists, thinkers, and athletes. What black also meant to Miles was supreme intelligence, elegance, creativity, and funk. Miles worked black culture encyclopedically—from the outhouse to the penthouse and back again, to paraphrase brother Stanley Crouch. He rolled up on symphony orchestras with greasy blues phrases and dropped Stockhausen over dopebeats. Like Bessie Smith, he wasn't ashamed to show his ass in high society, or to take his Issey Miyake gear to the toilet stool. (I'm proud to say I nearly bore witness to that shit.)

Accepting Clyde Taylor's definition of black music as "our mother tongue," no artist in history territorialized as many of its multi-accentuated language groups as Miles. And the way he worked those linguistic systems demands we interact as critically with his music as we do with the texts of Baldwin, Baraka, Morrison, or the slave narratives. The music of Miles Davis is the music of a deep thinker on African-American experience.

The reason black music occupies a privileged and authoritative position in black aesthetic discourse is because it seems to croon and cry out to us from a postliberated world of unrepressed black pleasure and self-determination. Black music, like black basketball, represents an actualization of those black ideologies that articulate themselves as antithetical to Eurocentrism. Music and 'ball both do this in ways that are counterhegemonic if not countersupremacist—rooting black achievement in ancient black cultural practices. In the face of the attempt to erase the African contribution to world knowledge, and the diminution of black intelligence that came with it, the very fact of black talents without precedent or peers in the white community demolishes racist precepts instantaneously. In this war of signifying and countersigning Miles Davis was a warrior king and we were all enthralled.

Paying tribute to the courtly airs of Jean Michel Basquiat, Diego Cortez compared Basquiat's noblesse oblige to Miles's, pointing out how important it was for black culture to have its own aristocrats. George Benson has spoken of how Miles made being a black jazz musician feel like the most exalted honorific one could achieve on this earth. In the business of reinvesting the devalued human stock of chattel slavery with a sense of self-worth, Miles was among the most bullish CEOs in the history of the company. Primarily because he's a blues people's genius.

Obviously, the notion of *black genius* is an oxymoron designed to send Eurocentrists screaming to the mat. Though considered an absurdity by academe, the artistry of a Miles or a Holiday or a Hendrix obliterates that prejudice with a vengeance. That Miles Davis ranks beside Picasso in the modernist pantheon has long been the stuff of journalistic cliché. All things being equal, Miles and Pablo will probably end up sharing a room together in a hell of mirrors being flogged by furies for all the women they dogged. That Miles looms as large as Warhol as far as postmodern thinkers go is an insight for which we can thank Arthur Jafa. Like Warhol, Miles came to use his visual presence and celebrity to manipulate the interpretation of his work and eventually made that stuff a part of the work as well, particularly in the '80s, when his cordial stage demeanor attracted more attention than his band or his horn playing.

Befitting his status as black aesthetic signifier in the flesh, Miles cannot merely be read as a fascinating subject. He's also for many of us an objectified projection of our blackest desires, a model for any black artist who wants to thoroughly interpenetrate Western domains of power and knowledge with Africanizing authority. For those who approach him as a generator of musical systems, metaphors, metaphysics, and gossip, Miles was the premier black romantic artist of this century. It's difficult to say at what point the legend of Miles enveloped his work. The mythologizing process began as early as the mid '50s. You can't interpret Miles's work if you don't acknowledge his syncretism of life and music. This has less to do with trying to read his music through his clothes or his sex life or his choice of pharmaceuticals than with him being, as his biographer Quincy Troupe says, "an unreconstructed black man," a Stagolee figure who makes the modern world deal with him on his terms if it's going to deal with him at all. Few black men receiving their pay from major white corporations could get away with saying they'd like to spend the last minutes of their life choking a white man and suffer no repercussions for it. No one else in jazz could have chucked a following built over a lifetime to pursue the wild and wacky musical course Miles took from *In a Silent Way* onward.

The funny thing is that as disorienting as that period was for his old fans, Miles stepped into the era of black power politics and hippie rebellion like he'd had a hand in creating it all along. He never seemed like the old jazz hand who was trying to get hip to the Youth and Soul movements of the day. Homeboy came off like he was redefining cool for that generation too. As in the '50s and '60s, in the '70s he emerged as chief prophet of musicality for the next 20 years. Punk, hiphop, house, new jack swing, worldbeat, ambient music, and dub are all presaged in the records Miles cut between 1969 and 1975. There's no other figure whose work can be said to have laid the cornerstone for the advances of Brian Eno, Parliament-Funkadelic, Prince, Public Image Ltd., Talking Heads, Public Enemy, Living Colour, Marshall Jefferson, and Wynton Marsalis. Miles? Yeah, they named that one right. Only thing more to the point might have been Moebius.

On the other hand, the reason Miles was always so fresh was because he was so rooted. When I met Miles for an interview in 1986 it immediately struck me that the person he most reminded me of was my late maternal grandmother. Like her, a barber who spent her last years cutting heads at an Air Force base, Miles not only seemed to be a country person thoroughly wise in the ways of cosmopolitans but the type of country person who seems to become even more country the longer they stay among so-called sophisticates. Not as a ploy, like you'd find in folktales, playing dumb in order to get over on city slickers, but more like recognizing countryness as a state of grace. I imagine this sense of transcendence comes from knowing you are of ancient, enduring, and obdurate stock and that the rest will soon fade.

Lester Bowie once countered Wynton Marsalis's line on the tradition by saying that the tradition in jazz *is* innovation. Perhaps the median between these poles is that you become an innovator by working your way deeper into the tradition rather than by working out of it, recognizing that there's gold in them haunted hills. If the trick is to advance the tradition without refusing, abusing, or deifying it, then Miles wrote the book of love there. You could reduce everything Miles ever played to an obsession with four elements: deep bass, open space, circular time, and blues falsettos. In a mystical or metaphorical sense you could read these constants as earth, air, water, and fire. No matter how avant his music might have seemed to the rear guard, Miles held to those constants. Miles is a nomad, and nomads are famous for being able to re-create their way of life anywhere. I think it was his clarity about where he came from that gave him his urgency to keep moving on, a fugitive for life.

Baraka says black musical tradition implores us to sing and fight. I disagree. I think we'd do that anyway, just out of human necessity. What I do think it teaches us is more Joycean in tenor: silence, exile, and cunning. Miles's music makes you think of Nat Turner, proud without being loud because it was about plotting insurrection. In this sense Miles never changed. His agenda remained the same from day one: stay ahead.

Writers only have their style to leave behind said Nabokov. Miles says he was always looking for musicians who had a style, a voice I think he meant, of their own. In a music built on celebrating democracy and the individual, Miles developed a voice that was not only singular, but critical of all who picked up the instrument afterwards. After Miles, you couldn't just be a good trumpet player. You had to sacrifice your soul and maybe give some blood in the process. Others might have played trumpet from the heart; Miles played it like he was having open heart surgery. At the same time, every note thanked God for putting Louis Armstrong on the planet. Miles's tight-lipped sound conveyed the gaiety of Armstrong's wide vibrato while conjuring up the calculating pockets of dark sarcasm and meanness that at times ruled his spirit.

These qualities were nowhere more apparent than in his treatment of women, if we take him at his word for the gloating accounts of physical and psychological abuse in the as-told-to Troupe biography. Much as I love Miles, I despised him after reading about those incidents. Not because I worshiped the ground he spit on, but because I'd loathe any muhfukuh who violated women the way he did and relished having the opportunity to tell the world about it. Miles may have swung like a champion but on that score he went out like a roach.

—1991

Call Me Abraxas: Santana

etragrammaton and Homeboy fell into high school reunion scoping for old band members and eventually lucked up on Bayray, Romeo, and Kidd Funkadelic. After an exchange of yo muhfuhs the conversation quickly turned to good sex and old girlfriends before Kidd canned the booty tales to give it up to his once-upon-a-true love.

"You all know who I was really digging on more than any dame back then was Carlos Santana."

Bayray: "Yep, *yep*, that's right, that's right—Santana used to be your *heart*, boy. Cold-blooded even."

Homeboy: "I swear. Couldn't *nobody* go over this wild muhfuh's crib without getting blasted right out of the joint by some *Abraxas* and doohickey."

Tetragrammaton, head mystic in the circle, mused: "Ah yes, Abraxas: signifying as Hesse learned from the gnostics that God and the devil may be one and the same, signifying as well Santana's coaxial synthesis of jazz, rock, and more ancient Abyssinian systems of polyrhythmic possession."

Picking up on this thread, Kidd ejaculated: "Oh yeah, buddy, oh yeah. Like you check how they threw that *Bitches Brew* on the top of that *Electric Ladyland* on top of that Santamaria *santeria* thang. Man, that music filled the serious *void*, you hear me?"

Romeo: "That Strauss ripoff they segued between 'Black Magic Woman' and 'Gypsy Queen' was baad, jim—twothousandandonespaceodyssey *down*."

Kidd reflected: "I used to know all them solos man."

"Yep, yep, that's right, that's right—you even be onstage gritting and squinting and clenching like Carlos too man."

'Remember when you wanted us to name the band Funkatana, Kidd? Like, what was you, in love with the bitch, or what was you gonna do, marry the muhfuh, take half his name and doohickey or what?"

"Yep, yep, like that Miles line 'bout Al Green where Miles say if Al had one tit I woulda married the motherfucker, ha-ha-ha!"

"Aw man, ya'll know it wasn't just me 'cause you used to be hearing Santana-style jams all over the place, like with War, Mandrill, Maurice and Verdine and them, Maxayn, Osibisa. Shee, Rolling Stones even."

"So what happened man, howcum they ain't into no more progressive Latin-jazz, like some *Caravanserai*. Why they coming out this lame AOR type groove nowadays?"

"Bayray, you remember when Carlos got all holy and big-headed behind discovering God and Mahavishnu and fired all them cats from the original band and then they put Journey together and so now Journey's making all that cash so Santana can't cut a record without jumping on board that Journey train, so they apartheid-orientedrock *down!*"

"Hey, Kidd, you know your boy Carlos got a new solo jam out and doohickey."

"Yep, yep, that's right, that's right, *Havana Moon* or some shit like that."

"Do it righteously jam Homeboy? Because that last one he did was a depressant to me."

"Well, I can't say it *jam*-jams, Kidd. I mean it don't get off like the whipping dick or nothing like that. I mean it's spozed to be a boogie-type jam but it sound to me like it could use a square kick in the ass. I like the feeling on it though, reminds me of Santana when they first hit, with that Latin blues feeling. Carlos got them white boogie boys outta Texas on it, the Fabulous Thunderbirds, but they be undercranking sound like to me. But in a way it's good 'cause look like Carlos going back to his roots for that feeling— 'cause they do some Chuck Berry, some Bo Diddley, even some of that Mexican mariachi shit. He ain't really into nothing new guitarwise but the, *huh*, album cover is real *purty*, ha-ha-ha."

"Check it: Even when that boy's music ain't shit his album covers always been the bomb—trulypsychedelic *down!*"

Kidd picked up on his vibe: "Santana used to have that mystique thang happening like Miles and Jimi."

Always the slow one, Bayray turned to Tetragrammaton and said: "So that's what *Abraxas* meant, huh? I always wondered 'bout that like I always wondered 'bout some Tetragrammaton like what kind of name is that for a . . ."

"Brother, I take my name from the Hebraic quadralineal which is the name of Jehovah deconstructed into the consonants JHWH, also known as Jahweh, or here in the Black Atlantic world as JAH, a triangular reconstruction which etymologically envisions Rasta-fari repatriation and the demise of the triangular slave trade now grown global as the Trilateral Commission. Further revelations on these matters are contained in my MS Tetragrammatonic Bica-meralism: A Breakdown of Tabloid Wildstyle and the Afro-Gonzo Aesthetic as It Relates to Other Subversive Vernaculars—such as neohoodooism, Ikonoklast Panzerism, P-Funkism, rappism, dubb-ism, and magic realism. All being systems wherein blood beating in Babylon become Babel-on brother, or deeper still, chant down Babylon to the beat, blood."

Lost in reverie, Kidd spoke: "Every couple years a band comes along that can't be labeled this or that, a band that plugs into all styles and systems. First it was the Beatles, then Sly and Jimi, then Santana, P-Funk, Stevie Wonder, Weather Report, and Miles; now it's the Police and Talking Heads you know."

"Tell me something Kidd, you still playing and doohickey?"

"I'm still waiting, man."

"For?"

"New Talking Heads."

"What they calling this one, *(not just) Knee Deep parts three and four?*"

"No brother," said Tetragrammaton. *"Speaking in Tongues."*

"How you know, chump?"

"Because dread eyes read the trades, muhfuh."

—1983

Beat the Message Too: Ramm-El-Zee vs. K-Rob

magine a rap that's such a hiphop horrorshow it makes "The Message" seem like a rerun of *Good Times.* Figure in enough sarcastic references to the Furious Five's routines to spell Brazen Parody and you might think "Beat Bop" is all in fun. Only when this two-man razz turns schizzy it gets real scary. So much so that you stop hearing a comfy routine and begin listening to a houserocking ritual killing instead. One walking that razor's edge between go-go jive and rap's flip side, the madness stalking the streets: "It doesn't matter to a thief if you're young or old, it's just money they want and they need it bad and to take another person's life makes them feel glad. So rock to the funky beat." Rapwise but on the for real side that's no B.S. from the mouth of K-Rob. "Beat Bop" really turns rappers and B-boys into jekyll and hydes when graffiti theorist Ramm-El-Zee comes on like a South Bronx rewrite of *Naked Lunch:* ".38 shooting real straight because I'm down like a doubledutch remanipulation on that beat Grandmaster make a move when I'm shooting to the boom-boom . . . death, death, death jam y'all."

The killer lines come with K-Rob's bad-boy-prays-for-absolution bit on the outchorus, which begins by begging for a second chance and a job and ends in resignation: "Whatever you say I must do, because you're the one and only and I trust you. Crime is going up. . . ." Now thang is, you don't know whether my man is talking about The Man upstairs or The Man; whether he's talking about going over to the Holy Ghost or giving it up to the Beast. Either way you can tell blood here is about some survival too. The message seems to be that you shouldn't play wordgames with life and death matters when you're rocking to the "beat from the depths of hell." Music by Sekou Bunch is a stripped down version of a recent thang 'bout some nasty gals. Bernie Worrell style splices and shock cuts float through the mix, so now go dig it, catch my drift.

—1983

I'm White!: What's Wrong with Michael Jackson

There are other ways to read Michael Jackson's blanched skin and disfigured African features than as signs of black self-hatred become self-mutilation. Waxing fanciful, we can imagine the-boy-who-would-be-white a William Gibson–ish work of science fiction: harbinger of a transracial tomorrow where genetic deconstruction has become the norm and Narcissism wears the face of all human Desire. Musing empathetic, we may put the question, who does Mikey want to be today? The Pied Piper, Peter Pan, Christopher Reeve, Skeletor, or Miss Diana Ross? Our Howard Hughes? Digging into our black nationalist bag, Jackson emerges a casualty of America's ongoing race war—another Negro gone mad because his mirror reports that his face does not conform to the Nordic ideal.

To fully appreciate the sickness of Jackson's savaging of his African physiognomy you have to recall that back when he wore the face he was born with, black folk thought he was the prettiest thing since sliced sushi. (My own mother called Michael pretty so many times I almost got a complex.) Jackson and I are the same age, damn near 30, and I've always had a love-hate thing going with the brother. When we were both moppets I envied him, the better dancer, for being able to arouse the virginal desires of my female schoolmates, shameless oglers of his (and Jermaine's) tenderoni beefcake in *16* magazine. Even so, no way in those say-it-loud-I'm-black-and-I'm-proud days could you not dig Jackson heir

95
•

to the James Brown dance throne. At age 10, Jackson's footwork and vocal machismo seemed to scream volumes about the role of genetics in the cult of soul and the black sexuality of myth. The older folk might laugh when he sang shake it, shake it baby, ooh, ooh or teacher's gonna show you, all about loving. Yet part of the tyke's appeal was being able to simulate being lost in the hot sauce way before he was supposed to know what the hot sauce even smelt like. No denying he *sounded* like he knew the real deal.

In this respect, Jackson was the underweaned creation of two black working-class traditions: that of boys being forced to bypass childhood along the fast track to manhood, and that of rhythm and blues auctioning off the race's passion for song, dance, sex, and spectacle. Accelerated development became a life-imperative after slavery, and r&b remains the redemption of minstrelsy—at least it was until Jackson made crossover mean lightening your skin and whitening your nose.

Slavery, minstrelsy, and black bourgeoisie aspirations are responsible for three of the more pejorative notions about blacks in this country—blacks as property, as ethnographic commodities, and as imitation rich white people. Given this history, there's a fine line between a black entertainer who appeals to white people and one who sells out the race in pursuit of white appeal. Berry Gordy, Bürgermeister of crossover's Bauhaus, walked that line with such finesse that some black folk were shocked to discover via *The Big Chill* that many whites considered Motown *their* music. Needless to say, Michael Jackson has crossed so way far over the line that there ain't no coming back—assuming through surgical transmutation of his face a singular infamy in the annals of tomming.

The difference between Gordy's crossover dream world and Jackson's is that Gordy's didn't preclude the notion that black is beautiful. For him the problem was his pupils not being ready for prime time. Motown has raised brows for its grooming of Detroit ghetto kids in colored genteel manners, so maybe there were people who thought Gordy was trying to make his charges over into pseudo-Caucasoids. Certainly this insinuation isn't foreign to the work of rhythm and blues historians Charles Keil and Peter Guralnick, both of whom write of Motown as if it weren't hot and black enough to suit their blood, or at least their conception of bloods. But the

intermingling of working-class origins and middle-class acculturation are too mixed up in black music's evolution to allow for
simpleminded purist demands for a black music free of European
influence, or of the black desire for a higher standard of living and
more cultural mobility. As an expression of '60s black consciousness, Motown symbolized the desire of blacks to get their foot in
the bank door of the American dream. In the history of affirmative
action Motown warrants more than a footnote beneath the riot accounts and NAACP legal maneuvers.

As a black American success story the Michael Jackson of
Thriller is an extension of the Motown integrationist legacy. But
the Michael Jackson as skin job represents the carpetbagging side
of black advancement in the affirmative action era. The fact that
we are now producing young black men and women who conceive
of their African inheritance as little more than a means to cold-
crash mainstream America and then cold-dis—if not merely put
considerable distance between—the brothers and sisters left behind. In this sense Jackson's decolorized flesh reads as the buppy
version of Dorian Gray, a blaxploitation nightmare that offers this
moral: Stop, the face you save may be your own.

In 1985 black people cherished *Thriller*'s breakthrough as if it
were their own battering ram against the barricades of American
apartheid. Never mind how many of those kerzillon LPs we bought,
forget how much Jackson product we had bought all those years
before that—even with his deconstructed head, we wanted this cat
to tear the roof off the all-time-greatest-sales sucker bad as he did.
It's like *Thriller* was this generation's answer to the Louis-
Schmeling fight or something. Oh, the Pyrrhic victories of the
disenfranchised. Who would've thought this culture hero would be
cut down to culture heel, with a scalpel? Or maybe it's just the
times. To those living in a New York City and currently witnessing
a rebirth of black consciousness in protest politics, advocacy journalism (read *The City Sun!* read *The City Sun!*), and the arts,
Jackson seems dangerously absurd.

Proof that God don't like ugly, the title of Michael's new LP,
Bad (Epic), accurately describes the contents in standard English.
(Jackson apparently believes that *bad* can apply to both him and

L.L. Cool J.) No need to get stuck on making comparisons with
Thriller, *Bad* sounds like home demos Michael cut over a long
weekend. There's not one song here that any urban contemporary
hack couldn't have laid in a week, let alone two years. Several of
the up-tempo numbers wobble in with hokey bass lines out of the
Lalo Schifrin fakebook, and an inordinate number begin with om-
inous science fiction synthnoise—invariably preceding an anti-
climax. *Bad* has hooks, sure, and most are searching for a song,
none more pitifully than the fly-weight title track, which throws its
chorus around like a three-year-old brat.

The only thing *Bad* has going for it is that it was made by the
same artist who made *Thriller*. No amount of disgust for Jackson's
even newer face (cleft in the chin) takes anything away from
Thriller. Everything on that record manages a savvy balance between machine language and human intervention, between palpi-
tating heart and precision tuning. *Thriller* is a record that doesn't
know how to stop giving pleasure. Every note on the mutha sings
and breathes masterful pop instincts: the drumbeats, the bass lines,
the guitar chicken scratches, the aleatoric elements. The weaving
of discrete details into fine polyphonic mesh reminds me of those
African field recordings where simultaneity and participatory democracy, not European harmony, serve as the ordering principle.

98
•

Bad, as songless as *Thriller* is songful, finds Jackson performing
material that he has absolutely no emotional commitment to—with
the exception of spitefully named "Dirty Diana," a groupie fantasy.
The passion and compassion of "Beat It," "Billie Jean," and
"Wanna Be Startin' Somethin' " seemed genuine, generated by
Jackson's perverse attraction to the ills of teen violence and teen
pregnancy. There was something frightful and compelling about
this mollycoddled mama's boy delivering lapidary pronouncements
from his Xanadu like "If you can't feed your baby, then don't have
a baby." While the world will hold its breath and turn blue in the
face awaiting the first successful Michael Jackson paternity suit,
he had the nerve to sing, "The kid is not my son." Not even David
Bowie could create a subtext that coy and rakish on the surface
and grotesque at its depths.

Only in its twisted aspects does *Bad*, mostly via the "Bad" video,
outdo *Thriller*. After becoming an artificial white man, now he

wants to trade on his ethnicity. Here's Jackson's sickest fantasy yet: playing the role of a black preppie returning to the ghetto, he not only offers himself as a role model he literally screams at the brothers "You ain't nothin'!" Translation: Niggers ain't shit. In Jackson's loathsome conception of the black experience, you're either a criminal stereotype or one of the Beautiful People. Having sold the world pure pop pleasure on *Thriller*, Jackson returns on *Bad* to sell his own race hatred. If there's 35 million sales in that, be ready to head for the hills ya'll.

—1987

The GOP Throws a Mammy-Jammy: Black Stars Bowl Over Bush at Blues Summit

T was a groggy morning in the new year when Mother Tate rang from D.C. to inform her son the music critic that the Republicans were putting on a rhythm-and-blues blowout for the inaugural. The elect were all black music standard-bearers if not outright royalty: Willie Dixon, Albert Collins, Steve Cropper, Duck Dunn, Billy Preston, Sam Moore, Koko Taylor, Dr. John, William Bell, Eddie Floyd, Chuck

Jackson, Ron Wood. A true daughter of Memphis, Mother Tate was ecstatic, and advised her son to come cover the mammy-jammy.

I wasn't so ready to jump. To these ears, such a chitterling circuit redux sounded like black pearls being cast before Reaganite swine. Worse, it seemed an opportunity for shameless Uncle Tomming. I feared the spectacle of seeing some once-conquering lion of soul going out like a roach. The response among my peers, a loose circle of post-Malcolmites, was also an automatic ugh. The very idea of African Americans entertaining Republicans goes down about as well with this generation as mixing snake oil with holy water. The sheer savagery of the Reagan Revolution toward black America speaks for itself. His peace and prosperity was bought by upping the black misery index with malice aforethought. When I hear of African Americans courting Reagan's kith and kin, I don't get happy, I worry. Big time.

While I was rolling over like Beethoven from this report on the setback of the race, Mother Tate hit me with another whammy. Namely, she had contacted the office of Republican National Committee chairman Lee Atwater about helping him achieve what he claimed was George Bush's prioritized goal: recruiting more blacks into the Grand Old Party. Jesus. Is nothing sacred?

This decision is not without its history. My mother has voted Republican in the last three presidential elections. She is not, however, a black Republican, a breed she respects as little as the party's hierarchy does: she's a race woman. Her activist résumé speaks for itself: veteran foot soldier with CORE during the Civil Rights movement, supporter of SNCC and the Black Panther Party when Black Power was in vogue, press manager for the first Marion Barry mayoral campaign and administration, national press secretary for Jesse Jackson during his 1984 bid for the presidency. She loves Public Enemy as much as anybody you know. Her personal favorite: "She Watch Channel Zero?!"

In each election, her ballot was cast not for the reactionary but against the Democratic Party, except in 1980, when she was protesting the "general feebleness" of the Carter administration. Mondale's freezing out of Jesse at the '84 convention cost him her swing vote in that slaughter. Need I spell out what effect Dukakis's dissing of Jesse and the entire African-American body politic did to turn her stomach? Call her an egotist, but Mother Tate is on a mission: to put the Democratic Party on notice that her black vote can't be held hostage to hysteria over the GOP boogie man. She believes African Americans should "be like the Jews and have somebody on all sides of every political question." (This, of course, assumes that all Jews are moles, and that blacks of whatever ideological persuasion can put a black agenda first—but if you think I'm opening that can of worms here, homeboy, it ain't happening.) Mocking those brothers and sisters who protest that them Republicans don't want us in their party: "Do they really believe the Democrats want them in theirs? All they want is your vote." Mother Tate describes herself as a lifelong political independent whose affiliations have always been based on who she thought could do the most for the largest number of African-American people. She takes the signals Bush has already sent out to black America as ample proof that now is the time for African Americans to renegotiate their place in American electoral politics.

And she is not alone. Jesse Jackson, seen in the presidential box on Inauguration Day, was invited to meet with Bush before Dukakis was, and came out saying it was impossible not to like the man and claiming that the rearing of the Willie Horton bugaboo was "not racist in its *intentions*." (Never mind the road-to-hell implications here—don't you just love the way nobody ever intends to be racist, it just happens, like an involuntary muscle spasm or an itchy trigger finger?) While the Democratic National Committee devises ways and means to deny Jackson a leadership role in the party, Jesse is floating the specter of a Republican rapprochement. But all this idle speculation can keep for now.

Chairman Atwater's all-star dream revue had been brewing in his mind from at least as far back as the Texas primary, when he contacted Joyce McRae, manager for Sam Moore (of Sam & Dave fame), about Moore's participation in the event of a Bush inaugural.

Appearances to the contrary, the big show was not conceived to entice African Americans into the party. The show was Atwater's way of paying homage to his beloved rhythm and blues, and a way of educating his fellow Republicans about the African-American musical tradition.

Once I decided I wanted to take on the Republican Rhythm and

Blues show, the matter of obtaining tickets presented itself as a problem. As it turned out, the event was an invitation-only affair and the deadline for press credentials had passed almost two weeks before. To the rescue comes Wondermom, whose contact in the Atwater office gave her not one but two tickets the man had held in reserve for himself. To appreciate the cunning magnanimity of this gesture you have to know that before she went to Atwater's office, Mother Tate enlisted the assistance of several high-ranking black Republicans who, to their chagrin, proved useless, clueless.

The event was not billed as a tribute to the blues but as a Tribute to Young America. Designed as a night on the town for the more toothsome party apparatchiks, it also cost considerably less per ticket ($35) than the more usual $1500-a-ticket fetes of the inaugural weekend. To make a short story shorter, come Inaugural Gala Saturday, there we were, Mom and me, two flies in the Bushwahzee buttermilk, taking our seats in the Washington Convention Center. Out of the 8500 attendees, there were probably more black folks working the stage than sitting in the house. My presumption that no more than a handful of these young (white) Americans could have passed an African-American cultural literacy test was borne out by the young Republican swinger behind me, who moaned that she hadn't heard of anybody on the bill and would have preferred to see Boston or the Beach Boys. Is it just me or are these people corny beyond redemption?

Because Mother Tate ain't one of them: in her mind this event would show these ignorant young people where rock and roll came from. Quite frankly, I don't give a damn when white people begrudgingly and belatedly have to give it up to the genius of my people. This is not to say that such acknowledgement doesn't have political use. But it's like when Doug Williams won the Super Bowl—I felt good for the brother, but it was another case of too little, too late, so what? Suffer my soapbox for a minute: African Americans are the cotton-picking base on which Western capitalism stands. We built this country twice over, first economically, then culturally, and remain an exploited and second-class citizenry. Tell me how much a white American loves our music and all I can think, per August Wilson, is, Joe Turner done come and gone—look what they done to my song, ma.

That night I was in a perpetual state of antipathy and ardor. Put cultural giants on the order of Willie Dixon and Bo Diddley before my eyes and the context cannot matter. From an African-American standpoint, we're talking icons. And as hypersensitive as I was to where I was and who I was there with, from the moment any of the folk hit the stage I was feeling groovy. On a certain level it would be antiblack to feel anything else. When Koko Taylor launched into "Let the Good Times Roll," my mother commented that this was the kind of Negroid sentiment that "had to leave white people wondering, 'What kind of people are these who can be singing let the good times roll after all we've put on 'em?' "

The taped preshow entertainment was educational enough to have been conceived for a Black Rock Coalition pep rally—clips of Jackie Wilson, Little Richard, Muddy Waters, Ruth Brown, and a young James Brown (ripping up the stage with more manic energy than a chocolate city on gooberdust) that devolved into the Rolling Stones, who are cool, but let's get real. Atwater introduced the program by announcing, "This is the music I've loved all my life. It's pure American music in its best form. Tonight isn't a night for politics. Tonight's a night for music and the blues." Stone cold African-American nationalist translation: politics is a white man's game but ya'll black folks sure can sing and dance. Atwater didn't say this as crudely as the ever-invidious Ed Koch did when he kvetched to a Brooklyn congregation on Martin Luther King Day how he wished we could get "politics out of the civil rights movement"—but that subtext was there nonetheless. Get this Lee: *everything* about being black in America is political.

Bandleader Billy Preston opened up the set with "Sweet Soul Music" and then introduced Dr. John, who may or may not have echoed feelings I've already expressed when he sang "Right Place, Wrong Time." Percy Sledge was the only entertainer of the evening who embarrassed me with coonery, dedicating his show "to one of the greatest and strongest men in the world" and closing out with "God bless you, Mr. and Mrs. Bush." Yeeech. (To be fair, Bo Diddley would later also wax patriotic before the crowd. Except when he professed pride in being born in the U.S.A., he came off like he was standing his ground rather than sucking up to the

103
•

Republicans—as always, his Rebel Yell, "I'm a Man," was neither a pleaded nor a bragged affirmation of self.)

Up next was Chuck Jackson, whose lithe elegance and open-hearted passion prompted my mother to take him as exemplary of "how through all the muck and mire we still come out beautiful. How we not only keep on going but keep on having a *good* time. And you know that Chuck Jackson is what you call *fine*." Testimony to her reading was Jackson getting happy in the sanctified church sense, engaging the crowd in a call-and-response interpolation of "It's all right" on "I Don't Want to Cry."

Willie Dixon, the Duke Ellington of Chicago blues, magisterially took the stage with Koko Taylor, propped up on a cane, dragging one leg behind him, and sporting this antique and seriously *fly* white velour hat wrapped with a silken band. When the music got Dixon going he forgot he needed a cane, and bopped around the stage spry as a spring chicken. Next up was the bowlegged Buddha himself, Bo Diddley, whose dance moves alone mark him as an original: a lateral hippity-hop augmented by these curvaceous turns that make you think of a sidewinder proficient with a hula hoop. Performing the hit he wrote for Albert King, "Born Under a Bad Sign," William Bell defied the downtrodden lyrics ("If it wasn't for bad luck and trouble/I wouldn't have no luck at all") with leonine ferocity and grace. Dressed in a sheared iridescent satin gown, Carla Thomas sashayed her opulent womaninity through "Baby."

Then Marvin Bush came up to introduce Mom and Dad to the tune of "Soul Finger," which may soon supplant "Hail to the Chief" if Atwater has his way. Bush was deferential, shook everybody's hand, stayed around long enough for Sam Moore to present him with a Yankee Doodle Dandy of a guitar and a framed poster from all the artists, and announced that he knew when to shut up. At this point Sam Moore invited a putatively reluctant Atwater to strap on a hot red guitar and perform a more than competent, even impassioned version of "Hi-Heel Sneakers." In this life, infrequently enough but enough to warrant mention, there occur occasions when some Caucasoid will compel you to say, the white boy can play. Atwater coulda been a contender, maybe even on the order of a Stevie Ray Vaughan, who shredded his guitar so viciously that night you'd have thought somebody was gonna beat him like he stole something if he didn't.

I can't say for certain that Eddie Floyd was making a statement when he grabbed a sultry young blond from the crowd and began singing "Knock on Wood" whilst fingering her tresses. Eldridge Cleaver might have interpreted this as saying to Atwater, "Yo, boy, if you gonna get all up into our music, then I can get all up into your women." My mother was jovial at the time. "If Jerry Falwell is watching this," she prophesied, "he's going to come snatch George Bush out the White House." Later she confessed to having been apprehensive too: black men used to get lynched on *suspicion* that they were thinking about such liberties.

Nothing was more electrifying than Sam Moore's rendition of Otis Redding's "I've Been Loving You Too Long," which drew from him the kind of pent-up bodysoaking ritual release that soul music was invented for. It gave me chills, and probably Sam too: for a few moments he stalked the stage without the mike, muttering under his breath. Albert Collins, Delbert McClinton, and Stevie Ray Vaughan closed the program and we're outta there, like Vladimir.

Come Sunday morning I buzz the artists at their hotel and manage to scare up Billy Preston, who could've been speaking for everybody when he said he had no feelings one way or the other about playing for Republicans because he considered himself an entertainer first. For him as for several others I spoke to, including musical director and Stax-Volt session man Michael Toles, Sam Moore, and William Bell, the high point of the show was watching Atwater perform and meeting President Bush. Toles was particularly struck by the Prez's cordiality toward the musicians, and all involved professed nothing but the highest regard for Atwater's devotion to their music. (For the record, however, Moore told me that both Robert Cray and Etta James refused invitations to perform; Cray because his agent had been a Dukakis workhorse, James because their suggestion that she perform old material made her feel she was being treated, Moore quoted her, "like a plantation nigger.")

In Atwater we have a man who runs campaigns for archracists

like Strom Thurmond but whose posture toward black culture is an abiding devotion, a man who did his graduate studies in the Machiavellian art of negative campaigning who's also a true-blue soul fan. Uh-huh. Well, Jefferson was a slaveholder who espoused the belief that all men were created equal, Hitler was a vegetarian, and Lenin turned to mush at the sound of Bach. In taking stock of Atwater's bedfellows, I'm reminded of a line by MC Hollywatts: why does everybody love black music but nobody love black people?

Sam Moore's manager McRae, who was Atwater's coproducer, told me that Atwater took a risk with this event, which so scared the bejeezus out of the party hierarchy that they refused to broadcast it live on cable out of fear it might embarrass the Prez. As the event was obviously a major success, Atwater has given them strong indications that he'd like to see it, or something like it, happen often during the Bush administration. According to Moore, Atwater has offered to make his office available to review proposals from the artists on how the government could further recognize their contribution, and provide things like health insurance and benefits so that a Willie Dixon wouldn't have to tour because he couldn't afford not to. McRae believes that after Reagan—who she believes set social relations in the country back to the Stone Age—this concert was a giant-step-for-mankind kind of thing. Per his inaugural speech, Bush has certainly come stumping a morally rehabilitated line when compared to his predecessor, the poor man's Galactus. Bush's symbolic gestures to the African-American community have been unsettlingly politic: the aforementioned conference with Jesse Jackson, his nomination of Dr. Louis W. Sullivan for Health and Human Services, his hiring of Constance Newman to head the Office of Personnel Management, and Barbara Bush's hiring of Anna Perez as her press secretary. For the record, Coretta Scott King and Dexter King shared a table with the Bushes at the concert.

While Atwater is certainly in a position to play Big Daddy, he doesn't come off like that. If he reminds me of anybody, it's Jerry Lee Lewis, a white-trash hellion who likes being licked by the tarbrush but is still a redneck through and through. Though seemingly a contradiction, I take it as a portent of Bush administration style. For African-American people, women, and the more disempowered segments of the Third World, the Bush era is already shaping up to be one that alternates lending a helping hand with a backhanded smack—where the abolition of affirmative action and the overturning of *Roe* v. *Wade* will go hand in hand with urban-enterprise zones, funding for the homeless, and drug treatment concentration camps rehabilitated from defunct military installations.

The state of poor black America hardly requires a paranoid-conspiratorial interpretation for us to adduce that poor African Americans have already entered the first stages of a holocaust.

We are entering into the most dire and opportune moment for renewed mass, militant activism that the African-American middle class will probably have in this century. The degree to which that class harbors feelings of alienation, resentment, and fear toward its poor will mightily determine whether solidarity or disengagement becomes the order of the day. We are at a precipitous crossroads where Bush's kinder, gentler overtures can easily slacken our resolve to seize the time. Only time will truly tell about the serpent in the wishing well. For now, don't, don't, don't, don't believe the hype.

—1989

Clitoral Madness:
A R Kane

Peace good woman
that once brought me home banana pudding in a jar
I could never conceive you
except as the eternal progenitor of dreams
Your vagina split asymmetrically
between the east and the west
Take this excannibal's kiss and turn it into a revolution
—*Archie Shepp*

will not wax lyrical over A R Kane. I will not wax lyrical over A R Kane. Am I lying? If I'm lying, I'm flying: Except for *Wings of Desire* and the death of Jean Michel Basquiat, no cultural phenomenon this year has inspired more rapturous prose than the music of A R Kane.

You have to read the British reviews to believe them: "A R Kane were oblivious figures, lost to the ecstasy of their own crackle, specks blown about by billowing dub, celebrating the amorphous, the white suspension, the death of origin and destiny. Just as desolate and sated as Miles circa *Bitches Brew*." That's a *typical* A R Kane review. Enough already.

Have a formal introduction: A R Kane are Alex and Rudi, two dreadlocked black Brits who moonlight as creative directors in Saatchi & Saatchi's ad department. Alex is the singer; both compose and play guitars. You may recall A R Kane's scraped-up guitars on M/A/R/R/S's "Pump Up the Volume." But if you come to A R Kane's album debut, *69* (Rough Trade), expecting hiphop, you're in for a dubwise, acid-fried loop.

For the longest time I couldn't stand their music. All I heard was lachrymose lullabies and, to quote Joe Levy, art-damaged blather. Only A R Kane's arrogantly Afrocentric way with inter-viewers impressed me. When they first came out last year, they were tagged a black Jesus and Mary Chain for having the gall to douse ditty pop with combustive feedback. A R Kane rebutted the hype, claiming they'd never heard the Mary Chain, hated rock and roll, and had been noise boys from way back thanks to Miles Davis and Sun Ra (whom they've recorded with). Now they claim all they listen to is A R Kane. I didn't realize they were geniuses until September 5.

On Labor Day, after years of resistance, I finally read Alice Walker's *The Color Purple*. Later I took a stroll through the Boogie Down Bronx with my gal in search of ake and saltfish done to Jahmaican perfection. The Bronx is another world. If Yankee Sta-dium hadn't landed in the Bronx, some other ETs would've colo-nized the spot. Land of the giants. Nothing is human scale, not even the sidewalk squares. Walk under the towering el on Jerome Avenue and you feel like you're little people and this is *Blade Runner*. The Concourse has to be the only promenade in the city where you're always as conscious of sky as you are of concrete jungle. Like I said: this is the land of the giants. Every corner of the Bronx is an epic narrative in search of an author. I tell homegirl the next García Márquez or Morrison is coming out of the Bronx. She looks at me like I must be on drugs.

109

Labor Day was a languorous day, perfect for tripping on the Bronx, *The Color Purple*, and A R Kane. Rereading Clarence Major's *Reflex and Bone Structure* had cleared the way for Walker. Something in the androgynous way Major's voice moves between masculine and feminine perceptions. "There are odors she lives with so closely she cannot intellectually deal with them, such as: the aroma of menstruation. Or the natural juices oozing from her vagina. They're so much a part of her *being*. She operates from the inside of such odors. But Cora never thinks of her own body as an instrument possessing what we have clinically termed a 'female sex organ.' "

Though surely I'm not the first, I read *The Color Purple* as a blues novel, a lyrical and optimistic rendering of personal tragedy and triumph. The Celie character's letters to God (really to the fiercely worried God within herself, to paraphrase Ntozake Shange) and her transgressive lesbian relationship with Shug Avery are peals of passion and personal revelation thrown up against a history of repression and violation. What I hear in the music of A R Kane are kindred transgressions of sexual propriety and the popular song. Excuse me while I kiss the sky. (I'm flying.) A R Kane make out-of-the-body music about sexual love and violence, New Age jingles for sadomasochistic swingers, celestial juke-joint selections for all those black angels gone to heaven who don't know how to stop doing the dirty grind. In short, A R Kane are Rilke's *The Duino Elegies* gone to Tartown. In power-chorded dub.

Before *69* A R Kane put out two EPs, *Lollita* and *Up Home*. The title cut on *Lollita* is music for a medieval spaghetti Western, or maybe surf music from Saturn. *Up Home* contains probably the only lyric that salutes both Marcus Garvey's Black Star Liner and "Stairway to Heaven," with music to match. *69* expands the terrain. The way A R Kane use the bass is weird, not as rhythmic propulsion but as undertow. Rarely do you hear backbeat you can't lose. The percussion counterpoints everything else. When they do give the drummer some, as on *Lollita*'s "Butterfly Collector," it's to exaggerated punk-amateurish effect, or, as on *69*'s "Suicide Kiss," it's as a liberated lead instrument à la Denardo Coleman. A R Kane's sound is heavy on dissolving or decaying overtones and faint arpeggios ringing up from the distance. *69* is where dub reggae meets its free-jazz and psycho-candy cousins.

A R Kane render punk and heavy metal dogmas about chops superfluous, creating a new school for guitar savagery. When they get deep into their white noise mode, liberating the guitar from tune, tempo, and tonality, they compare favorably to the anarchy of drummer Sunny Murray. Like Murray's, their din is so dense with definition you stop hearing cacophony and start seeing solid melodic abstractions swirling through the air. You wonder where this aleatoric symphony is hiding its conductor. But the A R Kane universe is as deliberately ephemeral as it is well ordered. Where Public Enemy dazzle us with their ability to convert any freaky sound into a dopebeat suitable for bumpin', A R Kane manage the opposite. Even their in-the-pocket song parts seem textured and poised to float up and away in a purple haze at any given moment.

If A R Kane were painters they'd be Basquiat. He melted Pop Art, semiology, and Abstract Expressionism down into his own mutant form, and so have they. For example, while Alex's plain-chant can be as compelling as Sting's, his voice is not A R Kane's emotional center. He ain't there to rule you, school you, or fool you. He's not even there to get A R Kane on pop radio. He's a compositional device who just happens to be drowning your ears in amorous self-absorption. Alex's vocals evoke swooning and suffering in the same breath, so much so that I sometimes hear him as a wimpy Billie Holiday. But while his cries and whispers more than adequately convey that loving feeling, even Alex's most impassioned atonalities register as structural beams first. A R Kane craft doowop Schoenberg might dig.

In *The Color Purple*, there's a scene where Celie goes to tears imagining Shug and Mr. cheating in the next room. In the same scene she revels in the pleasures of her recently discovered clitoris. Shug, who located it for her, describes it to Celie as "a little button" that gets so hot it melts when you're doing the nasty properly. This imagery got my sci-fi-damaged psyche to thinking: If Celie were a William Gibson cyborg, the button would be literal, and Celie would put on *69* while stroking her genetically engineered pudenda.

—1988

'Tain't Nobody's Business: Adeva

*W*hat becomes a legend most? A dope cover version by an inspired admirer. In 1967 at Monterey, Otis Redding referred to "Respect" as "a song that a girl took away from me." Aretha, if you're out there, give Adeva a holler. She's dying to hear your opinion of her "Respect" (Cooltempo), a club update of 'Re's civil rights protest. Adeva is a 23-year-old New Jerseyite and former school teacher who's made her own hit out of Aretha gold. The single has a solid grip on the dance charts, where the people vote with their feet. Given her propers in the way of material and production, Adeva could become major. The next Anita? Nah, the first Adeva. God bless the child who can hold her own.

She's a soul singer, one of the onliest her generation has popped. The proof is in the vocal tracks she lays on this Paul Simpson mix of a Rico Taylor arrangement for a Debbie Parkin and Smack Productions project. (*"Smack?"* quipped a comeback queen I know, "as in upside yo' head?") The score, an ambient romp, a slick and jazzy house suite, highlights Adeva's phrasing and reframing of the salient theme. In the chanted intro, she makes a resplendent mantra of needing respect, portraying a woman psyching herself up for tactful discourse with an asshole. When the ogre appears in the mix, demanding to be treated like doofus knows best, Adeva swoops down like a stealth bomber, hand on hip, that neck going quite viciously. True to her church roots Adeva doesn't stick to the text; she flubs lines deliberately and uses ellipses with abandon, scatting like 'tain't nobody's business if she do. In one verse, she slurs lines in a thrusting patter, pleading her case as if equal compensation and meaningful penetration were anything but estranged bedfellows. Adeva's voice arcs from bullfrog bass to ululations in the upper Ethiopian registers, with a midrange undaunted by early Chaka. Like Chaka way back in the day, Adeva's got It— that black woman t'ang to be exact—and got no inhibitions when it comes to flaunting it. On top of which, Adeva ain't no fake; she's skying a mean Cameo haircut, having rejected her record company's entreaties that she get a weave. Adeva is also the kind of sister who'll put a rudeboy in check pronto. When I called her up for basic info, she excused herself at one point to cold dismiss some meathead acting all loud in the background. *"Men!"* she gritted in my ear before pleasantly resuming our tête-à-tête.

—1989

Change of the Century: Ornette Coleman

113

t didn't take genius to flash on fashion as a suitably unorthodox topic to throw on Ornette Coleman: his visual style has long commanded more than a passing mention. In *Four Lives in the Bebop Business*, A. B. Spellman dotes on the "funny little waistcoats" Coleman designed for his quartet's New York debut and the leader's own eye-popping use of a white plastic alto.

The Coleman dress code can vary from wry accessories to exotichued monochrome suits, from subtle, many-colored thread-weaves to casual collegiate ensembles. The day we met, he wouldn't have been out of place as a croupier, his silver silk shirt draped by a black vest with muted paisley backing. For all that, I'm 'shamed to admit our conversation didn't stay on the fashion track long. Getting Ornette's pants and jacket measurements proved as fascinating as listening to the man whittle away on wisps of cosmological whimsy. Per his dictum that "a unison can be made of anything," everything Ornette says fits; i.e., fashion equals faith, freedom equals Ornette's democratic music system, harmolodics. "When you say music, that's a different sound. When sound is music, then we're talking about a different world. When music is a set territory, a set race, and a set pattern, then it just functions like shoes or anything else. I think sound is what gave the meaning to words and music is what gave feeling to hearing but I think categories is what has limited all of that. Taken the feeling out of hearing.

"I think feeling is really sacred. I learned that from the American Indians when I went on a reservation, that feeling is sacred itself. Feeling is symbolic to human beings of what God meant by putting breath in human beings."

Deal with it: Ornette Coleman is a conceptman, a man of ideas, one with his own oblique way with a phrase, granted, and therefore a philosopher, even if your mama might label him more a philosophizer, a Southern-bred shaman jes' a mite on the garrulous side. The originality of his syntax has often rendered Ornette indecipherable to some and sagacious to others, at times even both. One young pianist recalls an encounter that left him feeling that, even if he didn't understand Ornette, he was certain the man was a poet and that whatever he was saying, it was *deep*. Because Ornette is the kind of person with an answer or an anecdote for all queries; it might be thought that the reach of his philosophy far exceeds his grasp of the Western harmonic and harmolodic musical systems. You tell me: in a recent interview, Ornette was asked about the Heisenberg uncertainty principle as it related to music's effect on the human organism and instructed the interviewer that he was "no longer talking chemistry but alchemy"—as succinct a summary of the difference between the Newtonian and Einsteinian universes as you'll find outside of Lao Tzu. To some extent, Ornette reads like a crackpot genius, his discursive mind sweeping through its mental attic in search of the fabric connecting the cosmic and the mundane. At 57, Ornette holds his own not only in the African-American music pantheon, but among the ranks of all the free thinkers who've ever shaken us up by showing our prejudices and presumptions about class, culture, and the cosmos to be nothing but the emperor's new clothes.

Fashion figures into Ornette's ecumenical program as a way of seducing folk into getting on board his version of the freedom train. Ornette views even his sense of style as an extension of his humanist impulses. His interest in fashion extends to his designing his own duds, but he ain't no glamour boy.

"For me, clothes have always been a way of designing a setting so that by the time a person observes how you look, all of their attention is on what you're playing. Most people that play music, whether it's pop, rock, or classical, have a certain kind of uniform so they don't have to tell you what you're listening at. I always thought that if that was the case, why wouldn't I try to design from the standpoint of the opposite of that? Have the person see what you have on and have no idea what you were going to play. I'm not playing to represent what I'm wearing, and I'm not dressing to represent what I play. In Western society most successful public images have to do with how people want you to see them. A rich person goes around in jeans because he knows he's wealthy. Well, I don't dress to represent wealth, race, music, or nothing. It's more like religion, really. I would rather play in a setting that's going to allow the person that's listening to get into himself by distracting him from how I look in relationship to what he's hearing on stage. I don't want to go on a bandstand and have people try to imitate what I have on to get them closer to me. Like I don't try to see what kind of music they like to get them closer to me. I try not to think about either one of those things. Yet for some reason it has made people more interested in me. They say, 'Wow, those are some funny looking clothes, how did you come by those?' But I think that, in a world where I'm seeking to have an identity related to the universal person, my clothes have a universal appeal.

"I think the music is healing on many levels, whereas the clothes make the performer feel stronger before he even gets to the stage. The clothes enlighten the person to feel good. And with the playing and the music they both have this good positive effect on people.

"I heard that silk has something to do with making you less evil. I think it has something to do with light. I think from the time people began reading about human behavior in the Bible that someone had to invent fabric to cover all this evil up. But there is a light that is not related to electricity. If the sun didn't exist or if you took all the stars out of the sky that doesn't mean you wouldn't have light. It says in the Bible that in the beginning God created light, it doesn't say God created the sun, right? Maybe human beings are the real true light. Silk could be symbolic of that. There is something that flows in human beings that is close to what people call the truth, like when people say, 'See the truth in the light.' For some reason, in the Western world, though, silk has been related to pimps and preachers, people of high social imagery who manipulate people.

"The only time I'd seen black people dress up was going to church. Otherwise everybody looked like they just got out of a sandstorm or something. It made the male population appear to look sluggish, like they weren't interested in nothing. They had overalls and jeans, country stuff. Dressing up always seemed to me to have something to do with city living rather than country living and it's still that way. If you go somewhere dressed up and you're a black person, they usually don't tell you to take the package around to somewhere. Dressing up has a lot to do with not looking like your stereotyped black person that's looking for a job and can't do this and can't do that.

"When I see white kids walking the streets with their knees and their ass out, I wonder, do they want to be called bums? That's the style of clothes they wear, but they don't want to be called bums. But if they see a nonwhite person doing like that they call him a bum. If *they* do it it's called style.

"When a black person gets educated, such as myself, we have to find other territories to survive in. We can't survive in the territories we grew up in. If a young white kid decides he wants to play Chinese music in his apartment and finds something creative about it, he doesn't have to go to China to be successful. He can stay right there. But if a black person does that he has to change his environment and sometimes his attitude and be called Uncle Tom, but that's only because of the difference of being an individual person and being a racial person. I'm already black. I don't have to prove to anybody that I'm black and I don't have to act a certain way to get someone to like me because I'm black. I got a review in *down beat* by this guy who was listening to the Prime Time band as if it was just some black guys playing rhythm and blues. That's what he thought we were playing because we happened to be black and he heard some rhythm. But whatever problem a person has with the music they're playing has more to do with the results they want from it than the judgment of how they're being criticized. What I want from the music I perform is exactly the result I'm getting, no more, no less. And that result is for everyone to leave feeling themselves more of an individual."

Though Ornette has neither sought nor been granted the musical messiah-status bestowed on Coltrane, his characterization of his performance wardrobe as near-religious articles certainly intimates holy-man pretensions. But at Ornette's core is a notion of human salvation that seems to derive from both Jesus and Thomas Jefferson. It's a vision that considers self-expression synonymous with social responsibility, and individuality synonymous with spirituality—hence Ornette's belief that his personal style can service humanity. In discussing his harmolodics music system, where every player is free to take the lead at any time, Ornette poses it not just as a liberating paradigm for jazz performers, but for everybody.

"Everyone making their contribution in perfect unison. That is the most radical thing that has to do with human expression, not only in music, but clothes, cars, all things where you can bring your personal idea, see it making something better while everyone else is making theirs better. That has to be an advance."

—1987

Invisible Man Overboard: Marc Anthony Thompson

Who speaks for Marc Anthony Thompson—the most self-effacing Black man in the history of recorded sound? Who is Marc Anthony Thompson? When in journalese I tend to describe him as the Black Peter Gabriel, when not the North American Milton Nascimento. His music is as romantically technocratic as Gabriel's, his lyrics written with literate, loopy, and socially conscious adults in mind. I don't know what the funk they think of him at his record company, given that his second album *Watts and Paris* (Reprise) has been out for months, and they ain't done jack shit for it. My suspicion is that Thompson's too much his own man for them to peg, too damn oblique besides, and they're like, to hell with him. This when they could be jumping onboard a going trend: edgy, experimental Black songwriters. This Afrocentric avant-pop campaign has already given us Terence Trent D'Arby, Lenny Kravitz, Neneh Cherry, Tracy Chapman, Caron Wheeler, A R Kane, and Hugh Harris. Being more musically assured, less pretentious, and more colorful to boot, Thompson's record kicks a lot of their butts.

I discovered brother Thompson by a fluke. Back in 1985, I interviewed P-Funk guitarist Blackbird McKnight. At that time he told me he was on Thompson's 1984 debut, *Marc Anthony Thompson*. Figuring if 'Bird was on it I'm down with it too, I went to the closest cut-out bin and copped the mug for like, a $1.99. I played it once and forgot about it for a year. Next time I reached for the album I was going through heartbreak and keyed into this song called "Recover Gracefully." Never mind that in my cardiac-arrested state I converted the lyrics "Yes, I will recover gracefully" into "There's no way to recover gracefully," the song is a heavenward levitation on a par with one of Nascimento's ascents of the soul. Grounded enough to put the wounds of earthly love on exhibit, but metaphysical enough to believe break-up scars are evidence as much of a fall from grace as an ejection from the Garden. Thompson's song voice is from the dark side of the moon or maybe the light side of Miles Davis. Raspy, smoky, and sensuous but without a hint of come-on, it's a poet's voice, declarative rather than inviting. A this-is-my-world-if-you-can-deal-with-it voice, the sound of tenderized meat turned confessional. Only now, it may not be so easy to chew on.

Miles continually returns as a reference for Thompson vocals. Words fall from his lips in a guttural cadence, clearly meant to be felt as earthy sound and alienated presence before being lyrically dissected. And you do want to dissect them because Thompson's best songs read like worldly-wise metafiction. His first album got buried in 1984's Xmas glut; his new one has been thrown to the wind. Thirteen songs long, *Watts and Paris* owes little to anybody's idea of how to make a hit. It's a thoroughly modern mix of styles, sounds, and sensibilities. So that what you get is an upbeat number about wanting to change some girl's world, which then breaks down for a speech from Malcolm X about changing your thought pattern, your behavior pattern, and getting into some action. A slow burn **119** on the malingering time between relationships comes replete with a score that could have been from a Jean-Jacques Beineix movie. The song about two-legged dogs woofs so much bow-wow boo-hooing as to shame George Clinton out of any future canine muggery. But wait, there's more. Like "Monkey Time," wherein Thompson skewers Paul Simon as deftly as a Ginzu master: "I was Paul Simon in my dreams, woke up I was only Bruce Springsteen. My lips were gone, my weenie shrunk. Tried to dance I moved like a drunk."

How could you not love a song with lines that wicked and daring knowing that Thompson and Simon are label mates? Or lines wickeder still: "I taped the black man so let me be/South African been so good to me/I smile with you on the big TV/But don't you ever touch my Grammy." After the fade-out on the original mix of this song you heard the strains of "Hello darkness, my old friend" before a stylus is sent scratching across a vinyl surface. For some reason Thompson couldn't get permission to keep that little conceit. Sensitive, vulnerable, confessional type that Thompson is (sensitive, vulnerable, and confessional enough to write a song called "Pussywhipped and Blind"), Thompson has got balls and cheek in abundance.

So Thompson writes and orchestrates like a Hell's Angel on the road to Mecca, he sings like a low, hot wind blowing in from the Sahara on the way to a blind date with a sirocco, and I think he's three times dope even if his record company don't know what kind of private Idaho he blew in from. And you, you the public, should at least hear him out before his music vanishes like something out of H. P. Lovecraft. As in *The Coloured Man from Out of Space*.

—1990

Homeys on the Range: Public Enemy

*O*ther night (Dec. 23) Flip bade y'all's reporter to follow him not to the ends of the earth but damn near: the Stardust Ballroom, Boston Road between Seymour and Fish avenues in the Bronx. Take the 5 train to Gun Hill Road and hail a gypsy cab. That night Flip was hired-on moneytaker for brother-in-law Chuck Chillout (KISS FM) who produced the bill— Public Enemy, Schoolly D, Skinny Boys, emcees Special K and MC Lyte, comedian Chris Rock, and more. Think of how many half-weak shows you slept through.

I like to observe black teenagers in their natural habitat, the company of one another. Suck up on their language, humor, and energy; check out the latest in flygear and dance moves. Hiphop is like reggae in that the crowds flash as much (sometimes even more) star attitude than the stage acts. The Stardust crowd was flashing New York's most stylish (and tackhead-stylish) array of winter coats: furlined leathers, Avirex, Troop America. Chuck Chillout's security for the affair was some linebacker- and tight end–sized honchos with headsets. We're not talking goons though. His team was mobile, unobtrusive, and lighthanded. They efficiently quelled disorder and panic during the two minor altercations that broke out because of two assholes.

The girls made their entrance in pairs or threes, and so did the guys. Once down in the mirror-flanked hall that is the Stardust dungeon there was little interaction between the sexes. Out of a crowd that peaked at maybe 250, I never saw more than five dancing at any one time, and of those none danced for more than 30 seconds a pop. The latest floor craze is hyperkinetic—neck, head, elbows, and feet spasmodically jerking and shuffling every whichaway. Electric boogie meets lindy bop. I wondered what Barry Michael Cooper, who described the benign Wopp as "self-dismemberment," would make of these exploding gearshafts. Flip thought the frenzy and abruptness of their dancing analogous to the crack high. Into Cooper's metaphor and Flip's judgment comes the presumption that black-teen culture is overpopulated by violent crack junkies. Methinks the reason their dances live fast and die young is cause they're so used to having their parties broken up by disputes.

121
•

The prevailing atmosphere at the Stardust was fraternal, familial, even lounge-lizard casual. Other than ganging up in the Polaroid area to snap goofy group pictures, the dominant activity was milling and chilling, not illin'. There were few displays of black male posturing. That was reserved for stage personnel.

Schoolly D did not not move this crowd. His appearance and departure from the stage was met with an indifference bordering on obliviousness. Public Enemy was the only act of the night that got the people animated en masse, somewhere around 3 A.M. The crash collision thunder of their latest single "Bring the Noise" complemented the moves and gave them workout impetus. I dig these college-educated-and-proud-of-it homeys because they're stompdown and dissonant innovators of the form who promote black nationalism with panache. Pointman Chuck D could publish *The Quotable Chuck D* and it would fly in literate as well as pop-literate circles. To wit, "An antique fork, how long will it last?/We'll see in 12 minutes when he wants that blast."

The brother D has already chiseled more memorable quips into my head than any rapper in history. He also phrases his rolling polyrhythms melodically, a stride pianist of the mouth percussion school. Per his delivery, if Rakim is (pace Miles Davis) a rap ninja walking on eggshells, Chuck is the music's answer to the sheets-of-sound oratory Baraka bequeathed to the black poetry movement for love of Coltrane. Coltrane never had comic relief like Chuck's aide-de-camp Flavor Flav though. Chuck rides the stage like a wild stallion while Flav pogosticks. He's a surefire professor of ign'ance whose mismatch with the mainman derails the tradition of cult-nat loudmouths who don't know how to laugh at themselves. Meanwhile, DJ Terminator X speaks with his hands, a digital descendant of Malcolm. Some find Public Enemy too black, would rather they was rapping about boogers (to call a popular ditty of the day) than declaring themselves loud and proud supporters of Chesimard and Farrakhan. Public Enemy doesn't condescend to black youth. They talk at them and way over their heads, too, like the kids could stand to hear some race-conscious rabble-rousing. The Stardust crowd was totally down with the program. Black joy, sings Gilberto Gil, is the joy that warriors bring—Public Enemy in full effect, boyeeeee!

—1988

122
•

The Devil Made 'Em Do It: Public Enemy

Granted, Charlie Parker died laughing. Choked chickenwing perched over '50s MTV. So? No way in hell did Bird, believing there was no competition in music, will his legacy to some second-generation beboppers to rattle over the heads of the hiphop nation like a rusty sabre. But when Harry Allen comes picking fights with suckers adducing hiphop the new jazz, like hiphop needs a jazz crutch to stand erect, I'm reminded of *Pithecanthropus erectus,* and not the Charles Mingus version. B-boys devolved to the missing link between jazzmen and a lower order species out of Joseph Conrad. "Perhaps you will think it passing strange, this regret for a savage who was of no more account than a grain of sand in a black Sahara. Well, don't you see, he had done something, he had steered; for months I had him at my back—a help—an instrument. It was a kind of partnership." Page 87.

Hiphop being more than a cargo cult of the microchip, it deserves being debated on more elevated terms than as jazz's burden or successor. Given the near absence of interdisciplinary scholarship on the music, the conceptual straits of jazz journalism, and hiphop's cross-referential complexity, the hiphop historian must cast a wider net for critical models. Certainly Public Enemy's *It Takes a Nation of Millions to Hold Us Back* (Def Jam) demands kitchen-sink treatment. More than a hiphop record it's an ill worldview.

Nation of Millions is a will-to-power party record by bloods who believe (like Sun Ra) that for black folk, it's after the end of the world. Or, in PEspeak: "Armageddon has been in effect. Go get a late pass." In *Roll, Jordan, Roll: The World the Slaves Made,*

Eugene Genovese offers that the failure of mainland blacks to sustain a revolutionary tradition during slavery was due to a lack of faith in prophets of the apocalypse. This lack, he says, derived from Africa's stolen children having no memories of a paradise lost that revolution might regain. Machiavellian thinking might have found its way into the quarters: "All armed prophets have conquered while all unarmed prophets have failed." But the observation that blacks were unable to envision a world beyond the plantation, or of a justice beyond massa's dispensation, still resonates through our politics. Four decades after Garvey, the cultural nationalists of the '60s sought to remedy our Motherland amnesia and nationhood aversions through dithyrambs, demagoguery, and a counter-supremacist doctrine that pressed for utopia over reform pragmatism. Its noblest aim was total self-determination for the black community. For PE, that, not King's, is the dream that died.

The lofty but lolling saxophone sample that lures us into the LP's "Black Side" could be a wake-up call, a call to prayer, or an imitation Coltrane cocktease. Since we're not only dealing with regenerated sound here but regenerated meaning, what was heard 20 years ago as expression has now become a rhetorical device, a trope. Making old records talk via scratching or sampling is fundamental to hiphop. But where we've heard rare grooves recycled for parodic effect or shock value ad nauseam, on "Show Em Whatcha Got" PE manages something more sublime, enfolding and subsuming the Coltrane mystique, among others, within their own. The martial thump that kicks in after the obbligato owes its bones to Funkadelic's baby years and Miles Davis's urban bush music. But the war chants from Chuck D and Flavor Flav that blurt through the mix like station identification also say, What was hip yesterday we save from becoming passé. Since three avant-gardes overlap here—free jazz, funk, hiphop—the desired effect might seem a salvage mission. Not until Sister Ava Muhammad's tribute-to-the-martyrs speech fragments begin their cycle do you realize Public Enemy are offering themselves up as the next in line for major black prophet, missionary, or martyrdom status. Give them this much: PE paragon Farrakhan excepted, nobody gives you more for your entertainment dollar while cold playing that colored man's messiah role.

124

PE wants to reconvene the black power movement with hiphop as the medium. From the albums and interviews, the program involves rabble-rousing rage, radical aesthetics, and bootstrap capitalism, as well as a revival of the old movement's less than humane tendencies: revolutionary suicide, misogyny, gaybashing, Jew-baiting, and the castigation of the white man as a genetic miscreant, or per Elijah Muhammad's infamous myth of Yacub, a "grafted devil."

To know PE is to love the agitprop (and artful noise) and to worry over the whack retarded philosophy they espouse. Like: "The black woman has always been kept up by the white male because the white male has always wanted the black woman." Like: "Gays aren't doing what's needed to build the black nation." Like: "White people are actually monkey's uncles because that's who they made it with in the Caucasian hills." Like: "If the Palestinians took up arms, went into Israel, and killed all the Jews it'd be alright." From this idiot blather, PE are obviously making it up as they go along. Since PE show sound reasoning when they focus on racism as a tool of the U.S. power structure, they should be intelligent enough to realize that dehumanizing gays, women, and Jews isn't going to set black people free. As their prophet Mr. Farrakhan hasn't overcome one or another of these moral lapses, PE might not either. For now swallowing the PE pill means taking the bitter with the sweet, and if they don't grow up, later for they asses.

Nation of Millions is a declaration of war on the federal government, and on that unholy trinity—black radio programmers, crack dealers, and rock critics. ("Suckers! Liars! Get me a shovel. Some writers I know are damn devils. For them I say don't believe the hype. Yo Chuck, they must be on the pipe, right?") For sheer audacity and specificity Chuck D's enemies list rivals anything produced by the Black Liberation Army or punk—rallying for retribution against the Feds for the Panthers' fall (Party for Your Right to Fight"), slapping murder charges on the FBI and CIA for the assassinations of MLK and Malcolm X ("Louder Than a Bomb"), condoning cop-killing in the name of liberation ("Black Steel in the Hour of Chaos"), assailing copyright law and the court system ("Caught, Can We Get a Witness?"). As America's black teen population are the core audience for these APBs to terrorize the state, PE are bucking for first rap act to get taken out by Washington, by any means necessary.

Were it not for the fact that *Nation* is the most hellacious and hilarious dance record of the decade, nobody but the converted would give two hoots about PE's millenary desires. One of the many differences between *Nation* and their first, *Yo! Bum Rush the Show*, is that *Nation* is funkier. As George Clinton learned, you got to free Negroes' asses if you want their minds to bug. Having seen *Yo! Bum Rush* move the crowd *off* the floor, it's a pleasure to say only zealot wallflowers will fade into the blackground when *Nation* cues up. Premiered at a Sugar Hill gala, several *Nation* cuts received applause from the down but bupwardly mobile—fulfilling Chuck D's prediction on "Don't Believe the Hype" that by treating the hard jams like a seminar *Nation* would "teach the bourgeois and rock the boulevard." But PE's shotgun wedding of black militancy and musical pleasure ensures that *Nation* is going to move music junkies of all genotypes. "They claim we're products from the bottom of hell because the blackest record is bound to sell."

PE producer and arranger Hank Shocklee has the ears of life, and that rare ability to extract the lyrical from the lost and found. Every particle of sound on *Nation* has got a working mojo, a compelling something *other*-ness and that swing thang to boot. Shocklee's reconstructive composition of new works from archival bites advances sampling to the level of microsurgery. Ditto for cyborg DJ Terminator X, who cuts incisively enough to turn a decaying kazoo into a dopebeat on "Bring the Noise." Putting into effect Borges's rule that "the most fleeting thought obeys an invisible design and can crown, or inaugurate, a secret form," PE have evolved a songcraft from chipped flecks of near-forgotten soul gold. On *Nation* a guitar vamp from Funkadelic, a moan from Sly, a growl abducted from Bobby Byrd aren't just rhythmically spliced-in but melodically sequenced into colorful narratives. Think of Romare Bearden.

One cut-up who understands the collage-form is PE's Flavor Flav. Misconstrued as mere aide-de-camp to rap's angriest man after *Yo! Bum Rush*, he emerges here as a duck-soup stirrer in his own right. Flav's solo tip, "Cold Lampin with Flavor," is incantatory shamanism on a par with any of the greats: Beefheart, Koch, Khomeini. "You

126
•

pick your teeth with tombstone chips, candy-colored flips, dead women hips you do the bump with. Bones. Nuthin' but love bones."

Those who dismiss Chuck D as a bullshit artist because he's loud, pro-black, and proud will likely miss out on gifts for blues pathos and black comedy. When he's on, his rhymes can stun-gun your heart and militarize your funnybone. As a people's poet and pedagogue of the oppressed, Chuck hits his peak on the jailhouse toast/prison break movie, "Black Steel in the Hour of Chaos." The scenario finds Chuck unjustly under the justice ("Innocent/Because I'm militant/Posing a threat/You bet it's fucking up the government"). Chuck and "52 brothers bruised, battered, and scarred but hard" bust out the joint with the aid of PE's plastic Uzi protection, "the S1Ws" (Security of the First World). Inside the fantasy, Chuck crafts verse of poignant sympathy for all doing hard time. ("I'm on a tier where no tears should ever fall/Cell block and locked I never clock it y'all.") His allusion to the Middle Passage as the first penal colony for blacks is cold chillin' for real. Chuck's idea of a lifer, or career soldier, is also at odds with convention: "Nevertheless they could not understand that I'm a black man and I could never be a veteran."

As much as I love this kind of talk, I got to wonder about PE's thing against black women. And my dogass ain't the only one wondering—several sisters I know who otherwise like the mugs wonder whassup with that too. Last album PE dissed half the race as "Sophisticated Bitches." This time around, "She Watch Channel Zero?!" a headbanger about how brainless the bitch is for watching the soaps, keeping the race down. "I know she don't know, I quote/ Her brains retrained by a 24-inch remote/Revolution a solution for all our children/But all her children don't mean as much as the show." Whoa! S.T.F.O.!* Would you say that to *your* mother, motherfucker? Got to say, though, the thrash is deadly. One of those riffs makes you want to stomp somebody into an early grave, as Flav goes on and on insinuating that women are garbage for watching garbage. In light of Chuck's plea for crack dealers to be good to the neighborhood on "Night of the Living Baseheads," it appears PE believe the dealers more capable of penance than the

*Step the Fuck Off!

sistuhs. Remember *The Mack?* Where the pimp figures it cool to make crazy dollar off his skeezes but uncool for the white man to sell scag to the little brothers? This is from that same mentality. And dig that in "Black Steel in the Hour of Chaos," the one time on the album Chuck talks about firing a piece, it's to pop a *female* corrections officer. By my homegirl's reckoning all the misogyny is the result of PE suffering from LOP: lack of pussy. She might have a point.

—1988

Diary of a Bug

128

1. Greil Marcus knows what time it is, even if my inspiration for this format is F. Scott Fitzgerald's *The Crack-Up*.
2. Cuban novelist Guillermo Cabrera Infante interrogated about his favorite readings. "Fragments, any sort of fragments."
3. "In this journey, you're the journal, I'm the journalist. Am I eternal, or an eternal *list* [eternalist?]?" That's from Rakim's "Follow the Leader," though it could be Roland Barthes convincing us that authors are the creations of texts and that texts are the recreation of closed cultures and close readers. That the *author*, after Levi-Strauss, is a mythic figure, just a sign of narrativity. The crisis thrown up in Rakim's rhyme—the poet pondering whether he's a modernist or a postmodernist, a creative God or a revised body of texts—is rendered moot in the next line: "I'm about the flow, long as I can possibly go. Keep you moving because the crowd says so. Dance!"

Here Rakim locates his immortality in African culture's call-and-response continuum.

4. Public Enemy's Chuck D has as formidable a poetic mind as African-American literary tradition has ever produced. Purely in terms of polysemous invention, you got to give it up to the brother for a line like, "My plan said I had to break north. Just like with Oliver's neck, I had to get off." Breaking north alludes to the direction in which fugitive slaves hauled ass from the plantations. But the willful confusion of the freedom road with Oliver's neck rings from sea to shining sea how justice is dispensed along color lines. And of course getting off is slang that has one meaning in the jury box and quite another in a dance-fever sweatbox.

5. *You don't need to bring sand to the beach.* What your boys tell you when they find out that your woman is traveling with you to Bahia, Brazil.

6. *I can't dance.* A bluesy expression my man T.P. uses when he's had a fucked-up day.

7. *I can't get no rhythm from so-and-so.* My mellow Sheila's way of saying she can't get somebody to do right by her.

8. Cecil Taylor quizzed as to what he thinks the West will never understand about African culture: "The magic of rhythm."

9. In the October '88 *Musician* Randy Newman extols rap lyricists as his favorites, then says it's easier to rap than to set words to *music*. Somebody refer his monkey ass to Cecil. "The thing that frightened people about hiphop was that they heard people enjoying rhythm for rhythm's sake. Hiphop lives in the world— not the world of music—and that's why it's so revolutionary," Max Roach says.

10. "I Wish U Heaven," Prince 12-inch: "Take this beat. I don't mind. Got plenty others. They're so fine."

11. The sampling-is-theft allegation has been taken up recently by at least three rap groups: Public Enemy, Stetsasonic, Eric B. & Rakim. All three defenses are also aesthetic manifestos. On "Caught, Can I Get a Witness?" Flav laughs off the Eurocentric limits of copyright law, scowling that beats can't be copyrighted. Chuck conceives of dem ole funky beats as power-packed minerals, consigned like black folks to a position lower

than low, though better than gold. Eric B. & Rakim define the beats as family heirlooms. "Static? I don't cling. I got a tip of my own, and I don't sing. Don't understand, here's an example: a *rhyme sings* [emphasis mine] and a DJ samples. Because we don't have a band, it's just my voice and his hands. That's what hiphop was and still stands. The records we use from mom and pop's collection, find a break from a dope selection."

In "Talkin' All That Jazz" Stetsasonic eschew the oblique for outright confrontation. James Brown was old, until Eric and Rak came out with 'I Got Soul [sic].' " Music belongs to the people, and sampling isn't a copycat act but a form of reanimation. Sampling in hiphop is the digitized version of hiphop DJing, an archival project and an art form unto itself. Hiphop is ancestor worship.

12. "Talkin' All That Jazz," starring Stetsasonic, directed by Fab Five Freddy: read this video as a sampling defense, as another broadside proclaiming hiphop the new jazz. What it also extols is rappers' delight in putting a metrical foot up the ass of anybody who dares to play the dozens on this music. Stet's aggressive play-acting of every line translates each verse into a physical threat. Fab Five's editing gives expression to the knowledge that the camaraderie and cajolery of black-male bonding can be converted in a minute to combat uses by a posse. Fab choreographs movement in a way that's as polyrhythmic as the music without being slavishly cued to the beats and breaks.

13. "Night of the Living Baseheads," starring Public Enemy, directed by Lionel Martin. As you'd expect, PE's first video expends as much energy terrorizing the medium as it does delivering the word. Set in a near future that utopianly envisions a PE public-access channel, the video is a "scratch mix" of visual newsfeeds of which Chuck D's performance is but one sample among many. You'll be hard-pressed to find another music video that so freehandedly treats the "product" (band and song) as collage material. Some of the vignettes, like the ones depicting crack zombyism as an update on the

Middle Passage, are suggested by the lyrics. Others, like Chris Thomas's Geraldo-like invasion of a black family brought low by a basehead father, or MC Lyte's expose of Wall Street basing, are brilliant spin-offs. Flavor Flav emerges as the most irrepressible and eye-popping comedian since Al Sharpton. PE's legerdemain at packaging problack radicalism for musical consumption is becoming legendary.

14. "I'm Your Pusher," starring Ice-T, directed by Rick Elgood and Howard Woffinden. L.A. rapper Ice-T says his tag came from reciting passages from Iceberg Slim's black-on-black crime novels in the playground. At a time when every other rapper around wants to play gangster, here's one who's done prison time. This video glamorizes hiphop's outlaw status among the young and criminal-minded, pushing "dope beats and rhymes" *and* "just say no." In yet another near-future scenario, you got rap banned and contraband, a black market music sold on street corners where rap merchants like Ice-T vie with crackdusters for clientele. Shot like a Michelob commercial, full of quick cuts, color-saturated club life, and neon flash, it's the new jack's first successful blaxploitation movie.

15. I spend November 10 with Ice-T and Big Daddy Kane on a promotional trip. They do a morning assembly at I.S. 10 in Harlem, lunch at Copeland's, and the afternoon in 125th Street record stores. At one point Ice-T and Big Daddy Kane are lamping by a limo outside the Parker Meridien Hotel when a brother slides up to hand Ice a manila envelope containing a gift of Sun Tzu's *The Art of War*—another of those Zen combat manuals somehow universally applicable to late-stage capitalism and feudal China.

16. In the October *Spin* there's an interview with Max Roach and Fab Five Freddy in which Roach calls writer Frank Owen a racist white cocksucker before throwing him out of his house. This scene, we're told, was provoked by Owen's assertions that hiphop isn't a "purist" black art form due to rappers sampling riffs from white rock groups like Mountain, Kraftwerk, and Led Zeppelin. Never mind that their tired-ass riffs were heisted from black folks in the first place. This is like

131
•

saying that when black teenyboppers name a dance the Pee-Wee Herman, Pee-Wee can then go to their mamas and claim them as branches off his family tree. You tell me what appropriation has to do with genetics? Did Picasso become a mulatto after *Les Demoiselles d'Avignon?*

17. Stanley Crouch once queried me as to which rappers I thought were literate. I remember I mumbled something about Public Enemy. When I told this to Harry Allen he thought that by definition they'd *all* have to be. By which Harry meant able to read and write while Stanley meant as well-read as me. One thing I admire about Harry is that he refuses to have hiphop shoulder the burden of proof where its critics are concerned. I get defensive. Like hiphop needs me to prove it has a brain. Who do I think I am—Dr. Funkenstein?

—1988

132 *Posses in Effect: Ice-T*

Swarms of aggressive, Africanized bees will reach the United States within one and a half years, and they appear to be a more formidable threat than originally predicted. The bees are descendants of 20 to 30 African bees that escaped after being imported to Brazil for research purposes. The bees tend to be more defensive around hives and tend to more aggressively attack and pursue people than the gentler bees of European descent raised in the Americas. Scientists had assumed the Africanized bees would become Europeanized by mating with the gentler variety, and thus lose their propensity to sting in potentially

deadly swarms. But in the most surprising finding of the conference, researchers reported that the dilution of Africanized bees
appears only to be temporary. Researchers said one way to reduce
the Africanized bees' influence is to kill colonies they have infiltrated.

—Associated Press, October 16, 1988

Two California gangs fanning out along the interstate highway
system are spreading a sophisticated pattern of violence and drug
dealing across the country. Law enforcement officials say the
gangs have reached as far east as Baltimore and Washington,
staking out claims along the way in middle-size cities like Omaha.
The gangs, the Bloods and the Crips, have abandoned some of
the flamboyant hallmarks of their West Coast dealings. Officials
say their tactics mimic the entrepreneurial enterprises of newly
minted M.B.A.s "But we are not seeing the same kind of gang
activity as L.A.," Captain Barton said. "When they leave California they become a drug organization, not a gang." In Kansas
City the police say the California gangs have moved in to fill a
vacuum created since vigorous enforcement forced Jamaican
gangs either out of town or underground.

—*New York Times*, November 25, 1989

"The gangs of L.A. will never die, just multiply."

—Ice-T, "Colors" (Warner Bros.)

A. B. Spellman once said the outcast status of jazz had everything
to do with the music's creation by "the most despised and feared
group of people on the face of the earth—the black working class."
Hiphop is now the dominant cultural expression of the most despised and feared segment of that class: young black men. The
music has become a means for male bonding outside the control
of white-institutional America. It is the song and dance routines
of an incipient warrior culture. Hiphop represents the black male
treating his pariahhood as if social vilification were a superheroic
emblem.

Down here on the ground though, the reality is that young black
men are more endangered than dangerous. Recent statistics on our
mortality and numbers in prison affirm that we're the most *con-

certedly targeted population by the powers that be bar none. Hiphop alternately serves as the black man's battle cry and mediator. Analogous to the role Jesse Jackson plays as black America's ambassador, hiphop performs a defensive and diplomatic function for the young black male. This is not to say Jackson or hiphopsters make black men seem any less threatening, just that their eloquence, intellect, and organization show white supremacists how much they really have to fear.

Every successful rap group is a black fraternal organization, a posse. Ice-T is the first gold rapper to emerge from a bona fide black criminal enterprise, the gangs of Los Angeles. His trade-in of a life as a career criminal for pop careering measures the degree to which hiphop and the new jack crime syndicates are good and evil twins. One brother redeems, the over ravages. Ice-T's background gives him an advantage over all the wannabee gangsters in East Coast hiphop. When he steps into the killcrazy heads of the Bloods and the Crips, as he did with harrowing results on the theme song for *Colors*, he sounds scarier than hyperbole because you know he's talking reality.

The problem with Ice-T's *Power* (Sire) is that the rhymes don't have the poetic head-charge of his East Coast comrades, and his phrasing is too one-beat. He's rhyming too hard, popping evil shit gratuitously to keep up with the Kanes and whatnot. These days, the best hiphop lyrics posess what Ntozake Shange once identified as the relaxed virility of the black *Uebermensch*, the sound of a cool head attached to a hot body.

The mordant wit hiphop likes to show off with these days not only makes it our most quotable pulp, but the only one whose exegesis requires ballistics. The dope measure of a new jack lyric is whether it blows into the ear like a dum-dum bullet, indelibly stains the brain, and frequently exits the victim's mouth in the form of a conversation piece. On *Power* Ice-T rises to this standard only on "I'm Your Pusher," where he appropriates drug lingo to play the reformed hiphop moralist. "Drama" is a close second, finding Ice in my favorite mode for him, that of storyteller. It's a tale of thinking you know how to get over and finding yourself going under (the criminal justice system). Otherwise, I get the impression Ice is straining for badassedness. A tune like "LGBNFT" ("Let's

Get Butt Naked and Fuck Tonight") is an embarrassment for not even being smart enough to smack up the Beastie Boys. Then there's this pimp's last mack oration that sounds like rehashed *Hustler's Convention* bullshit. Ice finds his voice when he's dealing with the coast. He needs to just lay there and let the Apple come to him.

Gangbanging in the ghetto, on the other hand, has exploded since 1984, in rough synchronization with the rerouting of the cocaine trail from Florida to Southern California via Mexico, and the emergence of crack. This epidemic of youth violence has been inflated by law-enforcement agencies into something quite phantasmagoric. In a numbers game that ceases to distinguish the authentic high rollers and stone killers of the gang world from the wannabees, estimates of hardcore gang membership have risen from 10,000 to 50,000. Sheriffs' "gang experts" have invoked a spectre of 100,000 "rotten little cowards" overrunning Los Angeles County. Meanwhile an Andromeda Strain of Crips and Bloods is reported to have infiltrated the entire West, with accounts of local spores from Seattle to Denver, even white mutant variants in Tucson (such, at least, is the fantasy of hysterical parents).
 —"Los Angeles: Civil Liberties Between the Hammer and the Rock," Mike Davis with Sue Ruddick, *New Left Review*

135
•

The Emancipation Proclamation provoked lurid Democratic descriptions of an impending black inundation of the Midwest. In Indiana, one group of Democratic women paraded before an election with banners emblazoned: "Fathers save us from nigger husbands." Often it was remarkably direct. "Slavery is dead," the *Cincinnati Enquirer* announced at the end of the war, "the negro is not, there is the misfortune."
 —*Reconstruction 1863–1877*, Eric Foner, Harper & Row, 1988

When I see this wildness gone in a person, it's sad. This special lack of restraint is best typified in certain black men. They may give him bad names and call him "street nigger," but when you take away the vocabulary of denigration what you have is somebody who is fearless and who is comfortable with that fearlessness. It's not about meanness. It's a kind of self-flagellant resistance to certain kinds of control. Opposed to accepted notions of progress, the lock-step life, they live in the world unreconstructed and that's it.

—Toni Morrison in Claudia Tate's *Black Women Writers at
Work*

A language is on the hither side of Literature. Style is almost beyond it: imagery, delivery, vocabulary spring from the body and past of the writer and gradually become the very reflexes of his art. Thus under the name of style a self-sufficient language is evolved which has its roots in the author's personal and secret mythology. Its secret is recollection locked within the body of the writer.

—Roland Barthes, *Writing Degree Zero*

Tonight we pick 'em up for anything and *everything*, said an LAPD spokesperson before Operation Hammer, in which 1453 black men were arrested at random in southcentral Los Angeles, April 9, 1988.

—Mike Davis, *New Left Review*

—*1989*

Yabba Dabba Doo-Wop: De La Soul

*O*ut, out, out my face talking about *dope*. Man, your shit is tired in a daisy age. The operative word in hiphop today is *freestyle*. Well, at least in your big chucklehead mind if you want it to be. It's your thing, do what you wanna do. I can't tell you how to sock it to. But if I could, I'd advise don't be redundant. By now the will to dopeness ought to be as paradigmatic among hiphopsters as that don't-mean-a-thing reminder was to swing or if-you-ain't-gonna-get-it-on-then-take-your-dead-ass-home was to P-Funk. With outer colonies of the hiphop nation like L.A., Oakland, and the dreaded Miami weighing in heavy with escapist product for the hard-rock market, the New York posses continue to take it to the next phase, producing street-credible hiphop that literate adults can chew on. What's hip in New York 'hop ain't just doing the wild thing, but doing it your way, boldly rhyming where no one has rhymed before, coming off with lines and delivery as unbitably yours as a graffiti tag.

No constituency of the hiphop nation has done more to create auteurist headroom in the music than the posses of Long Island— Strong Island, as affectionately dubbed by the once-defensive natives. There is as much innovation going down on the Island as used to go down in the Boogie-Down, the Bronx that is, way, way, way, back in the day. Strong Island hiphop's different from hiphop elsewhere, and the groups coming out of there are remarkably dissimilar to one another. Public Enemy, Eric B. & Rakim, EPMD, and this year's deus ex machina De La Soul form hiphop's vanguard, alongside the equally avant KRS One, Hurby Azor, and Big Daddy Kane. Strong Island hiphop sticks more in your earhole, bedazzling bookish types, retaining mass-ass appeal to the max. The Islanders are also the ones who render Harry Allen's hiphop-is-the-new-jazz riff more than provocative hype, because in Strong Island hiphop, as in jazz, you have to develop your own way of singing and your own way of swinging, your own voice and your own *vounce*—or else move to Miami.

While too many rappers run the same cadence into the ground album after album, Strong Island rappers are liable to switch up the rhyme-flow midsyllable. That magic that used to be in jazz, when brothers routinely blew chorus after chorus of stupid-fresh riffs, snatching the music out the air like they had mental telepathy cosmic ray antennae, crystal radios in they cap-fillings or sumpin', has at last made its cultural comeback. Give me that old-time religion, this year's Chinese music by any other name, and somebody alert the jazz police. Future-shock just rode in on the LIRR.

You have to understand, black people from Strong Island are different from you and me. They have all the funk of inner-city ignays, an African villager's sense of community, preppy educations, and the bicultural savvy of a 'burb upbringing—a black middle class who went from ghetto barbarism to prefab apartheid without stopping to become bourgeois in the process. Try and find the Roosevelt, Elmont, Babylon, Hempstead, Wyandanch (pronounced *wine dance*, dig?), or Amityville chapters of the Jack and Jills, I dare you. On the other hand, since Strong Island's rappers also come from a land of lawnmowers, chaise-longue leisure time, and aluminum siding, it was only a matter of time before some Island posse emerged secure enough in their manhood to make hay of their white-picket roots.

Enter De La Soul, the first Strong Island hiphop band not too proud to lay bare their handiness with garden tools. Like Public Enemy's first strike *Yo! Bum Rush the Show*, De La Soul's debut *3 Feet High and Rising* (Tommy Boy) premieres a trio of high-IQ B-boys on a mission of redemption, sloshing a musical cup runneth over with neophilia. Chuck D has proclaimed De La Soul his favorite group, because the differences between PE and De La Soul are several, most of them whimsical. Compare the weaponry: Uzis and daisies.

PE are shock troops, De La Soul are flower children. Don't see them as in opposition though, given the black man's condition in America today. It's like Malcolm and Martin, Amiri and Jimi, Marley and Clinton, keeping in balance the way of the sword and the way of the hoe. One brandishes the mad-man theory; the other spreads the love oh sweet Jesus yes yes yes. Imagine your brain a fertile plot of virgin land wanting to be a seedbed of righteous black consciousness. To PE it appears in need of a scorched-earth policy. To De La Soul it looks like a swell spot to prune a strictly paisley and purple sage botanica, a cauliflower crown-cut barbershop, or the De La Soul version of *Pee-Wee's Playhouse*.

This is not to say De La Soul shy away from social protest. On "Say No Go" they develop worry lines over the baseheads to a tongue-in-cheek mesh of Sly Stone's "High on You" and Hall & Oates's "I Can't Go for That (No Can Do)"; *A baby is born into a world of pits/And if it could'a talked that soon in the delivery room/ It would have asked the nurse for a hit/The reason for this?/The mother is a jerk, excuse me, junkie/ . . . a way of today/Anyway/ Push couldn't shove me to understand the path into a basehead/ Consumer should have erased it in the first place*." On the whole, though, De La Soul come off more bugged out than teed off. Greenpeace should adopt their funny animal song "Tread Water" as its theme song. In it MC Trugoy the Dove imbibes life wisdom from Messrs. Monkey, Fish, Squirrel, and Crocodile to what sounds like incidental music from a *Peanuts* TV special.

De La Soul's delivery is passionate, playful, and plainspoken in the same breath; singsongy and so lacking in bluster, bravura, or braggadocio some will hear it as laid-back, lackadaisical. You thought EPMD had a relaxed rapping style? De La Soul make EPMD sound like Mickey Mouse. The light touch is also present in De La Soul's musical arrangements. You thought Eric B. was a deft and mellow mixer? De La Soul make Eric B. sound like Bachman-Turner Overdrive. On the love-smitten "Eye Know" a verse from Steely Dan's "Peg" becomes a romantic chorus, a snatch from the whistling solo in Sweet Otis's "(Sittin' on) the Dock of the Bay" a hornish obbligato. If PE advanced the art of sampling-and-stitching to the level of microsurgery on *It Takes a Nation of Millions*

139
•

to Hold Us Back, De La Soul take that knowledge to the bridge and drop it off in Toontown.

In jazz they say that ballads are what separate the men from the boys. By this rule De La Soul's Trugoy, Posdnous, and PA Pasemaster Mase are the he-men of hiphop. They do it to you slow and more bodaciously than any hiphop band I know, longer and more lovingly too. De La Soul are to hiphop sex what PE are to hiphop guerrilla warfare. On "Jenifa Taught Me (Derwin's Revenge)" De La Soul bow down to a horny female without passing judgment, showing a promiscuous biddy more respect than any brothers in hiphop history. On "Buddy" lusty male-bonding is done a solid, returning a certain charm to that irrepressible if disreputable enterprise. "Buddy" is either a euphemism for womens or the P word, but what the song really gets deep into is how tight De La Soul are with their dicks. More specifically about how tight De La Soul, the Jungle Brothers, and Q-Tip are with every man's favorite flopalong toy.

Surprisingly enough, this is not a song about how big their jimmys is or how many girly-girlies say ow! when the Soul comes around. This is more a me-my-jimmy-and-I kind of song, an I'm OK, jimmy's OK confession. Plying a convenient piece of sexist mythology, the Jungle Brothers advise (as studio guests of De La Soul) *on the lap jimbrowski must wear a cap, just in case the young girl likes to clap,* but on the whole, there has never been a more benign and beatific ode to walking around with a hard-on. "Buddy" is a sexy groove, De La Soul's smooth operator song, smoother than Spoonie Gee Big Daddy Kane Julio Iglesias combined.

There are 22 tracks on *3 Feet High and Rising,* 24 on the CD, and a whole bunch of them will make you wise up, bust a gut, go Gucci rolling in the aisles. I don't know whether it'll be "Take It Off," where the Soul pleads for the defetishization of brand name status symbols of every stripe, from Lee jeans to Afros, or their Chad and Jeremy style tip "The Magic Number," or their home porn video "De La Orgee," but one way or another De La Soul got something for you. They extend the tradition of *We're All Bozos on This Bus, Funkentelechy vs. the Placebo Syndrome,* and *There's a Riot Goin' On,* none of which represent well-trodden paths.

When he was booking for Chocolate City's 9:30 Club, my brother

Brian once returned ecstatic from auditioning a band of 14-year-olds he'd fallen in love with because they had the greatest love of all: Fear of No Music. They'd listen to and play anything. De La Soul got that polyglot ardor for music too, and unlike Fishbone they know that being an off shade of black does not mean you got to be afraid of the funk.

—1989

141

Yo! Hermeneutics!

Yo! Hermeneutics!: Henry Louis Gates, Houston Baker, and David Toop

> If you can't dazzle them with your brilliance then baffle them with your bullshit.
>
> —*Afro-American folk wisdom*

> In a war against symbols which have been wrongly titled, only the letter can fight.
>
> —*Ramm-El-Zee*

Word, word. Word up: Thelonious X. Thrashfunk sez, yo Greg, black people need our own Roland Barthes, man. Black deconstruction in America? I'm way ahead of the brother, or so I think when I tell him about my dream magazine: *I Signify—The Journal of Afro-American Semiotics*. We talking a black Barthesian variation on *Jet*, itself the forerunner of black poststructuralist activity, given its synchronic mythification and diachronic deconstruction ("Soul singer James Brown pulled up to court in Baltimore in a limousine and wearing a full-length fur coat, but convinced a federal magistrate he is too poor to pay creditors $170,000. Brown testified that although he performs regularly, he has no money. . . . U.S. Magistrate Frederick N. Smalkin agreed. 'It appears Mr. Brown's financial and legal advisors have surrounded him with a network of corporations and trusts that serves as a moat to defend him from the incursion of creditors,' Smalkin said"), not to mention its contribution to the black tradition of the encyclopedic narrative (cf. Ellison, Reed, Delany, Clinton, and Ramm-El-Zee).

Merely conceiving a poststructuralist version of this deuteronomic tribal scroll is enough to make me feel like a one-man Harlem Renaissance—at least until Thelonious asks if I'm hip to Henry Louis Gates, Jr., blood up at Yale (Cornell by the time you read this) who guest-edited two issues of *Black American Literature Forum* on the subject of semiotics and the signifyin' monkey. Turns out I vaguely recall hearing about an appearance the brother made at a Howard University Third World Writers' Conference a few years back. Rumor has it Gates shook up the joint talking about the relationship of structuralism to Booker T. Washington's *Up from Slavery:* folk wanted to know what all this formalism had to do with the struggle. Now, unless I'm mistaken that was the same year Barbara Smith nearly got run outta town on a rail behind delivering a radical lesbian-feminist reading of Toni Morrison's *Sula* (one sister proclaimed Smith had ruined a beautiful book by bringing her sexual perversion into it) and the same conference where Addison Gayle went off on Ishmael Reed for not being a social realist. (Bo Schmo meets the Loup Garoo Kid live and in living color like a mother-fer-ya.)

Reason I bring all this up is Gates has now published *Black Literature and Literary Theory*, 14 ground-breaking essays by an assorted lot of literary academics—black, white, African, Afro-American, feminist, structuralist, poststructuralist. The contributor notes confirm that these furthermuckers here are off into some brand new funk. Jay Edwards, for example, is author of a forth-coming two-volume *Vernacular Architecture of French Louisiana*. Barbara Johnson, professor of romance languages and literature at Harvard, has written *Désfiguration du Langage poétique*, translated Derrida's *Dissemination*, and is working on a book about Zora Neale Hurston. Anthony Appiah, formerly of the University of Ghana and Clare College, Cambridge, now at Yale, is editing and analyzing 7000 Twi proverbs and doing a book on those aspects of philosophy of mind most relevant to the interpretation of language.

In his introductory essay, "Criticism in the Jungle," Gates rhetorically asks, "Who would deny us our complexity?" and defends rigorous formal (as opposed to polemical) readings of black texts. Which isn't to say his program lacks sociopolitical baggage: "The essays collected in *Black Literature and Literary Theory* share a concern with the nature of the figure, with the distinctively 'black' uses of *our* English and French language and literature. . . . How 'black' is figuration? Given the obvious political intent of so much of our literary traditions, is it not somewhat wistful to be concerned with the intricacies of the figure? The Afro-American tradition has been figurative from its beginnings. How could it have survived otherwise? I need not here trace the elaborate modes of signification implicit in black mythic and religious traditions, in ritual rhetorical structures such as 'signifying' and 'the dozens.' Black people have always been masters of the figurative: saying one thing to mean something quite other has been basic to black survival in oppressive Western cultures. . . . 'Reading,' in this sense, was not play; it was an essential aspect of the 'literacy' training of a child. This sort of metaphorical literacy, the learning to decipher complex codes, is just about the blackest aspect of the black tradition."

And white folks thought black people only had the edge on them in primitivism; uh-huh, brothers and sisters got deconstruction racing through their veins too. Matter of fact, one of the hippest essays in the collection, James Snead's "Repetition as a Figure of Black Culture," gives the granddaddy of dialectics (that's Hegel, y'all) a run for his modernism, demolishing G.W.'s racist belief that European history is progressive and African history "primitive" by demonstrating that Western modernism's debts to The Continent are *conceptual* as well as formal. Roll over Picasso, tell William Rubin the news. Whole lot of signifyin' of that order goes down in this book; polysyllabic Western theories got to throwdown to the beat of polyphonous black aesthetic discourse. Says Gates: "The challenge of black literary criticism is to derive principles of literary criticism from the black tradition itself, as defined in the idiom of critical theory but also in the idiom which constitutes the 'language of blackness,' the signifyin(g) difference which makes the black tradition our very own. To borrow mindlessly, or to vulgarize, a critical theory from another tradition is to satisfy de Gaultier's definition of 'bovaryism'; but it is also to satisfy, in the black idiom, Ishmael Reed's definition of 'The Talking Android.' " Gates's notion of a black tradition built only on figurative language seems a bit text-bound and bookwormish to me, but this tropism can probably be read as a rhetorical ploy in pursuit of academic equality for the study of Afro-American literature. While we all know who really bears the burden of proof of "civilization," survival often bids us act otherwise.

Maybe the most admirable (and subversive) thing about the essays in *BLALT* is that they explain, question, argue down, revise, signify on the theories they consort with in the interest of integrating black culture into the postmodern world. Could be black culture been there and gone, considering the Art Ensemble of Chicago and especially Miles Davis (his schizzy public statements on jazz seem to epitomize the canon-rearing and canon-razing that lie at the heart of the entire postmodern deconstruction project), but who would deny these professors their shot at contributing to the state of the race? Black culture doesn't lack for modernist and post-modernist artists, just their critical equivalents. And now that, like Spielberg's *Poltergeist*, they're here, might as well face up to the fact that there's no avoiding the recondite little suckers.

Although if, like every other liberal arts–damaged bibliophile I know, you bring to the semiotics enterprise more than latent hostility, you may get into this book purely on account of the lucidity these interlocutors break the shit on down with. Take, for example, Anthony Appiah's "Strictures on Structures: The Prospects for a Structuralist Poetics of African Fiction," which manages, against the odds, a droll exegesis of Saussure and Lévi-Strauss. Believe it or not, Appiah actually makes fun reading out of his deadpan definitions of Saussure's *langue* and *parole*, not to mention Chomsky's ideas about linguistic *performance* and *competence:* ". . . how is it that we are able to find in the inchoate mass of ordinary utterances which Saussure called *parole*, that abstract system of rules he called the *langue?* It is because the Chomskyan notions of *performance* and *competence* provide an answer to this question that they are often mentioned in the same breath as the *langue/ parole* distinction. Chomsky's claim is that speakers have an implicit grasp of the rules of the abstract system of *langue*, which grasp constitutes *competence* and guides their actual *performance* in *parole*. Differences between what the *langue* prescribes and the raw stuff of ordinary speech are to be explained in terms of the failure of psychological processes which actually apply the rules. Analogously, we can claim that driving is governed (in Britain) by the rule 'Drive on the left in two way traffic,' while allowing that some people drive on the right when they aren't concentrating."

Appiah is damn near sidesplitting taking Lévi-Strauss and Saussure to task for claiming that a *langue* for decoding myth structure and literary structure exists in the collective unconscious: "I think that Levi-Strauss's view is that the decoding does occur, but that it is unconscious: this is an interesting thought, for which, if I may speak for myself and the myths of Asante, there does not seem to be much evidence. . . . For a breed so given to drawing on a linguistics whose privileged status seems to derive only from the scientism of our culture and times, literary theorists seem peculiarly resistant to even the most modest form of empiricism. We can acknowledge that all theory is underdetermined by the evidence, that a flourishing undergrowth of theory can subsist on the most meagre evidential terrain and still require of ourselves that we root our theorizing in the dry earth of experience."

Signifyin' on the signifiers is a running theme of this collection, but those whose butts get signified on aren't just Hegel and the formalist frogs. Barbara Johnson's "Metaphor and Metonymy and Voice in *Their Eyes Were Watching God*" makes strange bedfellows of black male activists and white feminists (both are culpable, Johnson believes, for denying black women's inner voices) in a remarkable essay that widens the significance of Jakobson's famous study on aphasia by appreciating Hurston's synthesis of public and private voices in the rendering of Janie Starks. Ostensibly, Appiah's essay is a debunking of the foremost African structuralist Sunday O. Anonzie; Houston Baker's "To Move Without Moving: Creativity and Commerce in Ralph Ellison's Trueblood Episode" manages to be equally Oedipal albeit more genuflectively. Baker produces a dialectical parallel between trickster Trueblood's exploitation of American racial myth for personal gain and Ellison's own careerist use of same: ". . . the 'critical pronouncements' in Ellison's canon that imply his devaluing of Afro-American folklore hardly seem consistent with the meanings implicit in his Trueblood episode. Such utterances may be regarded, I believe, as public statements by Ellison 'the merchant' rather than as incisive, affective remarks by Ralph Ellison the creative genius. Trueblood's duality is, finally, also that of his creator. For Ellison knows that his work as an Afro-American artist derives from those 'economics of slavery' which provided conditions for Afro-American folklore. . . . Joyce and Eliot taught Ellison that, if he was a skillful enough strategist and spokesman, he could market his own folklore. What is bracketed, of course, are the economics that dictated that if Ellison wished to be an *Afro-American* artist he could only turn to Afro-American folklore as a traditional, authenticating source for his art. Like his sharecropper, Ellison is wont to make 'literary value' out of socio-economic necessity."

In this assessment of Ellison, Baker could of course be remarking on the peculiar tautologies of slanguage and formal language black academics like him and Gates have to deploy to keep up a good front. I mean this is a slick game the bloods are running here, making with all the right poststructuralist references and verbiage to translate black folk's linguistic thang into some doodah dem buckra can relate to while at the same time being true to black culture's version of semiotics, namely signifyin'. Gates's closing essay, "The Blackness of Blackness: A Critique of the Sign and the Signifying Monkey" is a masterpiece of such duplicity. Through an appreciation of Ishmael Reed's *Mumbo Jumbo* Gates manages to viciously signify on all of black and Western discourse. (By the way, Henry, we got to figure out some other distinction besides this black and Western stuff, being as how blackness is a Western category in itself, and all that's black ain't purely African or non-Western even, semantic convenience notwithstanding. Robert Farris Thompson's notion of a Black Atlantic tradition is one solution, but you know, you start bringing bodies of water into it and folk get to signifyin' Negroes can't swim. Anthony Braxton's riff on the Trans-African tradition is another possibility but that could get confused with the antiapartheid organization. Hmm, mebbe semantic convenience will have to stand.)

Gates reads Reed's satire on all Sacred Texts as a parody of received ideas about "blackness" in the Great Black Novels of the past. He traces the incestuous intertextuality of the black literary tradition, citing Hurston's revision of Toomer and Du Bois; Ellison's of Wright, Toomer, and Du Bois; Reed's of Hurston, Wright, and Ellison. Then he pronounces them all examples of black literary signifying. What Gates finds in Reed's pastiche of definitively "black" texts (somewhat akin to writing the Great American Novel) is a highhanded version of that peculiar form of signification known to black folks as signifyin'—which to us does not imply merely decoding the symbolism of a thing but calling it out of its name and talking bad about its mama. (One of Gate's colleagues, Kimberly Benston, has coined a phrase for such literary versions of playin' the dozens as Reed's: tropes-a-dope.) In the final analysis what Gates's essay seems out to provoke is an acknowledgment of black folks' capacity to deconstruct and refashion Western culture in our own image. As proof, Gates draws on Ellison, Reed, and Richard Pryor and does some fine signifyin' of his own, taking examples from the black tradition to explicate Big Ideas—so what if he betrays a need to show off a little ed-ja-mi-ca-shun to cover his ass in the process. To wit: "Another kind of formal parody suggests a given structure precisely by failing to coincide with it— that is, suggests it by dissemblance. Repeating a form and then inverting it through a process of variation is central to jazz—a stellar example is John Coltrane's rendition of 'My Favorite Things,' compared to Julie Andrews's vapid version. Resemblance thus can be evoked cleverly by dissemblance. Aristophanes' *Frogs*, which parodies the style of both Aeschylus and Euripides . . . Lewis Carroll's double parody in Hiawatha's 'Photographing,' which draws upon Longfellow's rhythms to parody the convention of the family photograph, all come to mind." (Yessuh, I just snaps my fingers **151** and dere dey is.)

    I'm not the only one who has a few bones to pick with Gates— as I found out when I read Houston Baker's *Blues, Ideology, and Afro-American Literature*. You wouldn't know they had any differences at all from reading *Black Literature and Literary Theory*— where, excepting Appiah's spat with Anonzie, the critics don't signify on each other. Baker's disagreements with Gates are certainly as substantial as the Africans'. Seems that back in 1979 Gates appeared in a tome titled *Afro-American Literature: The Reconstruction of Instruction*, which sought to dictate formalist ground rules for the teaching of Afro-American writing. In his essay, Gates attacks the critics of the '60s Black Aesthetic movement. (Baker was a constituent, alongside such good brothers as Stephen Henderson, Larry Neal, and Lorenzo Thomas, whose absence from discussion in *BLALT* almost gives you the feeling Gates thinks black literary criticism began with him and his crew. Shee, as a colleague reminded me, wouldn't be no Afro-American studies at Yale or anywhere else if it hadn't been for these Aesthetic types and the black student rebellions of the '60s.) Gates thinks you shouldn't read black texts with regard for such extraliterary concerns as race politics and culture, he argues instead for a semiotic reading of the literature, with texts seen as a closed system of signs and black folk culture, like the blues say, allotted value relative to use by black writers. In rebuttal Baker writes, "When, therefore, Gates proposes metaphysical and behavioral models that suggest the literature, or even a single text exists as a structured 'world' ('a system of signs') that can be comprehended without reference to 'social institutions,' he is misguided in his claims, appearing only vaguely aware of recent developments in literary study, symbolic anthropology, linguistics, the psychology of perception, and other related areas of inquiry. He seems, in fact, to have adopted without qualification, a theory of the literary signs . . . that presupposes a privileged status for the creative writer." Baker records that by the time Gates wrote *The Signifying Monkey: Towards a Theory of Afro-American Literature,* he'd realized his debts to the Black Aestheticians for exploring the social and vernacular resources of black literary language but that the apolitical nature of his acknowledgments betrayed "overly professional or careerist" anxieties.

Only Lord knows Baker ought to be the last one to talk about overly professional anxiety, given his own relentless use of paragraph-length quotes from Foucault, Barthes, White (Hayden, not Bukka), and the like. Not to mention treacly passages that read like so: "Rather than a rigidly personalized form, the blues offer a phylogenetic recapitulation—a nonlinear, freely associative, nonsequential meditation—of species experience. What emerges is not a filled subject but an anonymous (nameless) voice issuing from the black (w)hole. The blues singer's signatory coda is always *atopic,* placeless." Besides the fact that this leaves me wondering what to do with blues verses about going to Kansas City and that Sweet Home Chicago, Baker seems to be underrating the contribution of the colorful personas (and nicknames) of the bluesmen— in pursuit, it appears, of an ontogenetic and hermeneutical *langue* for decoding black folks' blues consciousness, but what the hey, Baker actually becomes worth his weight in jargon by emphasizing the impact of economics on the blues and black literature. This emphasis in fact serves as the linchpin of Baker's formalist critical inquiries and race-man politics. His study of Richard Wright is especially provocative. Not only does it rescue Wright from the social realist stigma put on him by heirs apparent Ellison and Baldwin, it locates in his language a liberating critique of bourgeois Western literary practices (akin to Barthes's *Writing Degree Zero* project, according to Baker), which finds them impoverished when confronted with expressing black oppression and desire.

Gates's failure to select Baker's Wright essays over the one on Ellison is lamentable; apparently the author of *Shadow and Act* is deemed more worthy of membership in the Gates canon than the author of *Twelve Million Black Voices*. In this lapse Gates nearly condones the inability of the white body politic to conceive of differences between black people. On the other hand Baker seems equally nearsighted when he cites the blues (and the Southern rural form at that) as the only definitive arena for conjugating black economics and aesthetics.

Perhaps the supreme irony of black American existence is how broadly black people debate the question of cultural identity among themselves while getting branded as a cultural monolith by those who would deny us the complexity and *complexion* of a community, let alone a nation. If Afro-Americans have never settled for the racist reductions imposed upon them—from chattel slaves to cinematic stereotype to sociological myth—it's because the black collective conscious not only knew better but also knew more than enough ethnic diversity to subsume these fictions. As Amiri Baraka writes in his autobiography, we might laugh at Amos and Andy without losing sight of the fact that that aberration on the screen was not us. The line between individual identity and ethnic identification explodes the black community into factions of opposing race philosophers. Sadly enough, in these times, what sense of community there is derives more from the collective sense of a racist societal surround than from the ethnic affirmations available through black cultural communion.

Per Harold Cruse I believe there may be remedial and revolutionary implications to black cultural nationalism considered as a political strategy. These derive from black culture's proven capacity to re-invent capitalism's cannibalization and commodification of revolutionary ideas. By necessity our radical aesthetic tendencies have evolved within a context where commercial exploitation and excommunication from the mainstream went hand in hand. Afro-American music provides the paradigmatic model for this analysis: consider that the four-year period when George Clinton's Parliament-Funkadelic Thang accrued estimated profits of $40 million (roughly between 1975's apocalyptic *Up for the Down Stroke* and 1979's *Gloryhallastoopid: Pin the Tale on the Funky*, a synthesis of Genesis and the Big Bang Theory) was not only their most creatively fertile but one in which they could not get played on white radio. On black radio they functioned as active opposition to a form of record industry sabotage dubbed "disco"—or as I like to pun it, disCOINTELPRO, since it destroyed the self-supporting black band movement which P-Funk (jes) grew out of.

Obviously, the advent of hiphop can be said to have contributed even more radical acts of counterinsurgency, turning a community of passive pop consumers into one of procreative producers. (Consider the way freewheeling deejays put their signature to mixes composed from industrial materials, approximating in music Duchamp's notion of the readymade.) Hiphop's seizure of the means of reproduction has now led us to a Human Beat Box, who replicates the automated banging of the drum machine with his hamboning mouth, converting a tool of disCOINTELPRO oppression into a new form of black vernacular expression. (It can be said that when the film *Wild Style* leads us to believe Queen MC Lisa Lee of the Zulu Nation left the scene because of impregnation by rapper Lovebug Starski, reproductive rights of a whole other kind were brought into play—but these belong to another discussion.)

Gates's and Baker's advocacy of black signification echoes but does not exceed that of the Human Beat Box. Primarily because their sense of critical play operates out of a more static sense of black expression than the Fat Boys'—not to mention graffiti and hiphop theoretician Ramm-El-Zee, whose formulations on the juncture between black and Western sign systems make the extrapolations of Baker and Gates seem elementary by comparison. Asked why he spelled Ikonoklast with a "k" when he named his practice of armored graffiti writing "Ikonoklast Panzerism" (after the tank), Zee said: "Because the letter 'c' in its formation is an incomplete cipher: 60 degrees are missing. A 'k' is a formation based on the foki of it; a certain kind of science based on the knowledge of formation mechanics . . ."

In an *Artforum* feature, Zee added: "The infinity sign with the fusion symbol (x) in its middle has been wrongly titled Christian (+) and thus it has to be assassinated or the x has to be removed. The infinity sign is a mathematical, scientific, military symbol. It is the highest symbol that we have and you know there isn't even a key on the typewriter for it. 'Ikonoklast' means symbol destroyer, it's a very, very high word militarily, because the two Ks are the only two letters that can assassinate the infinity sign, remove the X . . . I'm going to finish the war. I'm going to assassinate the infinity sign. You have the gladiators, the freestyle dancers, warring on the ground, you have the graffiti writers warring in the air or in space. You have the translators, the DJs, the MCs. The DJs make the sounds of the pistons inside the graffiti element, or the tank. Their sound is the perfect tuning of the engines, the engines in the tank that go bambambam. That is beat culture."

Since beat culture née hiphop derives from a more visceral rap-prochement with the tradition of black signification than that possessed by the brothers from the academy, it's not surprising streetwise semioticians would offer more thought-provoking theories than those slaving away in Ebony Towers. David Toop's new book *The Rap Attack: African Jive to New York Hip-Hop*, works up a detailed history of the culture which produced the Fat Boys and Ramm-El-Zee, documenting rap's origins in Gulla abusive poems, Yoruba song contests, and the vocal virtuosity of those West African verbal assassins known as griots—as well as in such Afro-American language rituals as the dozens.

"The dozens contests were generally between boys and men from the ages of 16 to 26—a semi-ritualized battle of words which batted insults back and forth between the players until one or the other found the going too heavy. The insults could be a direct personal attack but were more frequently aimed at the opponent's family and in particular at his mother. According to linguist William

155
•

Labov, who studied these verbal shoot-outs in Harlem in the 1960s . . . the dozens seem to be even more specialized, referring to rhymed couplets of the form: *I don't play the dozens, the dozens ain't my game, but the way I fucked your mama is a god damn shame.* . . . The distance between talking rough with the dozens on the streets and moving it inside a roots club like Disco Fever with some beats for dancing is very small. It leads to the contradictions of Melle Mel, lyricist for the Furious Five, onstage in his ultra-macho metal warrior outfit trying to preach convincingly for an end to machismo and a beginning to peaceful co-existence."

From there Toop proceeds with a copious account of word-gaming in Afro-American music, citing Cab Calloway, "Bubbles" Whitman, Slim Gaillard, Eddie Jefferson, Babs Gonzalez, the black radio deejays of the '50s and '60s, Daddy O Daylie, Poppa Stoppa, and especially Douglas "Jocko" Henderson, the Ace from Space, whose influence on Jamaican sound system pioneer Coxsone Dodd would make possible the work of Jamaican-born Bronx immigrant Kool DJ Herc, usually credited as the father of hiphop deejaying and rapping. In between, Toop gives some play to black comics like Redd Foxx and Moms Mabley, and scores of black pop recordings with raps of one kind or another in them; from those of Barry White, Isaac Hayes, and James Brown, to others more obscure or forgotten, like Richard "Dimples" Fields's "She's Got Papers on Me" and Barbara Mason's response, "She's Got the Papers but I've Got the Man."

All of which effluvia only makes for intriguing sidebars to Toop's principal interest here, namely telling the tale of hiphop's genesis in fertile uptown environs like the Audubon Ballroom and Broadway International where Grandmaster Flash and Afrika Bambaataa, the Teller and Truman of hiphop's Manhattan Project (inasmuch as they engineered and advocated war and peacetime use of the fusion funkbomb Einstein Clinton's theorems made possible) began bringing the black masses into the Information Age by performing feats of digital computation on the wheels of steel. Says deejay Flash: "Bob James was like 102 beats-per-minute to 118, so from there it was like Bob James, James Brown, Donald Byrd, Roy Ayers to John Davis and the Monster Orchestra, 'I Can't Stop,' and that's like the ultimate you know. . . . I would like break the shit down to eighth, sixteenth notes. It amazed me sometimes."

Unfortunately, at these urban Los Alamos affairs, pure research in pursuit of critical mass-ass appeal could be overwhelmed by initiatives favoring mob rule. Toop records Flash on how the Audubon became an inhospitable environment for black technological innovation, once overtaken, like the Island of Dr. Moreau, by atavistic direct-action advocates: ". . . other b-boy groups were going in there and tearing the place up, breaking out the windows and then the news media and the cops started talking bad about it. . . . We was doing it with just us and other DJ. Other groups that didn't have the heart to go in by themselves were going in there with six or seven DJ groups. Seven or eight different sound systems—it was too confusing. This person was taking too long to turn on or this person's system was fucking up and once you've got that big mass of people you have to keep them entertained. So after a while motherfuckers was getting shot and this and that, so by the time we went back after the third time our clientele was getting kind of scared so we gave it up."

Toop historicizes hiphop culture, constantly referring it back to its antecedents in the wider black tradition: "According to Afrika Bambaataa, breaking started as a dance to James Brown's 'Get on the Good Foot.' . . . The word *break* or *breaking* is a music and dance term (as well as a proverb) that goes back a long way. Some tunes like 'Buck Dancers Lament' from early in this century featured a two-bar silence in every eight bars for the break—a quick showcase of improvised dance steps. . . . Many of the dances used in current freestyle hark back to American dances from the past. In Marshall and Jean Stearn's *Jazz Dance*, Pigmeat Markham recalls the dancing of Jim Green in A. G. Allen's Mighty Minstrels tent show during the early 1920s. 'Green had a specialty I'll never forget. He'd dance awhile and then fall on the floor and spin around on his backside in time with the music.' " Elsewhere, on graffiti: "Herbert Kohl's essay 'Names, Graffiti and Culture' is an analysis of both the reasons behind graffiti and the tags used by artists in place of their legal names. Kohl noted the changes taking place in graffiti as anti-poverty programmes in the late '60s legitimized

157
•

wall writing by bringing together the youthful black and Puerto Rican artists with socially motivated painters. This sanctioned outdoor art led to more elaborate forms growing out of basic chalk or Magic Marker scribbling."

Because Gates's and Baker's works betray insufficient interest in these futuristic black contemporary variants on the blues and signifying tradition, there's a sense of cultural closure to them voided by the vertiginously metamorphic nature of Afro-American culture as recorded in Toop's book. Leading one to concur, in the final analysis, with Afro-American folk wisdom that the half ain't yet been told.

—1985

Ghetto in the Sky: Samuel Delany's Black Whole

> Semiotics attempts to make explicit the implicit knowledge
> which enables signs to have meaning, so it needs the reader
> not as a person but as a function: the repository of the codes
> which account for the intelligibility of the text. The reader
> becomes the name of the place where the various codes can
> be located: a virtual site.
>
> —*Jonathan Culler*
> The Pursuit of Signs: Semiotics,
> Literature, Deconstruction

> Yes, this is the ghetto.
>
> —*Donny Hathaway*

Everybody's hip to what a B-boy is, right? Well, one night I'm out with my friend Pam from Los Angeles, part-time starlet and TV newswriter on leave from her slave (read: gig) with ABC News. When I relate to her that these two Negroes barreling up Sixth Avenue like to knock somebody down are called B-boys, she cracks that out in El Lay, B-boy is a Sunset Boulevard drag queen. Then she claims her B-boys are as deep into hiphop as ours. The moral of this tale is: pan across what seems to be a world of difference and you'll find as many connections as disjunctions. This in turn leads us to the subject at hand: the science fiction of Samuel R. Delany, which for a quarter century now has explored what happens when alien world views intersect, collide, or mesh. Take *Stars in My Pocket Like Grains of Sand*, homeboy's new novel (him being black and Harlem-born, mind you), in which humans share a society with an alien race known as the evelm. Scaled, six-legged, taloned, winged, and blessed with multiple tongues, the evelm live alongside cloned descendants of a human settler colony. In this social system, termed a nurturing stream culture, human and evelm children are brought up by a mixture of human and evelm mothers.

I asked Delany if this conception of cooperative childrearing was based on an African communal model. Turns out instead it was inspired by the Harlem he grew up in, and his own extended family. Sure enough, any number of dialogues between the protagonist Marq Dyeth and his mothers seem full of the kind of warmhearted upbraiding feisty old black grandmothers and aunts like to hand out. Not coincidentally, almost all the major characters in this intergalactic epic are black. Delany told me, rather devilishly, that there's only one white character in the book and that the trick is to spot whitey. How much of a smile this conceit brings to your lips depends on your sensitivity to SF universes full of a zillion species of extraterrestrials and only caucasoid humans. Delany plays with this convention even more explicitly when Dyeth reflects on the strange-looking boy who turned up one day in his stream's sandbox: "At that age, I did not know that at one time perhaps a fifth of the human race had such pale skins and such colored and textured hair—and were called caucasian . . ." Thinking back on that scene from a perspective deeper in the text, you have to wonder whether Dyeth's fascination with this boy had to do with his race or with his nail biting, a trait Dyeth finds arousing in potential sexual partners—who in his constellation are always male.

Besides being black Delany is gay, and in his books sexual preference figures as prominently as racial identity, if not more so. Dyeth's love interest in the new novel is Rat Korga, former slave and lone survivor of a mysteriously annihilated world, who has been computed by the Web to be Dyeth's perfect erotic object out to a few decimal places. The Web, by the way, is one of three political factions waging the Information Wars over the 6000 planets in the novel's galaxy. The Family and the Sygn are the other two. Their enmity stems from a long-standing dispute: "The Family trying to establish the dream of a classic past . . . on a world that may never even have existed in order to achieve cultural stability, . . . the Sygn, committed to the living interaction and difference between each woman and each world from which the right stability and play may flower." And the Web, an arm of the Sygn, being the interstellar agency in charge of the general flow of information about the universe. The Web manages this flow through a technique called GI—General Information—which maps and circuits synapses, then accesses them to a vast galactic computer library. Among the features of this system are instantaneous reading and comprehension of poetry and the option of calling up data to fill in the gaps when communication bogs down between you and an alien.

That all this makes the book seem less like some futuristic homoerotica, or Toni Morrison in the 28th century, and more like the science-fiction novel as semiotics enterprise will come as no surprise to those readers who know that besides being black, gay, and a feminist to boot, Delany is a structuralist critic. He speaks of science fiction not as a genre but as a form of *paraliterature*, and has written a book, *The American Shore*, that's a 300-page exegesis on a 20-page short story by Thomas Disch. (When I told him various philosophies convey the sense that he's out to become the ultimate ghetto writer, he replied that his mother always said he had a ghetto mentality.) Delany uses the cold war between the Family and the Sygn to signify on two systems of dictatorship—one authoritarian, one libertarian—and how they structure human and alien possibility. Asked if he felt a kinship with Eastern European writers because of their treatment of cultural alienation, Delany said he was more intrigued by their depiction of how social engineering inevitably leads to social decay. He felt this brought a sense of reality to their fiction missing from traditionally utopian American SFs.

Given his concern for the dialectics of social organization, a case can be made for Delany the Marxist. His work has always seemed to play with one of Uncle Karl's more famous dicta—to wit, the future of woman will be a future of class struggle. My favorite Delany novel, *Nova*, besides being a space-opera reworking of *Moby Dick* and the quest for the Holy Grail, presents future societies full of class divisions and class antagonisms. Following his own belief that SF doesn't so much represent reality as misrepresent it, Delany makes cultural rather than economic oppression the cause of those antagonisms. He envisions a 31st century where the inequities and alienation brought on by class division of labor and relative work-value have been handily dispensed with:

"The entire sense of self-control and self-responsibility that man acquired during the Neolithic Revolution when he first learned to plant grain and domesticate animals was seriously threatened. The threat had been coming since the Industrial Revolution and many people had pointed it out before Ashton Clark. But Ashton Clark went one step further. If the situation of a technological society was such that there could be no direct relation between a man's work and his *modus vivendi*, other than money, at least he must feel he is directly changing things by his work . . . technology had reached the point where it could do something about what Ashton Clark was saying. Souquet invented his plugs and sockets, and neural-response circuits, and the whole basic technology by which a machine could be controlled by direct nervous impulse, the same impulses that cause your hand or foot to move. And there was a revolution in the concept of work. All major industrial work began to be broken down into jobs that could be machined 'directly' by man. . . . Now a man went to a factory, plugged himself in, and he could push the raw materials into the factory with his left foot, shape thousands on thousands of precise parts with one hand, assemble them with the other, and shove out a line of finished products with his right foot, having inspected them all with his own eyes. And he was a much more satisfied worker . . . Ashton Clark, it has been said, was the philosopher who returned humanity to the working man. Under this system, much of the endemic mental illness caused by feelings of alienation left society. The transformation turned war from a rarity to an impossibility and—after the initial upset—stabilized the economic web of worlds for the last eight hundred years."

The flipside of this futuristic Marxist kingdom come is revealed when the gypsy minstrel, Mouse (kind of a cross between Jimi Hendrix and Huck Finn), tells how on Earth gypsies were hunted and slaughtered for refusing to literally plug in to the homogenizing cultural mainstream. Which you can read if you choose (and I do) as Delany's way of saying that even in the 31st century it'll be open season on niggers of one kind or another.

162
•

Considerations of work, race, and place in society don't take a backseat in Delany's new novel either. The bulk of it is Dyeth's first-person narrative about his work as an Industrial Diplomat (someone who facilitates exportation of industrial materials between alien cultures). Dyeth gets to travel to other worlds and meet interesting new extraterrestrials in a universe where fewer than 3 per cent of the inhabitants of one world ever set foot on another because both the Family and the Web frown on interstellar travel. (Otherworldly curiosity has to be satisfied by a technique known as vaurine projection, which functions as a kind of interactive travelogue experience.) Dyeth's favorite rumination is on how alienating an alien culture remains no matter how much GI you got going for you. He discourses on things like how on one world it's taboo not to accept a gift *offering* yet tantamount to asking for a death sentence to accept the *gift*, or how humans in the Family-controlled part of his world are involved in violent conflict with the evelm because they don't care to make genetic distinctions between them and the lower-order flying dragons and therefore consider relations between evelm and humans bestiality. Family members also consider relations between humans of the same gender to be a form of perversion. The evelm, by the way, have three sexual types—male, female, and neuter—all of whom are capable of bearing children, though for the males this reproductive rarity often proves fatal. The humans in Dyeth's stream aren't products of direct egg-sperm relations but of cloning. Stream culture is matriarchal and personal pronouns refer to both males and females in the feminine gender. (Human/evelm mutation has not been experimented with, case you were wondering.)

The specter of racism rears up in the book's third-person prologue, which describes Rat Korga's years as a slave on Rhyonon before the planet was immolated. One of the intriguing things about this chapter is how similar Delany's satirical handling of slavery and slave mentality is to Ishmael Reed's and Ralph Ellison's. Just check the book's opening—"Of course, you will be a slave . . . but you will be happy with who you are and with the tasks the world sets before you." Korga hears this from the doctor who gives him the synapse snipping operation known as Radical Anxiety Termination, which not only makes for happy slaves but slaves in-

163

•

capable of reasoning, information processing, or self-preservation. Korga nearly incinerates himself walking across the hot side of his planet when one of his masters misdirects him there. He also lets two other slaves fester and die because RATs can't handle inductive reasoning or emotional identification with other slaves. For his negligence he's beaten unmercifully with a steel pipe by one of his female masters, while sympathetic males cower in revulsion. A scene which ain't exactly what you'd call an endorsement of the sexually liberated female—but then one of the subtexts of the novel is that black women are going to be the folk who conquer the stars and gonna bust some balls along the way to doing it. (Hence on Rhyonon the terms "bitch" and "dog" are reversed, women deploying bitch as a trope of sexual power, men wearing the dog collar as a mark of impotence and shame.)

These extrapolations on postfeminism move from the high dramatic to the high satirical when Korga is "liberated" by a bohemian who has designs on him. She frees the seven-foot, herpes-scarred Korga to stud for her but doesn't realize that he's gay. This turns out to be of minor consequence since she doesn't really desire a sex slave; what she wants is mastery of a man who's read everything she's read—"I want to control such a man, make him lie down in the sand and suck my toes." She gives Korga a glove which imprints reams of interstellar texts on his brain (we're talking apocryphal and Borgesian volumes of the stuff here, like *The Mantichorio* with its 137,000 lines of alternating heptameters and hexameters and "the complete extant work of the twenty-two-year-old prodigy Steble, her five multicharacter dialogues, the handful of papers on algebraic algrammaticalities, the surviving fragments of her journal for the '88–'89 concert season, and the final impassioned letters sent from her deathbed in the disease-infested Jabahia Prison complex . . .") and for a brief time allows Korga a cosmic sense of his mind and the universe. When his liberator is captured for making off with a slave, Korga loses his glove and all his newfound consciousness. Returned to slavery, he is less content, and even begins instructing other slaves to point their hands to the stars.

Reading this reminded me of the passage from Frederick Douglass's autobiography where he talks about how his master didn't believe slaves should learn how to read because it would only make them unhappy. Douglass didn't regret literacy, but came to realize that his master was right: an intelligent slave is a more unhappy slave. Delany's SF variation on Ellison, Morrison, Reed, and the slave narrative confronts American racial history more directly than any of his other work, even *Dhalgren*. If you've read that 879-page opus, this statement may strike you as rather skewed: *Dhalgren*, after all, is set in an American city after an apocalyptic black uprising has driven its white citizens away and left the run of the town to black gangs and the various countercultural types who wander in to slum around. Delany savvily realized that a science-fiction novel about blacks doesn't have to be set in another galaxy far far away—here and now is weird enough. But the blacks in the book are peripheral to the walking dream state of his amnesiac antihero Kidd, who experiences them more as products of his interior landscape than as characters with lives outside of his head. Rat Korga's prologue is different because it dramatically parodies the victimization of blacks by American racism.

In his criticism, Delany often mentions that he wants to imagine futures where the race question has been resolved. As an adolescent, he had an epiphanic moment reading Heinlein's *Starship Troopers;* it came when the hero of the book, whom Delany had assumed was white, is described in passing as a person of color. I told Delany I received a similar jolt reading *Starboard Wine* when I came across a speech he gave at the Studio Museum of Harlem. "We need images of tomorrow," he said, "and our people need them more than most." The "our people" business surprised me because it was the first time I'd come across anything in his work that indicated he openly identified with, well, the rest of us colored peoples.

I've always found Delany's racially defused futures problematic because they seem to deny the possibility that the affirmative aspects of black American culture and experience could survive assimilation. By which I mean not just the obvious things like the genius present in black music, speech, and style but the humanity and range of personas born of black people's sense of communion. Until I read that passage, I figured Delany for if not an Oreo then somebody who wasn't interested in being labeled black. And while his fiction is full of black and other protagonists of color (Rydra

Wong, Oriental poet, linguist, and starship commander of *Babel II;* Lorq Von Ray, the interstellar mulatto of *Nova;* Kidd, the native American antihero of *Dhalgren;* Lo Lobey, black mutant Orpheus of *The Einstein Intersection*) the race of these characters is not at the core of their cultural identity. Which used to bug me out like a mug because what I expected from our one black science-fiction writer was SF which envisioned the future of black culture as I'd define it, from a more or less nationalist stance. (That Delany was for so long the only black science-fiction writer reminds me of Eugene Genovese's observation that black Americans have tended toward pragmatic rather than prophetic leadership.) The trick thang about Delany is that while his black characters don't wear their negritude on their sleeves, they're not exactly upstanding members of tomorrow's black bourgeoisie either. Consider how many of them have been poets, musicians, and/or outlaws whose art and intelligence have gained them social mobility within the dominant culture and the option of rejecting its values whenever it suited them.

One thing I've learned from Delany is that black writers need to address not only the complexity of the black community but the complexity of the world. By sidestepping the race question, he's been able to criticize sexual, racial, and economic oppression in America and depict a wider range of human, alien, and mutant characters than you'll find in books by other black writers—not to mention books by other American writers, except for Pynchon and DeLillo. And as in *Gravity's Rainbow* and *Ratner's Star,* some of the most lyrical and stirring passages in Delany's work fuse the juncture between art, technology, and social science. Here's one from the chapter in *SIMPLGOS* where Dyeth describes Korga's rescue by the Web: "The synapse-jamming technique first surfaced on a moon of Rhyonon's cousin world, Jesper, here in the Tyon-Omega system, as a medical method for dealing with certain social intractables. It was squelched by the Web as inhuman and was finally superseded, on that moon, by a program of drug therapy . . . it resurfaced as part of the practice of an extremely violent art form: for some twenty-five years during Rhyonon's second century many of the artists in various geosectors of Rhyonon's southern hemisphere, when the emotional stringencies of their craft became too great, would voluntarily subject themselves to this form of mental suicide—during which time the practice gained great social prestige. . . . At some time in the past Korga had apparently been offered, by a benevolent society, a chance at what had been up till recently, on his world, the *ave atque vale* of artists and priests: the chance to have the paths in the brain through which worry forces us to grow closed over forever and detours about those troublesome crossroads left permanently open. . . . It's precisely those "anxiety" channels which Radical Anxiety Termination blocks. . . . Rat Korga will never get all those little neurological transmitters wired in the crevices in the top five vertebrae that will hook into whatever local GI system happens to be around."

This means that Korga's mind can't be controlled by the Web, a typical Delany bit of irony: the same operation which made Korga a slave gives him freedom in an overdetermined universe. Korga gets access to GI's computers without allowing them access to his brain through a batch of hand rings made for Vondramach Okk, legendary dictator, poet, world-conqueror, and bohemian sybarite. Her connection with Korga sets up messianic possibilities Delany will undoubtedly deliver on when the second volume of his SF diptych appears late next year and, needless to say, I can't wait.

—1985

167

•

Growing Up in Public: Amiri Baraka Changes His Mind

Reading Amiri Baraka's memoirs, I had to laugh like a mug when I came to his first encounter with Albert Ayler. If only because the crack Ayler lays on him behind one of his holy writs on the music succinctly sums up my own take on Baraka's head. Pulling rank on the self-appointed scribe of the jazz avant-garde, Ayler puts him in check with a rhetorical question. "You think it's about you?" Humbled, our omnipotent critic does some hasty soul-searching: "I did and did not think I knew what he meant. In some ways I did think it was about me. Albert meant it was really about Spirit and Energy. . . . Albert was always jumping on folks by saying of corny people, 'He thinks it's about him. And it ain't about him!' " Reading that, I wondered whether Baraka meant to call himself corny for once. Then got morbid thinking he oughta have it paraphrased for his epitaph. Like, here lies Amiri Baraka, he thot it was abt him.

The beauty as well as the bullshit of Baraka has always been how eloquently he's managed to confuse his head with the Godhead, his mental problems with the world's ills, his identity complexes with those of all black people.

In his sharpest and his shoddiest work, the subjective wars for space with the sociological, the political with the personal, the existentialist with the engagé. In the autobiography Baraka jokingly (perhaps) points up how his sense of good and evil came from radio mystery plays—like to say the evils of his imagining and the evils of the world were but one and the same, both disposable at will. Beneath his desire to have his morality plays go gate-crashing reality, to have art change society, lies Baraka's need to do his growing up in public—to have the world take heed of what changes it's been putting him through.

Portrait of the artist plotting revenge on society: Take *Dutchman*—which we all thought was an allegory on the seduction of the black man by white America. No, says its author; he only wanted to get back at his first white girlfriend for running mindgames on him when he were just a naive young colored boy flush from the Air Force. Which again, however, points up the beauty of the cat: his ability to turn his navel observations into a mirror of society. Baraka's gift for converting introspection into racial commentary probably derives from his moments of alienation and communion with both the black and white worlds.

Consider the road traveled by this black boy, who grew up middle class in Newark with two civil servant parents, flanked by the Italians on the hill and running with the bloods in the valley. Realizing he ain't slick enough to work the hustlers convention, he readied himself for college by opting for an Italian prep school. Then flunked out of the university because he ain't ready for prime-time in the black bourgeoisie either. And so joined the Air Force in search of him Self and on leave lucked up on it staring out from a volume of Joyce in a bookstore window. After which he became a voracious reader in pursuit of intellectual status—a course of action that procured him an undesirable discharge, prophetically enough, for subscribing to subversive literature (the *Partisan Review*).

Our pilgrim then progressed to the Apple, circa 1957, holing up in a drafty Lower East Side garret in pursuit of the poet's life. Eventually fell in with the hip literary crowd of the day, Olson, Ginsberg, O'Hara, Sorrentino, that crew, and established himself as an Afro-Edwardian presence on the New York bohemian scene. A state of grace which lasted until he got invited to Cuba in 1960 and got ranked on for his bourgeois individualism and poetic solipsism. The Cuban trip made him renounce his art-damaged apolitical ways. Malcolm X and the death of Malcolm caused him to declare all gloves off between him and the downtown world that had schooled him in the ways of the white intelligentsia. Now in search of him *black* Self, he scooted to Harlem to found the historic Black Arts Repertory Theater/School, which spawned the cultural wing of the Black Nationalist movement.

Having become a member-subscriber to this program through his influence, I also owe Baraka one for turning me on to the music (jazz, that is) and writing through his tomes *Blues People* and *Black Music*, which not only made me run out and cop my first Trane, Dolphy, and Miles sides but taught me music could be made with words and ideas as well as notes and tones. Then I discovered his poetry. Lord, how can I begin to tell how in love I am with this man's poetry! Not only for its scope, sweep, and invention, but for the voodoo it runs on modernism's icons (Pound, Williams, Joyce, Eliot, Genet, et al.), and its empathy for life—the sort you'd expect from some versifying naturalist rather than a product of this concrete jungle:

> *Harlem is vicious*
> *modernism. BangClash. . . .*
> *Can you stand such beauty?*
> *So violent and transforming.*
> *The trees blink naked, being*
> *so few.*
>   —"Return of the Native"

> *Flesh, and cars, tar, dug holes*
>   *beneath stone*
> *a rude hierarchy of money, band*
>   *saws cross out*
> *music, feeling. Even speech,*
>   *corrodes.*
>   —"A contract. (for the
> destruction and rebuilding of
>   Paterson)"

The black poetry circuit Baraka sparked in the '60s practically made John Coltrane a national hero in the black community. And if Baraka has been dubbed the Father of the Black Arts Movement it's because, as poet Mae Jackson recently related, he gave young black artists a place to go outside of white bohemia and black academia, a place more open to communion with black working-class culture (though some of us still landed back up in those two purgatories to stay that one month's scratch ahead of the snatch man).

The most valuable lesson I've learned from the breadth, depth, and volume of Baraka's work is not unlike the one I learned from Langston Hughes. Which is: Yes, my sister/brother, you can actually make a career out of vexing the King's English until it speaks in tongues. Even more instructive has been Baraka's recombinant splicing of black life and Western literary modernism, which sez yo, homegirl/homeboy, you can talk that arty talk and walk that walk, slide in your stride, zip in your hip; so go on 'head with your baad self, mix that intellectual shit in with a few healthy doses of yang and you'll still be cool. Reminding us always, as he admonishes his bohemian incarnation in the autobiography, "Be careful in giving up the provincial that you don't give up the fundamental and the profound."

In Baraka's case, this warning also begs the inverse: Be careful in celebrating the provincial that you don't cast out the cosmopolitan and the complex. Because the tragedy of Baraka's writing, for a lifetime reader of the mug like me, is that in what critic Werner Sollors has termed his quest for a populist modernism Baraka hasn't been able, like García Márquez, Cortázar, and Cabrera Infante (not to mention Sembene, Césaire, and Ngugi wa Thiong'o, if we really want to up the ante), to radically fuse his comprehensive knowledge of Western literature with his need to address the condition and complexity of his people. Least not lately, though if you go back to "The Screamers" you got my man laying the groundwork for a modernist black novel which evokes the provincial and the cosmopolitan, the political and the personal without ever leaving the scene of a screamin' and honkin' Newark cabaret.

The Cabrera Infante of *Three Trapped Tigers* got nothing on this Baraka when it comes to making orchestra music out of adolescent memory; nor the Cortázar of *Hopscotch* if we're talking about mapping the interior city; nor the García Márquez of *Chronicle of a Death Foretold* if we want to study up on how journalism can be surrendered to magic realism without missing a beat.

That was the night Hip Charlie, the Baxter Terrace Romeo, got wasted right in front of the place. Snake and four friends mashed him up and left him for the ofays to identify. Also the night I had the grey bells and sat in the Chinese restaurant all night to show them off. Jay had a social form for the poor, just as Bird and Dizzy proposed it for the middle class. On his back screaming was the Mona Lisa with the mustache, as crude and simple. Jo Stafford could not do it. Bird took the language and we woke up one Saturday morning whispering *Ornithology*. Blank verse.

And Newark always had a bad reputation, I mean, everybody could pop their fingers. Was hip. Had walks. Knew all about the Apple.

172
•

Only like I said, that was a whole 'nutha Baraka ago y'all. And much as I love my main mutha, I got to say his output over the past decade ain't been nothing but a muthafunkin' disappointment, give or take a few gems he stole out along the way, like the poems "Das Kapital" and "In the Tradition," the liner notes for Woody Shaw, a few other scraps of verse here and there. Because otherwise we talking about some diatribe disguised as literature. Stuff so lame I sometimes had to do the serious doubletake and ask myself, is this the same cat made me want to throw down on a typewriter in the first place? Sheee, you lying to me. Which isn't to say hearing Baraka recite some of this mess couldn't make your ass snap to, 'cause he's still one of the meanest rap acts around. (So mean in fact you wish somebody would lock him and Duke Bootee up in a 24-track; bet they'd come out with some agitprop hiphop make LKJ and Dennis Bovell sound reactionary.)

Popular opinion likes to tell you how Baraka's politics, first those of black nationalism and later those of Marxism, fucked up his writing; that as he got more race and class conscious he got progressively less craft conscious. And there's truth to that. Reading and listening to some of the more polemical work, you do feel yourself in the presence of a revolutionary shaman, out to chase his devils away with rhetorical spells and incantations rather than artful literary strategies. This conceit doesn't beg reviving that dead dialogue of whether art and politics mix (because we know how well art of a kind mixes with the politics of racists, capitalists, and imperialists, given the proposed NEA guidelines which seek to insure that the nation's art doesn't contradict the nation's foreign policies), but does point up Baraka's need to be identified through his work with having seen the error of his former ways and come to the correct ideological position.

The strangest thing about the memoirs is that they formally and structurally recreate the process of Baraka's literary degeneration, the book tracking his personal, political, and literary changes in a way that's very schizzy, to say the least. The various sections read like lost pages from former works, almost as if in writing them he was reliving not just their historical occurrence but their point of literary origin as well. The chapter on his Newark upbringing reads like parts of *The System of Dante's Hell,* sometimes fractured and associative, other times given over to straight narrative about his childhood. My favorite of his remembrances is of going to black **173** baseball games and the sense of ethnic communion and celebration he took from them.

> The Negro league's like a light somewhere. Back over your shoulder. As you go away. A warmth still, connected to laughter and self love. A collective black aura that can only be duplicated with black conversation or music.

The sections on Howard University, the Air Force, and Greenwich Village remind me of *Tales* and *Home,* full as they are of angst and intellectual awakening:

> I had been reading one of the carefully put together exercises *The New Yorker* publishes constantly as high poetic art, and gradually I could feel my eyes fill up with tears, and my cheeks

were wet and I was crying, quietly softly but like it was the end of the world. I had been moved by the writer's words but in another, very personal way. . . . I was crying because I realized I could never write like the writer. Not that I had any desire to, but even if I had had the desire I could not do it. I realized that there was something in me so *out*, so unconnected with what this writer was and what that magazine was that what was in me that wanted to come out as poetry would never come like that and be *my* poetry.

The Howard section of the memoirs won me out because of how fluidly it reads and because like my mentor I dropped out first chance I got. It also proves the Tombstone of Negro Education ain't changed in 30 years and points up Baraka's genius at crystallizing the Northern urban black male experience—his gifts for making prose poetry out of the body of cultural attitudes toward music, speech, style, and women which bind and shape big city brothers:

> I was a member of the mob, of really great guys, in the sense of those times. We were great bullshitters, and we spent hours, months, years, sitting round bullshitting. . . . We had our own language, on campus generally, but inside the group there was a sharper focus to it. Some of the stuff was even made up by us. Pretty girls were "phat" pronounced *fat*, ugly ones were "bats." We would even go to elaborate metaphors to let people know what we thought about their companions if they wasn't up to snuff. We'd call somebody with an ugly girl Bruce Wayne (meaning Batman) . . .

174

•

Narratively, the memoirs began to take a turn for the worse (and let me add that this is one of the worst edited and proofed books in years) in recounting the nationalist period, reading as it does exactly like the hipty dip rhetoric he was printing back when he was under the gun, trying to juggle double lives in art and politics and beginning to let art take the fatal plunge. And as much as the book reworks Baraka's literary descent, there's also something to be said for how unreconstructed it reveals his ideas to be about the revolution that never came, black supremacy, homosexuals, women (ever the ideologue, he comes off good on "the woman question"; it's the spiteful way he deals with old flames that rankles), and high yella nigras. While, remarkably, there's not a trace of anti-Semitism, the caste aspersions are really vile.

After giving one whole chapter over to divvying the world up into his version of the good, the bad, and the ugly (read: the black and brown, the yellow, and the white) Baraka does a pretty fair job throughout the rest of the tome convincing us how little love is lost between him and fair-skinned black folk. In places where he gets to accusing some high-browns of being Toms he even makes reference to that being the yellow in them coming out. Now who he means to be cracking on, I think, is the black petite bourgeoisie. But only once does he say that. Besides which, I don't know where he got his color-caste census from, but far as I know they ain't never all been high yellas. And even if they had, nobody who fancies himself a good Marxist needs to be running that kind of ism-schism on black people here in 1984.

Baraka is obviously full of contradictions, emotional and intellectual, that no party line is ever gonna resolve for him. Not to say he hasn't spent a lifetime trying to make good the attempt. I once asked a friend of his why Baraka had gone through so many changes. He replied it was because, more than anyone he'd ever met, Baraka was tortured by always wanting to do the right thing. More cynical folk would tell you the negro just likes being contrary, more hard-nosed analysts would tell you while his literary gifts border on genius his powers of reason tend to fail him miserably when it comes to choosing ideologies and ideological partners. (There's a recurring pattern in the book of Baraka being swayed to one position or the other by the dynamism of some tougher black male—Malcolm X, Robert Williams, Ron Karenga. Malcolm and Williams I got no problems with, but that wild and crazy guy Karenga, no way.)

It's to laugh twice over when Baraka says early on he realized change would be a constant in his life and when he cops a plea that folk understand he is now what he has always been, a revolutionary committed to change. Making you wanna just go street on his ass and crack, like yeah we know you need to be committed,

175
•

negro, the question is, to what? And you wonder if he'd even get the joke, this cat having made such a virtue of his vices. T'aint his changes per se which have made Baraka so hard to take seriously as a political person, but the vociferousness with which he proclaims himself a true believer in one dogma only to just as vociferously vilify it when he's ready to move on to the next. So that we find the ultimate bohemian literati only publishing his white fellow travelers, the ultimate nationalist becoming a devout believer in black separatism, the ultimate Marxist gleefully declaring the death of black nationalism upon deliverance of his first pro-Marxist speech. Somehow the ultimate revisionist fails to mention the devout who got left in the lurch when he changed his line from get-whitey to workers of the world unite, the lefty version of "We Shall Overcome." Growing up in public again, only this time leaving a mess of young minds trapped and confused, and wiser colleagues doubtful about his commitment to the cause of black liberation. (Though if you talk to some of these citizens, they'll tell you how of late he's come back to black. And certainly the excellent essays he's been writing in *Black Nation* bear this out.)

Reentering the black nationalist period through the memoirs is like stepping into the twilight zone for real. When you consider what black folks' mass energy level was then and what it is now you feel like that era maybe never happened at all, like bebop and the Harlem Renaissance even were more recent and likely occurrences in African-American history. The fire that time, where'd it go, up in smoke? The din having died down from all those readings, riots, and rebellions, you could almost think black folk just packed up the circus one day and went home. But only if you wanted to be ahistorical about it and forget that we shared the bill with FBI, CIA, and COINTELPRO—the empire striking back against our romance with revolution (almost like we were some upstart Asian or African nation). And then there was the internecine shit that went down, sometimes provoked by double agents, sometimes by star-tripping political egos at war. And when you reconsider the procession of demagogues Baraka drags out from under the rug of history, Carmichael, Cleaver, Karenga, himself, and the trips they put us through, you relive the tension and intensity of a people caught in a crossfire between shamanism and hard struggle, outraged emotion, and wasted energy, and wonder why in the hell did we go through all of that. Did it get us where we are today, Jesse dreaming on at the Democratic national convention, or Farrakhan running mindgames on Ted Koppel, or did it accomplish something more?

I know the answer is affirmative. These characters really did raise the consciousness of people a lot more naive, sincere, and committed than themselves, and while you can question their political and intellectual depth (which pale before that of Du Bois, C. L. R. James, and Walter Rodney), the movements they initiated raised critical questions of culture and identity among black people which have yet to be resolved. Certainly they have something to do with the way my head turns when I see the fine sisters in the braids or dreads, check their ebony elegance (yeah, nationalism really turns me on), what I feel when I listen to Trane or wade through the crowd at Harlem day, or try to get somebody to understand that South Africa needs to be abolished as much as nukes do.

Something to do with black art and style on one level and deeper still with a sense of community, culture, and love for self. And since Baraka helped precipitate a big part of that transformation in my consciousness, I can overlook some of his failings and end up respecting him. Not so much for the stands he took, but for taking them when he could've been America's next most beloved Negro author. And then again for things like taking on the mafia and getting Ken Gibson elected in Newark (in the ultimate act of faith in black power of whatever stripe), for putting his life on the line to save a brother shot down in the Newark riots, for always having continued to write in the midst of so much madness, violence, and struggle. See, you can take comrade Baraka to task, chump him for cuttin' the fool growing up in public, but can't nobody say he grew up to chump out on black people. Not unless, of course, you're a bookworm like me who thinks highbrow culture matters in the struggle too and wishes he'd finished what he started with "The Screamers."

177

·

—*1984*

Guerrilla Scholar on the Loose: Robert Farris Thompson Gets Down

U p at Yale, Robert Farris Thompson's courses in African art have become legend behind the man's cutting up in class like there wasn't a world of difference between scholars and shamans, secret initiates and structural anthropologists, professors and priests, enthnographers and extraterrestrials. Thompson's lectures are tour de force performances, involving adept drumming and dancing, color-saturated slides, and a stage delivery derived from prayer meetings with a dash of Irwin Corey on the side. The message behind this song and dance isn't so different from what's in Thompson's fourth book, *Flash of the Spirit: African and Afro-American Art and Philosophy*. Whether experienced in oral or text form, his work contains a multitude of revelations about the aesthetic, social, and metaphysical traditions of Africans and their New World descendants in Cuba, Brazil, Haiti, Trinidad, Mexico, and the United States. What Thompson has to say about these black cultures is encyclopedic enough to make you think one day he'll go sign up for membership. He has in fact advanced to varying stages of initiation within several African religions—and given how the data reel off his tongue, he either has a microchip for a mouth or a degree from a griot academy.

Now understandably some of the brothers and sisters out there got problems with Thompson, seeing as how he's a white guy.

Severed from your heritage by slavery and oppression and all that shit, how do you put up with one of your oppressor's progeny trying to come off hip reclaiming it for you? Regardless, I have to give it up to Thompson on three counts: his perspective is Afrocentric rather than Western academic; it's more informed by genuine reverence and enthusiasm than by the savage arrogance we've come to expect as the Anglo-Saxon norm when pondering Africa; and he knows too much to be ignored. Period.

Centuries of racist assumptions go packing it in in *Flash of the Spirit*, as in Thompson's other books (*Black Gods and Kings*, about the Yoruba; *African Art in Motion*, from his 1974 exhibition on visual, social, and choreographic systems; and *Four Moments of the Sun: Kongo Art in Two Worlds*, a book-length essay and catalogue from a 1981 exhibition he curated at the National Gallery). Thompson doesn't play the charge-countercharge game—he never dignifies running dogs of Eurocentricity with an argument. What he's created is a multidisciplinary systems analysis of African cultures, complete with information overkill, visionary vocabulary, revolutionary reinterpretations, and scrupulously sensitive word selections. Thompson has excised such vandal obscenities as "tribalism," "fetishism," and "black superstitions" from his lexicon, and replaced them with discussions of neighboring civilizations, cosmograms, and Black Atlantic philosophy. He refers to African **179** civilizations by regional ethnic names rather than those imposed by imperialist borderlines (Nigeria becomes Yorubaland when not the land of the Ejagham; Mandeized architecture, not Maliized, crops up in Mexico after the slave trade) and sees all New World blacks as kin by virtue of specific Yoruba and Kongo resurgences throughout the cluster of cultures which make up the African diaspora.

Thompson figures into this web as mediator between world views, celebrating African ideas in an evocative and provocative Western tongue. Though loaded down with the tools of Western scholarship, he seems to have the incantatory powers of a Yoruba priest when explaining how divination is used to counter uncertainty, or of a Kongo sorcerer when explicating the moral of a medicine bag whose elements cohere in a miniaturized cosmos rife with metaphors of chaos and composure. By his own admission a believer in Black Atlantic philosophy, Thompson can be an immensely poetic proselytizer as he bridges not just European and African concepts but those of Afro-Americans and their African progenitors as well. In a section on Ejagham women, Thompson provides knowledge of a feminism born of a feminine mystique not far removed from passages you find in Toni Morrison's novels:

> Nnimm women moved as the forest moves, as the sea moves, in a swaying, chiming mass of fibers, bones and shells. Beyond use, beyond disruption, the image of the Nnimm women was a multitextural manifestation of potentialities, resisting the pigeonholing of women as purely instruments of labor. Fear of what these women had intuited and stored within their objects provided checks against injustices that might have been committed by other men or women.

Describing South Carolina artist Henry Dorsey's pun-filled home of ready-made decorations and electrokinetic sculptures, Thompson finds roots for these improvisations in Kongo-American grave art, which outstrips dada in suggesting that shock therapy and slapstick can heal the modern spirit. And his analysis of the complex Nsibidi script system of the Ejagham reveals a codification of morality which ought to be familiar to anyone who's ever witnessed legalese in the service of justice:

180
•

> The Ejagham developed a unique form of ideographic writing, signs representing ideas and called Nsibidi, signs embodying many powers, including all that is valiant, just and ordered. Nsibidi in the Ejagham means roughly "cruel letters." . . . Consider Nsibidi writing then as justifiable terror in the service of law and government.

Thompson believes that the Black Atlantic tradition, contrary to common ignorance, has conceived civilizations with as much intellectual and aesthetic significance as any in the West and Far East. Not for nothing does *Flash of the Spirit* open with a discussion of Yoruba urbanism, which dispels the myth of Africa as bush country, and close with a dissertation on Nsibidi, which counters the lie that Africans have no forms of writing; the book thereby completes a circle of affirmation over negation, just as Osanyin's bird-and-daggers staff represents the triumph of mind over the forces of annihilation. The kinship of Thompson's thinking to that of black radical historians like C. L. R. James, W. E. B. Du Bois, Chancellor Williams, Cheik Anth Diop, Josef ben Jochanan, and Ivan Sertima is startling enough to run up on in print. But in speaking with Thompson, what seems even more surprising are his allusions to blackness as a transcendental state of being. Even for those of us convinced of that by our mamas from day one, Thompson's hyperbolic eloquence can seem a bit romantic.

Rapping with him, I heard myself laughing wholeheartedly in agreement while also thinking, this is one *out* white mother-fucker here boy. Accusations of white Negro yearnings that pursue Thompson have some credibility. But while his tales of an El Paso boyhood spent learning to play the blues from the local brothers do swagger a bit with that hipty-dip tone, and his stories of conversion to the faith by mambo and Abakua in the '50s give off a faint aroma of Jungle Jim ("So there I was, this lone gray in a courtyard with men dancing in the name of the stars and twirling this way and that and making a hundred ideographic signs and so I decided fuck everything else, I must devote myself to this"), Thompson's mammoth body of scholarship transmutes those frivolous untutored impulses into work of universal significance. Intergalactic, even.

"When I start my spring course I take old Neil Armstrong's photograph of planet Earth but of course what you see is the noblest of all continents, Gondwaraland, our first continent, our Mother continent, Africa, where we all come from. And I ask my students, just suppose you were coming from the eighth galaxy and you were trying to figure if there were sentient beings on this sphere and you sent a ray down to the West Indies and boom, you get reggae and you sent a ray down to Tokyo and you get maybe not the hippest jazz but Tokyo reggae or Tokyo jazz or some vaguely black-influenced music. I don't think they'd be playing too much classical Japanese music on the AM stations there. Well, what I'm trying to say is that blacks control the airwaves here and the message

181

•

those beings from the eighth galaxy would have to send back is I don't know who's running this planet but to judge from the music this planet is *baad!* Blacks of the Atlantic world have creatively altered the shape of the planet permanently, have created the sounds which have shook the whole of the 20th century by the scruff of its neck. Politically I don't even want to think about how horrible things are but I mean culturally the conquest is complete. And the act of making those creative sounds is indication that existential gaps are being filled by black people and that existential stances are taking place all over the Western world.

"This has to be explained to people in ways that will get them out of the old bag that it's just entertainment or athletic energy. You know there were always these myths that people feared blacks for their supposed sexual superiority or athletic superiority but I think the real fear is elegance, the elegance of the black mind. A couple of people reading me have felt there has to be something wrong here because I'm talking about elegance and *we know* elegance in 19th century, New York, Paris—and so we can't possibly have this kind of artistic, critical elegance going on in mere Yoruba forms or in a mere hamlet on the top of a hill in Kongo. People say how can you claim the Yoruba are as elegant as we are, these people are rustics—as if rustics can only read and write in rustic. The blues to most people is music to complain by or music to fuck by or music to complain to with a fuck beat and I mean my God, we could do the same thing with Shakespeare if we wanted because he was into entertainment too. But we don't handle it that way. We don't handle Chaucer say from the perspective of the farts and dirty jokes.

"But these people cannot sit down and study the full dimensions of blackness like they study the Torah or the road map to Jerusalem. Because for every inch of musical, percussive savor there's just bottomless layers of philosophy, ethics, and shortcuts to right living. There are a lot of sinister forces out there who don't like to believe that God forbid there could be an alternative Atlantic tradition to the great Greco-Roman, that contrary to what we've been taught to believe, all of the Western hemisphere doesn't just derive from Europe. But all that's about to be detonated because there are a lot of people working on this now and we're headed for a showdown of scholarship which is going to be a preshadowing to other final showdowns."

Flash of the Spirit seems designed to take its stand in the upcoming Dodge City of dueling dogmas as a primer for the whole Black Atlantic World, and for the Thompson corpus. One problem I have with the book is that it's sometimes too dense (as in the chapter on the Yoruba gods and goddesses and their respective attributes) and in others too underdeveloped or abrupt (as in the chapter on Nsibidi, which should probably be a book in itself). Thompson is also such an adept, such a convert, he's lost any sense of alienation and any need to provide anecdotes of personal revelation and transformation from his field encounters. For all its popularizing intentions, *Flash of the Spirit* is not subway or supermarket fare, and one reason is the absence of a narrative thread to loom a spiritual journey from the rich raw data and poetic analysis. Being one of the converted myself and having Thompson's other more exhaustive books under my belt and his booming drill sergeant delivery in my head, I could bring more context to *Flash of the Spirit* than is actually there. The book also suffers from a shortage of visual material—no illustrations in color and not enough in black and white, leaving you hungry for the spectrum of correspondences you can feast on in Thompson's talks and books of exhibitions past. The beauty of the book, though, is that it often arrives at epiphanies like the passage on the Ejagham women— passages which show African peoples producing sacred objects, dances, and songs that bring into focus the philosophy behind the morality and musicality of Black Atlantic civilization.

Thompson has plans for a book "showing New York for what it really is, which is an incredible African city," an exhibition on altars and meditation in the Black Atlantic world, and a film version of the new book done in conjunction with a major black independent filmmaker (Thompson says he'll disappear and give the floor to the tradition's real guardians, its priests and practitioners). While at 50 Thompson claims not to have enough decades left in him to complete all the work he'd like to do, I wouldn't bet against him going the distance. And while there probably are sinister forces out there who hold him in disfavor, his sizing up of the competition seems to pay no nevermind:

"You have people who say Thompson seems wedded to the notion of cool, perhaps because he wants to be popular or vulgar even. Well, man, I take that as a compliment because what I really hear them saying is 'don't mess up our art history with street nigger talk.' But there's no way they're going to stop the attempt to fuse so-called *high* art history with so-called street. Because I'm a guerrilla scholar, man, and I take my cues from what I hear and if someone tells me to stop emphasizing cool, then perhaps I'll start emphasizing *chill* if they like."

—*1984*

Harlem When It Sizzled

184
•

Reading David Lewis's and Jervis Anderson's histories of Harlem sent echoes of Countee Cullen through my head. Those with Black Lit 101 in their upbringing will probably recall Cullen's "Heritage." For those more culturally deprived, that's the one where Cullen waxes pathetic over whether Christian conversion has cost him an African soul. Put Harlem on my mind in place of the Motherland and similar concerns go off in my head. Only unlike Cullen I'm not worried for my soul. No, what I'm missing on account of dope, desegregation, and the new diasporan gospel, namely assimilation, is the Harlem they used to call Black Mecca. That Harlem ain't what it used to be is obviously no news: it's been the nation's handiest model of urban ethnic ruin for damn near three decades. Understanding that black folk once considered the place about as close as they were going to come to the promised land in this motherfucker here takes some leap of faith—especially if your fix on its present state is somewhere between gentrification and cultural decay.

Lewis and Anderson allowed me to connect with the mythic Harlem my mother grew up hearing about. In her day, says Mom, the living knew they wanted to go to Harlem just as surely as the dead knew they wanted to go to heaven. Still, after reading *When Harlem Was in Vogue* and *This Was Harlem, 1900–1950*, I'm less nostalgic for Harlem as the promised land than as a striving black community that once upon a time bristled with the daily discourse of poets, politicians, musicians, entrepreneurs, and day workers. If the geography of segregation was meant to keep blacks and whites out of each other's sight, it also made the black communities my parents' generation grew up in places where Afro-American ambitions weren't stifled by poverty before they even met up with overt racism. Principally because the most brilliant talents of the race didn't have any place else to go. Locked in the community, they kept a stiff upper lip and passed dignity around.

Jervis Anderson's look at Harlem from 1900 to 1950 arrived on the heels of David Lewis's tribute to the Harlem Renaissance, so I wonder how often these two tripped over each other doing research in the Schomburg collection or the National Archives. They certainly managed to run up on the same reference material. (In fact a few bon mots I'd thought were Lewis's turned up in Anderson too, spliced in from some other wise guy.) Lewis's book is a dashing, pithy read, Anderson's a long-winded tome. After gliding through Lewis's catty, chatty skeins of sarcasm and scholarship, Anderson's more prolix sophistries only benumb. This pollyannaish bit on Joe Louis being a prime example: "During what remained of his life, however—as in much of what had gone before—Louis showed by his conduct that his spirit was not confined to 'the colored section' but inhabited broader areas of American experience which were shared by all men and women of civility and good will." Brother, that's a mouthful and not too easy to swallow either.

The one major plus of Anderson's book is that wading through his section on Harlem's origins will put you on a more proletarian footing than Lewis's exposé. Lewis does such a diverting job of damning the effete snobs you hardly notice how peripheral the masses are. And what with the Talented Tenth and all running around forging the conscience of the race in the smithy of their souls, you kinda forget everybody in Harlem wasn't a poet or a race leader back then. While I wouldn't say Lewis lacks a common touch, he can't be said to do much with it.

What he does do brilliantly is bring to life the legends who made the Harlem Renaissance happen. In the '20s, Harlem emerged as the political and cultural locus of Afro-American urban life, the stronghold of the race's best and brightest. Within an intricate mural of this burgeoning black universe, Lewis sketches revealing narratives about the interactions and motivations of the community's most prominent artistic and political figures. The glittering roster of racial icons aren't names easily encountered without awe—particularly if you're a contemporary black artist, academic, or activist: Du Bois. Garvey. Hurston. Robeson. Star players in a cast of thousands.

Lewis is provocative because he doesn't hesitate to reduce these bronze figures to human scale—or even knock them down to size. In this sense, he has ushered in a genre new to the relatively genteel tradition of Afro-American belles lettres. Namely, literary

gossip. In some quarters of black intelligentsia, Lewis's divulgences of political backbiting, color-caste snobbery, and pederasty have brought him under fire for indiscretion if not blasphemy. Among the juicier of his intimations is that Alain Locke, Langston Hughes, Countee Cullen, and Harlem dandies Richard Nugent and Harold Jackmon liked each other more than they liked girls. Among the more dumbfounding is the revelation that protean egghead W. E. B. Du Bois married his befuddled, virginal daughter Yolande off to a known homosexual (Cullen)—and then apologized for her failings on the honeymoon.

While there may be some truth to the charge that Lewis only threw this stuff in to spice up the narrative, scholarship seems like his primary motivation. For all its tawdry tidbits, his cunningly phrased book contains the only portrait of the Renaissance that doesn't shy away from addressing the petty but crippling conflicts among Harlem's politicos and social hierarchies in the '20s. Be-

sides which, there's simply too much evidence of scrupulous research. He apparently read not only all the poetry and fiction of
the '20s but also every scrap of magazine and newsprint and personal correspondence he could dig up. Not to mention six years
interviewing witnesses. What he's managed to do is separate the
myth of Harlem from its history without making the truth read any
less glamorously than the legends.

Consider Harlem's '20s as a kind of funked-up Weimar Republic
for *bloods,* and you'll have a grasp on why that era has gone down
in Afro-American lore and literature as a time of grand cultural
renaissance. Which is to say, one where radical trends in Afro-
American art and politics converged with the black bourgeoisie in
a bacchanal of strident nationalism, new money, and bohemian
revelry. While whites who've written on Harlem's '20s have nos-
talgically recalled its carnal nightspots and darky entertainments,
Lewis describes how Harlem's black population saw their community as an oasis of racial salvation: "Quarreling bitterly among
themselves about the right road to deliverance, Garveyites, neo-
Bookerites, socialists, utopian cultists, and all manner of integra-
tionists shared in equal measure what might be called Harlem
nationalism—the emotional certainty that the very dynamism of
the 'World's Greatest Negro Metropolis' was somehow a guarantee
of ultimate racial victory. To a remarkable degree that collective
optimism touched everyone—the humble cleaning woman, the il-
literate janitor, even the criminal element."

Some of the more uppity brothers and sisters of the day went
around proclaiming themselves the New Negroes. They weren't
about to take shit off the white boy, and they tended to act and
dress the part. Black postwar militancy and spanking new brownstones gave this vanguard its initial social daring; the "Red Summer" of 1919 tempered it with political pragmatism. Home from
the French front, all the brave brothers, like those in Harlem's
valorous 15th National Guard, were talking about turning in some
of those dead Germans and decorations for jobs and justice or
picking up the gun. The response of more than a few racist white
citizens to this rebellious if romantic threat was a bucket of blood—
the Red Summer—a nationwide orgy of mob violence against
blacks that rampaged through two dozen cities and left thousands

lynched or burned out of their homes. As planned, this pogrom cured other survivors suffering from pre-Newtonian (Huey, that is) delusions of revolutionary suicide. What it didn't quell was Afro-American demands for the kind of social and economic gains anticipated as payment-in-kind for wartime patriotism.

In the aftermath of the Red Summer, moderate black leadership faced the problem of devising political strategies that were both vociferous and nonaggressive. An elitist cadre of liberal-arts damaged Afro-American intellectuals assumed the task of transforming this pragmatic paradox into praxis. Foremost among them was William Edward Burghardt Du Bois—W. E. B. to you—living embodiment of the nascent NAACP; editor and chief propagandist of the organization's influential organ, *Crisis* (under Du Bois's editorship it regularly sold 100,000 copies monthly—astounding in an age of predominant black illiteracy, astounding, in fact, today); and author of *The Souls of Black Folk,* a collection of essays that kindled intellectual ambition in a generation of young black artists and academics.

Du Bois's persuasive pamphleteering had almost singlehandedly rallied black men into the First World War—just as the feisty black brain trust's lobbying to integrate the American armed forces had eventually won blacks the right to serve. (Imagine that—back then brothers had to beg their way onto the front line. So thank god for integration, right?) Yet, for all his appeal to the masses to sacrifice life and limb for the advancement of the race, Du Bois was no populist. As formulator of the notorious Talented Tenth doctrine, W.E.B. believed equality should first be granted to worthy Ivy League educated blacks like himself. This dincty delusion put him at loggerheads with the ideologies of the three other leading black political strategists of his time: first with Booker T. Washington's plan to create a separate-but-equal class of Afro-American yeomen (a dream that inspired legions of southern black academics years after his death in 1905, and equally enthralled the patrician hearts of white philanthropists); then with Marcus Garvey's African repatriation movement and A. Philip Randolph's Black Bolshevikism (an ideology which got Randolph branded "one of the most dangerous men in America" by J. Edgar Hoover, so you figure he must have been doing something righteous).

Debate between these factions, and especially between Garvey and Du Bois, often got more mutually destructive than constructively critical. The barbed exchanges Lewis digs up between these two are hilarious, if embarrassing in the extreme. Du Bois once wrote an article branding Garvey either "Lunatic or Traitor." Garvey's reply to that was that he didn't have to ask whether the "crossbreed, Dutch-French-Negro Editor" was a traitor. For punishment Garvey recommended horsewhipping. Common in the Du Bois camp was the revulsion expressed by Robert Bagnall, who described Garvey as a "Jamaican Negro of unmixed stock, squat, stocky, fat and sleek." 'Course if that sounds like high yellow hijinks at their worst, Garvey's arguments for a pure black race purged of its blue-vein aristocracy aren't much closer to unity in the community.

Controversy rages to this day about how much of a hand the Talented Tenth's leadership had in the downfall of Garvey's United Negro Improvement Association, which at its peak claimed a membership worldwide of two million. The evidence Lewis presents about Du Bois and other black moderates asking to enlist in the government's campaign against Garvey is sickening stuff. But as Lewis also notes, J. Edgar Hoover had already assigned a specially recruited Uncle Tom to Garvey, and both the British government and the United Fruit Company had asked for U.S. intervention to curb Garvey's rabble-rousing in Africa, Central America, and the Caribbean.

189

•

Whatever the backstage machinations, Garvey's trumped-up tax fraud conviction and deportation in 1925 left Du Bois's Talented Tenth a clear shot at mandating the destiny of black America. Or at least the destiny of those Afro-Americans with college degrees or white philanthropists. This perspective gave them a comprehension of racism that was narrow, selfish, and skewed. "The error of black leaders like Du Bois," Lewis writes, "transcended skin color; they were rebels in America only to the degree and duration of their exclusion from it." To the Tenth's Oxford-educated aesthete Alain Locke, for example, the key to racial harmony was interracial elitism: "The only safeguard for mass relations in the future must be provided in the carefully enlightened minorities of both race groups."

Yet for all their selfishness when it came to race and caste, the Tenth's leadership made remarkable gains for blacks in higher education. At a time when many black colleges were generously endowed based on their adherence to Booker T. Washington's vocational training program, Du Bois and crew gained economic parity for black liberal arts schools. Behind this lobbying lay the belief that only through educational acculturation would the barriers to racial advancement be swept away. To this end, the NAACP and the Urban League enlisted culture as the first line of defense after charitable WASP guilt and circumspect Jewish benevolence. (Lewis throws his two cents into the ever-prickly matter of black-Jewish relations by producing evidence that the early 20th century Jewish leaders viewed blacks as a lower-on-the-totem-pole buffer between themselves and American anti-Semitism. Not exactly a novel notion in the black community.) Regardless of motivation, such patronage gave the NAACP and the Urban League the where-withal (and the time) to devote themselves to their dream: they would bring about integration by proving how sophisticated they were.

The artsy wing of the Harlem Renaissance was Charles Johnson's brainchild. Johnson, editor and chief sociologist of the Urban League's publication, *Opportunity*, understood that in the lynch-mad '20s art was the only haven of opportunity for blacks. Johnson, says Lewis, "gauged more accurately than any other Afro-American intellectual the scope and depth of the national drive to 'put the nigger in his place' after the war, to keep him out of the officers corps, out of labor unions and skilled jobs, out of the North and quaking for his very existence in the South—and out of politics everywhere. Johnson found that one area alone—probably because of its implausibility—had not been proscribed. No exclusionary rules had been laid down regarding a place in the arts . . . it was left to the Afro-American elite to win what assimilation it could through copyrights, concerts, and exhibitions."

Opportunity's May 1925 literary awards dinner put art on the barricades in the race war. White notables there to shore up the ranks included judges Fannie Hurst, Eugene O'Neill, Alexander Woollcott, Van Wyck Brooks, and Clement Wood. Among the winners, prophetically, were Countee Cullen, Sterling Brown, Langston Hughes, Zora Neale Hurston, E. Franklin Frazier, and Eric Walrond. Publicity from these awards brought publishing offers from major houses, and as Johnson hoped, attention from well-heeled whites. Support for the New Negro literature became highly fashionable, its authors' presence at downtown soirees de rigueur. The Lost Generation hoped New Negro blood would bring joy to a Caucasian race in its death throes.

Given proper encouragement, some black authors were more than happy to liven up the wake. A lot of black fiction from the '20s is unreadable today because it was geared to the tastes of such white primitivists as Carl Van Vechten or—like the writing of Du Bois's Sorbonne-grad girl Friday—it suffered from class preciousness. Lewis critically examines the stellar exceptions to these tendencies: Nella Larson's near-forgotten novels of psychic unmasking, *Quicksand* and *Passing*; Rudolph Fisher's Harlem satires; George Schuyler's comic sci-fi treatment of American color-mania, *Black No More*; Eric Walrond's *Tropic Death*; Langston Hughes's *The Ways of the White Folks*; and Jean Toomer's *Cane*. Published in 1923, *Cane* instantly won praise as the most sophisticated work of fiction ever written by an Afro-American and also as a major piece of experimental modern writing. Paul Rosenfeld ranked Toomer with Joyce and Proust, while critics as diverse as Allen Tate, Sherwood Anderson, Waldo Frank, and Kenneth Burke went equally gaga. A collage of poems, episodic sketches, short stories, and drama, *Cane* is an evocative rendering of a black pastoral South doomed to extinction and a black urban North characterized by schizzy surreality. It is also one of the few books by an Afro-American male that seriously addresses the psyches of black female characters.

The book's rescue from obscurity by the '60s Black Arts Movement is an irony Toomer probably wouldn't have appreciated: the author of *Cane*, you dig, never wanted to be known as a black author. A surviving letter to his publishers upbraids them for calling him a "promising Negro writer," and goes on to say, "If my relationship with you is to be what I'd like it to be, I must insist that you never use such a word, such a thought again." Well, la-de-dah. The critical success of *Cane* drew Toomer into the Lost Gen-

191

•

eration's inner circle, company more to his liking. Alfred Stieglitz and Georgia O'Keeffe became his friends (O'Keeffe's biographer hints of a short affair) as did Marianne Moore, Edmund Wilson, and salon maven Mabel Dodge (with whom Lewis suggests a strange sexual liaison). But if all this charismatic genius makes Toomer sound fast on his way to one helluva literary career, think again. Or better yet, think Gurdjieff. After a mesmerizing encounter with the Russian mystic, Toomer became a zealot and never published again.

Like Toomer, Claude McKay is generally recognized as one of the Renaissance's star products. And also like Toomer, McKay spent hardly any time in the thick of it. Sailing to Russia in 1923, the roustabout Jamaican émigré spent six months there as the black toast of the Bolsheviks, then a decade traveling Europe and North Africa. His contacts with the Harlem movement were maintained through correspondence and the publication of his poetry and fiction. McKay's politics were as contradictory as Toomer's racial identifications. The most politically educated Renaissance writer chose to live more like a free spirit than an engagé rebel and was a Socialist who espoused Garveyite nationalism—even though he found Garvey's central vision of African redemption "puerile." Which in itself may not be surprising, since as a Jamaican in exile McKay longed for the days of British paternalism. Equally confusing is the fact that while McKay was, for a time, co-editor of Max Eastman's *The Liberator,* he despised propaganda. His literary output was consistent with his political vacillations. The anti-propagandist wrote some of the most biting protest verse in the language—Churchill ripped off McKay's Red Summer–inspired "If We Must Die" for a wartime speech—while the man who left Harlem to escape its "sex and poverty" and "hot, syncopated fascination" and "color consciousness" shamelessly sensationalized all that tawdry stuff in his novels, which are perhaps the worst examples of the Harlem primitivist school.

As Lewis tells it, the young black writers who did hang out in Harlem during the '20s probably had more fun than either grumpy McKay or zonked-out Toomer. Being younger, Zora Neale Hurston, Langston Hughes, and their peers took to Harlem's fast lane as often as they took to their typewriters. They mockingly referred to themselves, in Hurston's coinage, as the Niggerati, and upon occasion left their elders aghast. *Fire,* a one-shot collaboration, brought hateful reviews from Talented Tenth guardians disgusted by its celebrations of black street life and folklore. *Fire* represented the younger writers' declaration of independence from the effete tradition of black literature favored by the Tenth. For Hughes and Hurston especially, life in the Black Bottom outranked life on Sugar Hill as source material. Though not just because life in the lowlands was more interesting—as literature it moved more product among a white audience looking for Negro exotica.

Well provided for by white patrons, they could afford to disrespect their elders and revel in rebellion and raunch. Charlotte Mason—Hughes, Hurston, and McKay called her "Godmother"—was a wacky Park Avenue widow of means who had thrown her lot in with the "Negro cause" to help save the world's primitives from contamination by Western civilization. Ironically, her chief bursar and head talent scout, Alain Locke—she called him her "precious Brown boy"—couldn't get civilized by the West fast enough. Oxford's first black Rhodes Scholar spent his summers soaking in the museums and spas of Europe. Occasionally Mason worried that Locke's overweaned intellect would cause him to lose his racial inheritance on the "slippery pond of civilization." But Locke and Mason learned to exploit each other with tolerance: she because he secured her the patronship of Hughes, Hurston, McKay, and sculptor Richmond Barthe; he because her dollars allowed him to influence these bohemian welfare cases.

In return, artists were required to write fawning poems and pay house calls. Hurston fell into the role with gusto, says Lewis, "delighting the old lady with ethnic capers and 'coon' stories that would have been the envy of Joel Chandler Harris." Even wildman McKay wrote picaresque narratives extolling the primitive. Prized pet Langston Hughes got ousted from Godmother's little acre when his muse drew him closer to the proletariat. An anti-capitalist Christmas poem he published in *New Masses* in 1931 so upset Mason that he couldn't get a chastened shuffle in edgewise. Soon, though, Hughes would have company; he wasn't going to be the only Renaissance man to find himself out on his ass in Depression America.

193
•

With the country declared an economic disaster area, racy Negro literature got unfashionable, and the sources of its patronage dried up. But it was a while before the Renaissance artistes found their misfortunes coinciding with those of less eloquent brethren and sistren on the breadlines. Hughes, for example, following his banishment from Mason's fold, toured Haiti and Cuba on a Harmon Foundation grant. A year later he joined a boatload of young black Com symps and sailed to Russia, where all aboard had been invited to star in a Soviet anti-slavery musical(!). (This project got stymied when the Soviets discovered that not all Afro-Americans could carry a tune as well as their beloved Paul Robeson.)

Inevitably the economics and politics of the '30s drastically reordered the Talented Tenth's program. Du Bois embraced a confusing new policy of socialism abroad and separatism at home that got him booted out of the NAACP. The organization's presiding leadership lost two potentially prestigious civil rights cases—the Scottsboro Boys' and Angelo Herndon's—to the Communists because of caste snobbery. As the economic and political state of black America grew dimmer, aristocratic integration schemes seemed like the product of minds more out to lunch than merely highfalutin.

Even as late as 1933, NAACP secretary James Weldon Johnson could write, "A little bit more here and a little bit more there and the dam will break and the waters will no longer be segregated." If Johnson believed racism only a nudge away from oblivion—well, he obviously didn't know his ass from a hole in the ground. Because, as Lewis observes, Harlem's impoverished majority was hardly living a stone's throw from Utopia: "For Afro-American urban dwellers the more things changed, the more they worsened. Despite its vaunted Renaissance and distinguished residents, Harlem was no exception. In this 'city within a city' almost 50 per cent of the families were out of work, yet a mere 9 per cent of them received government relief jobs. The community's single medical facility, Harlem General Hospital, with 273 beds and 50 bassinets, served 200,000 Afro-Americans. The syphilis rate was nine times higher than white Manhattan's; the tuberculosis rate was five times higher; two black mothers and infants died for every white mother and infant."

• • •

For Jervis Anderson, Harlem begins not with Du Bois but with how your average brother and sister got up there in the first place. Harlem's transformation from a haven for wealthy white New Yorkers into a black community is, in Anderson's narrative, a story of tragicomic intrigue. New York City's black population had been on the move uptown since the early 1800s, pushed out by every hostile immigrant group or business interest in need of space. The 1890s found most bloods settled in the Tenderloin, from the Twenties to the low Sixties on the West Side, which quartered moneyed blacks, southern immigrants, and a redlight district known as Black Bohemia. Two catastrophes in the first years of the century gave blacks the boot from there: the destruction of the Tenderloin for Penn Station, with its resultant commercial-property landgrab, and a mad dog police-led riot in Hell's Kitchen. After those two throwdowns blacks packed up and made out for the West Nineties quick.

What opened the gorgeous brownstones and wide boulevards of Harlem to this exodus was a combination of white greed and a hustling young black realtor named Phillip Payton. As legend has it, Payton ran up on two white landlords of adjacent buildings, in heated discussion. To settle the score, one gave Payton his property to fill with blacks. "I was successful in managing this house," Payton recalled later, "and after a time I was able to induce other landlords to . . . give me their houses to manage." Payton's parlay of his initial gambit into the creation of the hugely successful (even by today's standards) Afro-American Realty Company flooded Harlem with blacks. Remembered now as the father of Harlem, Payton also helped give rise to a host of other black property management firms. Their success had as much to do with business savvy as with white landlords' customary readiness to jack up rents for black clients.

Not all of Harlem's older residents were happy with the new neighbors. Anderson quotes one of them: "Can nothing be done to put a restriction on the invasion of the Negro into Harlem? At one time it was a pleasure to ride on the . . . elevated. Now you invariably have a colored person sitting beside you. . . . Why cannot we have Jim Crow cars for these people?" One white Harlemite suggested that his fellow landed gentry erect 25-foot fences to

195

•

protect them from the very sight of the invading black hordes. But as frequently happens here in the land of the uprooted and the home of the highest bidder, mean green won out over neighborhood purity in the end.

The community that transplanted itself to Harlem contained every human type imaginable. From the Tenderloin came your smugglers, scramblers, burglars, gamblers, your pickpockets, peddlers, panhandlers, thugs, pimps, and pushers; all your big moneymakers. With them they brought the nightclub owners and innovative musicians who were to make Harlem so chic and alluring in the '20s. What the nouveau bougies who represented Harlem's educated and/or mercantile classes brought with them besides new money was moral propriety and, when it came to the masses, an attitude. As in that expressed by black businessman John B. Nail, explaining why his class hired European servants: "If there is one thing the negro of the servant class doesn't know it is that the color of his skin doesn't make him the equal of his master. You know what a fresh colored servant is in a white family? Just imagine the hell that would be raised by a fresh colored servant in a colored family."

Anderson's digs unearthed tons of quirky quotes like these. But they also led him to irritating excesses. He heaps in whole paragraphs of reference material where a few quotes or a summary would do, and he favors the obit page when it comes to transmitting biographical information. And why are there so many *lists* in his book? I mean we're talking a building occupants list, a list of churches, a list of preachers, a list of boxers, a list of bars, a list of popular periodicals, a list of Harlem notables, a list of dead Harlem notables, a list of occupations, a grocery list, even a list of bootleg liquor ingredients, fer chrissakes.

As Anderson moves toward the '50s, his material gets skimpier, his aims more diffuse, his organization more scattershot. Fascinated by Harlem's cavalcade of celebrities, he ignores the everyday people of the community. Since more than a few folk who lived there in the '30s and '40s are still alive, I have to wonder why some of their stories aren't included. And Anderson's cutoff date of 1950 seems like a panglossian move to avoid tainting his glitzy portrayal of Harlem with what heroin turned it into—which is some horrorshow. By ignoring Harlem's present, Anderson has written not popular history but popular showbiz romance. And to a certain extent the same could be said of Lewis, even given his iconoclasm and sophistication.

The two books share a failing: both Lewis and Anderson refuse to analyze where the historical myth of Harlem fits within the context of Afro-American reality in the 1980s. For contemporary Afro-American professionals and intellectuals, the Harlem of legend is at best a Utopian cultural myth: about the segregated but self-contained black community of the past, isolated from white America but strong enough to sustain itself thanks to the talent caged within its boundaries. Unlike Du Bois and Johnson, however, today's black braintrusts don't have to work or live in the "black community"; thanks to affirmative action they can braindrain themselves out to the highest corporate bidder and cop a squat in the suburbs. Which is cool up to a point. Except that what remains unresolved for this generation's upwardly mobile blacks is just how much assimilation they dare risk at the expense of alienation from the Harlems of today, especially given that the terms of this assimilation are enforced only by fragile tolerance and easily eradicated legislation. Because in the face of Harlem's decay, the question is this: just where do you go when you can't go home again and baby it's cold outside?

197

—1982

Cult-Nats Meet Freaky-Deke

Somewhere along the road to probable madness or a meaningful life, I decided that what black culture needs is a popular poststructuralism—accessible writing bent on deconstructing the whole of black culture. Anybody who's read Harold Cruse's scathing dissection of black leadership, *The Crisis of the Negro Intellectual,* knows his argument that each generation of black leaders has failed from an inability to conceive black liberation totally and systemically. Meaning they failed to develop agendas that fused protest and reform politics with self-help economics, sophisticated cultural critiques, and a Marxian take on the political economy of capitalism. Twenty years later, the void Cruse railed against remains. If you think I'm going to try to fill it, you got another think coming. I'm bold but I ain't that bad. This whatchamajiggy here is about how black aestheticians need to develop a coherent criticism to communicate the complexities of our culture. There's no periodical on black cultural phenomena equivalent to *The Village Voice* or *Artforum,* no publication that provides journalism on black visual art, philosophy, politics, economics, media, literature, linguistics, psychology, sexuality, spirituality, and pop culture. Though there are certainly black editors, journalists, and academics capable of producing such a journal, the disintegration of the black cultural nationalist movement and the braindrain of black intellectuals to white institutions have destroyed the vociferous public dialogue that used to exist between them. Consider this my little shot at opening it up again.

Given the lack of debate and discussion among educated blacks today, Harold Cruse's remedies for the black intelligentsia's failings seem more quixotic now than 20 years ago—particularly because back then the civil rights and black power movements were producing a generation of artists and activists who could be provoked into getting hot and bothered. (You ask a buppy mofo his stand on the race, he'll tell you he favors Carl Lewis.) Cruse presaged the black cultural nationalist movement as conceived by Amiri Baraka and Ron Karenga. While the founding fathers have long taken deserved lumps for the jiver parts of their program (like the sexist, anti-Semitic, black supremacist, pseudo-African mumbo-jumbo, paramilitary adventurist parts), to their credit they took black liberation seriously enough to be theoretically ambitious about it. Perhaps their most grandiose scheme involved trying to transform a supremacist sense of black cultural *difference* into the basis for a racially bonding black American zeitgeist—one that would serve blacks as Judaism was believed to have solidified Jews. The plan was to convince 30 million people they constituted a nation, not only because they were an oppressed minority, but also because they were superior to the corny white man and his Western civilization.

A considerable amount of this philosophy was developed by Baba Baraka, formerly a prized black stepchild of Western modernism. Baraka has acknowledged that he derived his black supremacist gumption from African-American music, which definitely represents the one modernist arena blacks are the masters of. (It is our music, especially jazz, which confronts Western culture with its most intimidating and improbable Other: the sui generis black genius. But that's a whole other dissertation.) The leap from perceiving the genius of jazz to envisioning an Afrocentric master race is quite a doozy. Generously, it could be understood as an extremist's reaction to blacks being classified for centuries as subhumans without culture and history. Given that context, let's be generous. Two decades ago, Malcolm X implored blacks to cast aside their differences and unite against the common foe we all caught hell from, the white man. Yet that dream of black unity addressed racial oppression more meaningfully than it did the more crucial dilemma of cultural identity. (If being black meant nothing but being oppressed by white people, black liberation would have no

199

•

meaning. Like if white people weren't around to be mad at, people into being black would be out of a job.)

What the cult-nats made possible is a conception of black culture where anything black could be considered an aesthetic object of contemplation more beautiful than anything produced by the white man. In this sense the cult-nats were our dadaists. While the dadaists tried to raise anarchy to an artform and bring Western civilization down with style, the cult-nats figured a "black is beautiful" campaign would be enough to raze Babylon, or at least get a revolution going. The cult-nats' black-übermensch campaign obviously didn't do much toward liberating the masses, but it did produce a postliberated black aesthetic, responsible for the degree to which contemporary black artists and intellectuals feel themselves heirs to a culture every bit as def as classical Western civilization.

This cultural confidence has freed up more black artists to do work as wonderfully absurdist as black life itself. The impulse toward enmeshing self-criticism and celebration present in the most provocative avant-garde black art of the '70s and early '80s (cf. Miles Davis, David Hammons, Senga Ngudi, Art Ensemble of Chicago, Ishmael Reed, Charles Burnett, Pedro Bell, George Clinton, Samuel R. Delany, Richard Pryor, Charles Johnson, Octavia Butler, Jayne Cortez, Ntozake Shange, Toni Morrison) owes a debt to the cult-nats for making so much noise about the mythic beauties of blackness that these artists could traffic in the ugly and mundane sides with just as much ardor. (Admittedly, most of these artists have at one time or another confused a passion for black exotica with detached representation. On the other hand, we all know there's not a single freak in their work without a counterpart even more out-the-box somewhere in the kinky wilds of black America. Such is our mutant diversity.) What's unfortunate is that while black artists have opened up the entire "text of blackness" for fun and games, not many black critics have produced writing as fecund, eclectic, and freaky-deke as the art, let alone the culture itself. (Some exceptions: Henry Louis Gates, David Levering Lewis, Lorenzo Thomas, Nathaniel Mackey, Adrian Seaward, Clyde Taylor, Houston Baker.) For those who prefer exegesis with a polemical bent, just imagine how critics as fluent in black and Western culture as the postliberated artists could strike terror into that bastion of white supremacist thinking, the Western art world.

In *Art After Modernism: Essays on Rethinking Representation,* Brian Wallis laments that there's never been a serious study of the relationship of black culture to institutionalized art. (Like don't nobody know that since Cubism, black culture and Western modernism have been confused for conceptual kissing cousins; that since bebop's impact on Abstract Expressionism and the Beats, black modernism has been confused with white alienation and social deviance; that since Duke Ellington compared Picasso to Miles Davis, black genius has been confused with the formal exhaustion of Western art; that since Norman Mailer wrote "The White Negro," black cool has been mistaken for a figment of white heterosexual anxiety; that since Thomas Pynchon shabbily disguised Ornette Coleman as McClintic Sphere in *V.*, black alienation has gotten confused with existential parody; that since Ornette Coleman called Jimi Hendrix's "Star Spangled Banner" the most beautiful since Toscanini's, the power to impose cultural democracy has fallen into the hands of black people with strange ideas; that since I heard a snotty white DJ say he stopped thinking Parliament/Funkadelic was stupid disco when Brian Eno cited them as an influence, I've known George Clinton was right when he said that as soon as white folks figured out funk was intellectually acceptable they'd try to hop on board the Mothership.) To this postliberated black aesthetician, Wallis's whine sounded like an invite to bomb the white bastion rather than know my place relative to it. At first I thought I'd have to go it alone, but then I discovered a smart, empathetic white man I could cannibalize—one all ready to see MOMA collapse in the dust with an Air Jordan high-top at its throat.

201

A big round of applause, then, to my host culture-bearer, Hal Foster, senior editor at *Art in America*, editor of the postmod collection *The Anti-Aesthetic*, and now author of *Recodings: Art, Spectacle, Cultural Politics*, a primer in poststructuralist discourse and debate with its sights on bringing about the end of Western civilization in theory. Taking aim, he blasts away at those involved in rationalizing capitalism through the culture industry. For people who look toward critical theory as a way to outthink the powers that be rather than to disguise fuzzy thinking behind hermetic verbiage, Foster makes a lot of sense. He doesn't see theory as an end in itself, but as a "toolkit" to pry apart the hidden collusion between the corporate class and its artsy running dogs, like big bad MOMA and those messy Neo-Expressionist painters. Having arrived at the astounding conclusion that criticism is of marginal value to the art marketplace, Foster prizes his marginality as license to speak "out of place."

The margins from which Foster speaks are indeed extreme—so extreme that by book's end he's set himself up against not only pluralism, Neo-Expressionism, postmodern architecture, primitivist-modernism, and *The New Criterion* crew, but Barthes, Baudrillard, Hegelian dialectics, and the very idea of Western history. (The "enemy" identified throughout *Recodings* is "the white, patriarchal order of western culture and its pretenses of sovereignty, supremacy and self creation.") In the early sections Foster goes about exposing those postmodern artists who profess autonomy from corporate power or pretend to be political by acting like social outlaws. To this end he is such a thorough deconstructionist that not even artists he admires escape his powers of dissection. Though his demolition of Neo-Expressionism ("The Expressive Fallacy") comes as no surprise, it's unexpected when an infatuated appreciation of Robert Longo's work ends on the downbeat. "A utopian principle of hope may be evoked here but no actual community is engaged. This work has no social basis (other than the dominant class whose representations are collided). Its mix of archaic and futuristic forms attests to this absence—as does its apocalypticism, which is symptomatic of the failure of the dominant culture (and its 'artist guardian') to conceive social change in terms other than catastrophe. In the absence of such a social basis utopian desire may well become a will to power—or an identification with the powers that be."

Behind the facades of the postmoderns, Foster never fails to detect the presence of the corporate class. Echoing Baudrillard's crucial revision of Marx, *For a Critique of the Political Economy of the Sign*, Foster opines that the corporate class, having achieved mastery of accumulation, now desires mastery of "symbolic production," meaning mass media and modern art. The "penetration of the sign by capital" is a major theme of *Recodings*, along with the problems that penetration represents for those committed to "cultural resistance," Foster's favorite form of theory-mongering.

Where others find total freedom in the pluralistic postmodern marketplace, he finds no more than the franchised freedom of the commodity. Here artists suppress all desire for social change and are rewarded for producing consumable art, "safeguarding social inertia by participating in an illusion of democracy." Equally suspect is the return (through Neo-Expressionism) of the myth of the modern artist as bourgeois transgressor and last refuge of "humanist values." (This gets kinky when you consider how much transgressive shock value, and hence "humanism" in modern art, derived from the moderns' primitivist ideas about Africa.) Though these myths once served early modernism by making the artist an adversary of the bourgeoisie, today they serve the corporate class by making artistic transgression "a posture available to everyman." (Reading this brought to mind the Jean Michel Basquiat behind the bar in the Palladium's Michael Todd room.) Attacking postmodern architects for elitism, Foster finds in their vernacular revivals not a populist modernism but a supercilious lowbrowism, not a regeneration of modernist ideals but a regression to classic architectural forms for the myths of authority they sing to the powerful.

203
•

For Foster, the most provocative American art of today situates itself at a crossroads where representations of sexual identity and social life can freely intervene in critiques of institutional art, mass culture, and the corporate class. Barbara Kruger, Jenny Holzer, Hans Haacke, Cindy Sherman are artists Foster finds significant because they don't just make consumable objects but also manipulate signs, seeking to make "the viewer an active reader of messages rather than a passive contemplator of the aesthetic or consumer of the spectacular." The history of these artists' practices begins in the adversarial site-specific work done in the '70s by Hans Haacke and Daniel Buren. At that time their work centered on confronting the power of the museum to marginalize radical art, updating Duchamp's antiaesthetic. Yet Buren believed that the real perfidy performed by galleries and museums was not aesthetic but economic; they protected the very idea of the art market by supplying exchange-value to art. Foster notes that this critique became particularly crucial once the bourgeoisie had abandoned its classical culture for a consumerist one, and reinvested in the museum as modernism's warehouse. Barbara Kruger, Jenny Holzer, and other feminist manipulators of "sign-value" revise the work of these male artists by mocking the power invested in official language. In "For a Concept of the Political in Contemporary Art," Foster draws on Baudrillard's critique of a belief held dear by Marx, Walter Benjamin, and the Russian constructivists: that political art must be aligned with the production of the industrial worker. Baudrillard found that model faulty because it identified the white male worker as the sole force for social progress. This denied the significance of struggles by those outside or subordinate to production: students, blacks, gays, women. Because the site of their struggles is as much for representation, for significance and signification within academia and the media their active resistance of patriarchal and racist practices must take place there. The intent is not to segregate the struggles of blacks, gays, and women from those of the white male worker under capitalism, but to equalize them. Rethinking political art today means recognizing that per Foucault, power derives its authority not only from social consent and economic determinism but from those "disciplinary institutions" which control behavior and the body through "social regimens" (at work, school, the corporation) and "structure our lives materially."

It is the realization that disciplinary institutions produce "socially adjusted individuals" which has brought poststructuralist concerns with representation, sexuality, textuality, and totalization to the foreground of contemporary political art. Baudrillard recognized that the commodification of culture has rendered obsolete the distinctions between art and commerce, culture and economy, and any reading of signs (art and media) as if they were impenetrable by capital. Since the corporate class dominates symbolic production, art has become a capitalist comprador, out to protect commodity values rather than those of classical bourgeois culture. "According to this position, the bourgeoisie no longer needs a traditional culture to impress its ideology or retain its rule; the commodity no longer requires the guise of a personal or social value for us to submit to it: it is its own excuse, its own ideology."

Traditionally, modern art has sought to resist collusion with capital or shock the bourgeoisie through either primitive transgression or formal elitism. But these strategies failed to be truly radical because they didn't intend to better society and may, says Foster, even have prepared society to consent in the "social transgressions of capital." He believes that the shock-of-the-new impulse of early modern art contributed to "subtly reconciling us to the chaos of the late-capitalist world." Nostalgia for avant-garde transgression Foster finds not only nihilistic but of little value to political artists today. What he proposes is a practice which views culture as an arena where "active contestation is possible." From this vantage point, capital would not be seen as a megalith to be shocked and liberated by, say, "primitivism," but as a network of disciplinary institutions and sign systems to be constantly targeted for adversarial deconstruction. Resistance, then, doesn't aim for transcendence of corporate culture's limits into some mythical liberated zone, but for critical intervention in the process by which capitalism is rationalized through mass culture and modernism.

Foster believes these interventions could become more than merely theoretical if Western political artists were able to forge cultural revolution alongside subcultural Others—those whose collective practices not only create new languages of representation but signify a disbelief in mass culture, modernism, and the West. Among these subcultural practices he cites reggae, black gospel, and Latin American fiction. Where others such as Barthes, Baudrillard, Deleuze, and Guattari have sought out subcultural codes to call the West's supremacist ideas of history and difference into question, Foster closes *Recodings* by pronouncing that Western theorists should chill, and open the field for blacks, gays, and feminists to command the critical foreground of cultural resistance.

What *Recodings* has to say about cultural resistance, commodification, representation, and Western supremacy is fascinating to mull over from a black perspective, particularly since so much black aesthetic and political debate has for years been concerned with these issues. If I'm so gung-ho about integrating Foster's

205

poststructuralist toolkit into a discussion of black culture, it's not because black culture lacks Foster's mind but because it lacks his bent for knowing and dissecting his subject in total. In the past, the sectarian nature of black art and politics has worked against a "unified field theory" of black culture. The person who seems to be moving most determinedly in that direction is, ironically, a white man, Yale's Robert Farris Thompson, whose books and lectures on African art and philosophy in the "Black Atlantic tradition" are milestones of comparative analysis on the continuum which runs between black culture in Africa and the New World, spiritually, aesthetically, and philosophically.

Thompson's work disproves and demolishes at every turn the myth that classical African culture doesn't derive from as systematic and highly evolved a tradition of critical thought as Europe's. (Yoruba sculpture, for example, is no less a product of conscious conceptualization than art in the Greco-Roman tradition. The difference isn't a matter of intellect but of intention.) Thompson articulates the critical infrastructure at work in classical African art, music, and dance, and its impact on the New World. Yet even that breadth of learning barely touches on what black culture has evolved to in 20th century America. I'm pushing for a popular black poststructuralism because we need theoretical and critical tools as exacting as those that produced a work like *Recodings:* writings which ask hard questions about where our culture stands in history, what total liberation means to black people living now, and how black art can continue to express that desire for freedom. Another reason, more self-involved in nature, is that I'm part of a generation of bohemian cult-nats who are mutating black culture into something the old interlocutors aren't ready for yet.

Though nobody's sent out any announcements yet, the '80s are witnessing the maturation of a postnationalist black arts movement, one more Afrocentric and cosmopolitan than anything that's come before. The people in this movement find no contradiction in deriving equal doses of inspiration from influences as diverse as Malcolm X and Jimi Hendrix, George Clinton and George Romero, Kareem Abdul-Jabbar and Lisette Model, Zora Neale Hurston and Akira Kurosawa, William Burroughs and Romare Bearden, Barnett Newman and Sun Ra, Jah Rastafari and Johnny Rotten, Toni Morrison and Laura Mulvey, George Jackson and Samuel Delany, Albert Ayler and Andrei Tarkovsky, Rudy Ray Moore and Nam June Paik, Black Elk and Bud Powell, Cecil Taylor and Joel Peter-Witkin, Chester Himes and Jacques Tati, Ishmael Reed and Maya Deren, Anthony Braxton and Bruce Lee, Jean Rhys and Nona Hendryx, Antonin Artaud and Amiri Baraka, Robert Farris Thompson and Professor Longhair, Julia Kristeva and Chaka Khan, Kurt Schwitters and Coptic scrolls, Run-D.M.C. and Paolo Soleri, Fredric Jameson and Reverend James Cleveland, Katherine Dunham and Meredith Monk, Darryl Dawkins and Ndebele beadwork, Ramayana and Elegba-Eshu, Kathy Acker and Nina Simone, Audre Lorde and the Maasai, Duane Michals and John Coltrane, Skip James and Bill Viola. Cornucopia for a New Negro Bohemia? Hey, every generation's got to have one. And that list of odd couples only represents those favored by the freaks I know about. (No telling what kind of black bizarro worldviews are being cooked up by members of the cadre still underground.) But even though quotation is the postmod thing to do, I'm not just namedropping here. The point is that the present generation of black artists is cross-breeding aesthetic references like nobody is even talking about yet. And while they may be marginal to the black experience as it's expressed in rap, *Jet*, and on *The Cosby Show*, they're not all mixed up over who they are and where they come from.

207

These are artists for whom black consciousness and artistic freedom are not mutually exclusive but complementary, for whom "black culture" signifies a multicultural tradition of expressive practices; they feel secure enough about black culture to claim art produced by nonblacks as part of their inheritance. No anxiety of influence here—these folks believe the cultural gene pool is for skinny-dipping. Yet though their work challenges both cult-nats and snotty whites, don't expect to find them in *Ebony* or *Artforum* any time soon. Things ain't hardly got that loose yet.

Black culture as these artists know it is a debased commodity within black and white popular media, and even within the avant-garde. Their targets for the kind of "cultural resistance" and "intervention in codes" Foster speaks of are complicated by the artists having to take on racist representations and black self-hate simultaneously. For these reasons Spike Lee's success, in both commercial and artistic terms, with *She's Gotta Have It*, represents a coup of staggering proportions. It is in fact a populist black post-structuralist's dream.

Not only does Lee overload his "joint" with black in-jokes and semiotic codes (I'm thinking now of the references to Zora Neale Hurston, Malcolm X, Eleanor Bumpurs, Edwin Perry, and Black Reconstruction that turn up, as well as things like using straight-ahead jazz to underscore hiphop humor, and the conjugation of "drugs" and "jheri curls" to mark them as equally vile) but he pushed such an uncompromisingly black vision to blacks through mainstream distribution, exhibition, and media channels. Lee's making a success out of a film shot for jackshit with a collectivist cast and crew demolishes Hollywood's megabudget mystique. Now, if all that's not culturally resistant, I don't know what is. And Lee's staunch raceman interviews have been even more rad, breaking on Whoopi's blue contacts, Michael's nose, *The Color Purple*, as well as threatening letters from Quincy Jones's office (not to mention the MPAA, which he says tried to give him an X because softcore black sexuality tweaked their uptight, racist nerves). The sweetest aspect of Lee's success is that the only formula it offers for those who'd desire to emulate or exploit it is faith in the brilliance of black culture. What we need now is black criticism as balls to the wall as *She's Gotta Have It*.

208

Because black people don't have institutions for serious, sophisticated study and advancement of our culture, my dream of a populist black poststructuralism is actually kind of loony, but every man needs his own Moby Dick. What I envision is an Afrocentric cross between MIT, MOMA, MGM, Macmillan books, and Motown, a self-supporting facility equipped to bankroll a braintrust of B-boys, feminists, philosophers, visual artists, musicians, athletes, scientists, theologians, historians, political activists and economists, and produce their findings and artifacts for mass audiences. Since I can't underwrite this black tower of Babel, I can at least target a few white whales for it to harpoon, a few black holes for it to get sucked up into. First off, if it were to take up the Brian Wallis project, a study of the relationship of black culture to institutionalized art, there'd be a need for an encyclopedic reference book on black visual culture.

Given the kind of money the de Menils are sinking into their Eurocentric project, *Images of the Black in Western Art*, I'd hire a staff of editors, designers, and critics (Richard Powell, Judith Wilson, Kellie Jones, and Rosalind Jeffries come to mind) to produce a multivolume bricolage of black images from every source conceivable: police mugshots, graffiti, Cubism, race riots, newspapers, hair product ads, comics, black independent cinema, advertising, music videos, lynchings, minstrelsy, breakdancing, iconic jazz photography, Bauhaus furniture, images of blacks in Western art, modern art by black artists such as Twin Seven Seven, Leroy Clarke, Skunder Boghossian, Calvin Reid, Al Loving, Senga Nengudi, Daniel Dawson, Charles Abramson, Janet Henry, Houston Conwill, Ed Love, Rikki Smith, Nelson Stevens, Selim Abdul Mubdi, Edgar Sorrells-Adewale, Emilio Cruz, Martha Jackson-Jarvis, Lorna Simpson, Jack Whitten, Randy Williams, Sandra Payne, Jules Allen, Pedro Bell, Jean Michel Basquiat, Albert Chong, Romare Bearden, Wilfredo Lam, plus the art of every black ethnic group in Asia, Africa, and the Americas. The text for these volumes would be drawn from as varied a collection of sources— all making for a veritable postmodern bible of black visual representation and critical difference. Publish that bad boy and all this bulljive we hear about the impoverishment of black visual culture would have to cease. Next on the agenda would be a series of symposiums on topics like Institutionalizing the Production of Black Musical Geniuses; the First Annual Conference on Black Mother Wit, Phylogeny, and Dub; Zen and the Art of Skip James; Harlem as Hyperreality: Reading Chester Himes; Rags, Hickeys, and Wops: The Etymology of Doo; Jazz and the Heat-Death of the Universe (A Comparative Analysis of the Death of the Author in Postmodern Painting and Jazz); Breakdancing as Telemetry; Genii in the Genome: George Clinton and Jeremy Rifkin's Rhythm Theories of Evolution; Race Mutation Theory and Quantum-Black Myth; The Mathematics of Graffiti: Ramm-El-Zee's Ikonoklast Panzerism; The Political Economy of Scratch; and Beat the System to Death: Bootstrap Capitalism and Guerrilla Warfare. The possibilities are frightening. You fill in the blanks.

Now I know some people are going to read all this and level charges ranging from silliness to rank sophistry to Bakuninism.

209

Let them come on with it. My mission is clear. The future of black culture demands that this generation bring forth a worldly-wise and stoopidfresh intelligentsia of radical bups who can get as *ignant* as James Brown with their Wangs and stay in the black. Give me such an army and we'll be talking total cultural black rule by the time the eco-system collapses, SDI bottoms out Fort Knox, the Aryan Brotherhood is officially in the White House, and Wall Street is on the moon.

—1986

Signs and Cymbals: Nathaniel Mackey's Postmod Pop

Bedouin Hornbook struck me as the most moving and intelligent fiction about modern jazz I'd ever read— probably because Nathaniel Mackey transcribes black music into my favorite kind of postmod narrative: part philosophy, part confessional folklore. Mackey, a poet who teaches at the University of Santa Cruz, uses jazz as the way into a hermeneutic vision quest full of existential rumblings and doubts. The first volume of a planned series called *From a Broken Bottle Traces of Perfume Still Emanate*, *Bedouin Hornbook* is a collection of letters written by the narrator, "N.," to a woman addressed as "Dear Angel of Dust," who may or may not be deceased.

N. is a multi-instrumentalist working with the "Mystic Horn Society"; he keeps Angel posted on developments with the group, also composed of Aunt Nancy Djamilla, Lambert, and Penguin. Like Sun Ra's Arkestra and the Art Ensemble of Chicago, they play an array of non-Western and European instruments and are concerned as much with theater and ritual as concertizing. In fact, *Bedouin Hornbook* has to be read as a thinly veiled homage to Ra and the AEC, and their adaptations of African, Asian, and European philosophy to the jazz vernacular. N.'s descriptions of the Mystic Horn Society in action read like excerpts from a mythographers' convention:

> By way of a flurry of 16th and 32nd notes, Penguin made it known that the Papyrus of Nesi-Amsu, repeating a legend reputed to be "older than the pyramids," reports that Temu "had union with himself" and thus produced the gods Shu and Tefnu ("air" and "moisture"). This legend comes down to us in a number of versions and the specifics of Temu's "union with himself" vary from account to account. . . . According to one of these, Temu showed up in Annu in a state of arousal, took his erection in his hand and masturbated. As a result Shu and Tefnu—whom we now know to have been of Nubian origin, Penguin pointed out in an aside—came into being . . .

211

A later Lambert solo ponders Zeus's punishment of Prometheus on the basis of color, riffs on Prometheus's brother Epidermis and the skin-game of history, then closes by asking, "could Mt. Caucasus have been the 'racial mountain' that Langston Hughes used to talk about?"

Off the bandstand, the esoteric bent of the group spills naturally into the streets, where even crude graffiti provoke semiotic debates about black culture:

> There, somewhat shakily written in pencil, were the words: "Mr Slick and Mister Brother are one of the two most baddest dude in town, and Sutter Street." . . . Penguin said he was struck by what he termed "its enabling confusion concerning the singular and the plural," that he saw its vacillation between the claims of the one and the counterclaims of the other . . . as the sign of

a deepseated upheaval in the consciousness of the folk, an insistent interrogation of the bounds between individual and collective identities, something like the "I and I" of Rastafarian talk in fact. . . . Aunt Nancy objected that Penguin, as she put it, had "put words in the mouths of the people," that he sold them short and gave them too much credit at the same time. What he said smacked of outmoded, condescending notions of the people's inability to think in individualist terms. At this point Lambert jumped in and asked how she'd explain, even if that were the case, the words, "Mr Slick and Mister Brown are one"— to which Aunt Nancy answered back, "Bad schooling." . . . Lambert came right back, though, raising his voice to compete with the laughter and insisting that anyone who chose to misread the handwriting on the wall did so at his or her own risk. He said it was obvious that the hand of whoever had written those words had been put upon, literally shaken by powers—whether artistic or autistic, he couldn't, he admitted, say—which were neither to be trifled with nor explained away by hard-headed sophistries disguised as common sense. He added that if anything the words were a summons, a call-to-arms as it were, an invitation into an area on *un*common sense, and that the dislocations they visited upon so-called proper English were manifestly of an invasive, mediumistic order. By the time he finished a heavy, uncomfortable silence had settled over everyone.

212

Bedouin Hornbook is packed with passages in which Mackey plays on poststructuralism and black arcana. Interpretations of Egyptian and Dogon cosmology are frequently interpolated with punning discourse that shows no mercy to either reader or trope. It's a testimony to Mackey's writing that he's sometimes able to construct arch and ironic dialogue out of such tendentious and pretentious language. Mackey also goes further toward presenting one man's philosophy (in the Western literary sense) of black music than any writer since Amiri Baraka in *Blues People* and *Black Music*, but thankfully *Bedouin Hornbook* isn't only an exercise in phenomenology.

Though music is the principal concern of N.'s letters, he's as likely to probe his frailties in them as his metaphysics. Fascinating volleys are constantly being exchanged between N.'s existential moments and the timeless continuum his musical improvisations claim to invoke. N.'s reportage sometimes prefigures his dreams, while his memories are often found to hold the key to his visions of the future. Like Ishmael Reed, N./Mackey engages in intertextual play among his characters and ideas. But the gamesmanship is always integral to the narrative moment, and even when the wordplay borders on the sophomoric, it provokes thought. (When, well into the book, N. pleads to Angel, "Forgive me for resorting to etymologies again, but therein, I'm convinced, lie the roots of coincidence," this enlightened if wordgame-weary reader considered it a gracious nod in *his* direction.) Mackey's punning and conceptual wordplay always suggests poetic implications. Mackey draws upon jazz's dialectical critique of Western culture (you know, the one that accounts for how jazz can represent both the Africanization and antithesis of Western classical music) in ways that transcend cultural nationalism to reach for the ineffable. In one letter, for example, N. declares that the political differences between blacks and whites have their roots in aesthetics and metaphysics:

> I'm troubled by the apparent fatalism intrinsic to form, the threat of a conservatism the centralness of "form" seems to imply. Music got pulled in not only because I'm a musician but because of the longstanding tradition which uses musical form as the symbol par excellence of a cosmic status quo, the so-called "harmony of the spheres." Any such harmony, if it exists, does so at our expense I'm convinced. This led a drummer I once had been with in a bar to say that if the harmony of the spheres ever came near him he'd "pop it upside the jaw." In this town you don't have to listen long to realize that the music coming down from on high can't be heard for the noise the police helicopters make.

213

•

Through the archetypal jazzman's search for the eternal now, *Bedouin Hornbook* shows Mackey attempting to come to terms with a host of binary opposites relevant to intellectually inquisitive African Americans everywhere—the schisms brought on by pondering ancestry and identity, folklore and book learning, mythology and modernity, ethnicity and multiculturalism, community and self. Mackey works wry passages of soul-searching into N.'s mytho-poeic and philosophical inquiries, enriching his book with equal parts compassion, intimacy, and intelligence. Though it's over-written and brainily purple in patches, Mackey's writing (much like the best of Ornette Coleman or country blues) rewards close reading with resonances of real experience. I don't think I could ask more of writing than that.

—1987

You Look Fabulist: Steve Erickson's Wild Kingdom

214

teve Erickson's writings belong to a venerable and arcane tradition in American letters that could be called Gothic Fabulism. This canon would accom-modate the morbid forefathers of our literature of the fantastic, Poe, Hawthorne, and Melville. The tradition they began was brought into this century by Faulkner, and carried forward by Raymond Chandler, Richard Wright, Ralph Ellison, Ishmael Reed, Cynthia Ozick, Toni Morrison, Louise Erdrich, John Edgar Wideman, and Don DeLillo. Central to Gothic Fabulist doctrine is the idea that the novel has enough authority to pass judgment on the sins of entire civilizations—to subject everything from ethics to eating habits to a retentive scrutiny bent on scraping clean a culture's moral crevices.

More often than not, GF books deflate the vainglorious puffery of manly rites of passage while celebrating the exacting ceremonies of such acts. In our homegrown existentialist library, the protagonist not only recounts nightmares out of American history (often through parables), but re-enacts the more tortuous nightmare of personal remembering—a passage of no small aching, not least because the typical hero has made the horrors of civilization his own drive-in monster movie, usually as a means to reckon with some private scar of shame. The Gothic Fabulists tend to see the novel as a handy place to go shedding buckets of cultural blood guilt.

So it isn't surprising that this is the one American literary lineage—apart from slave narratives and the testimonials of Native Americans—that persists in upping the spiritual costs to white American manhood of its genocidal history. Through Wright, Ellison, and Reed we are made aware of how much heroism and terror is involved in the black male's pursuit of an identity and a place in a white macho world; through Morrison's and Erdrich's excavations we are given an exhibition of the wounds that the fathers of three races have visited upon their daughters, and of the mythic power that resides in the ideas of female essentialism and woman as a creature of nature.

215

Erickson is the baby of this bunch. For my money, he is the only heavyweight contender around among American novelists under 40, excluding genre-specialist William Gibson. Erickson's three novels—*Days Between Stations, Rubicon Beach,* and *Tours of the Black Clock*—are at once illuminating and irritating, deeply moving and deeply unsatisfying. The irritation and dissatisfaction generally derive from the fact that Erickson, like all Gothic Fabulists, is an unrepentant allegorist who, unlike the luminaries of his breed, has so far lacked the patience to create a strong sense of place, that necessary evil his forebears and contemporary betters have carried over from the 19th century social novel. In Erickson's case, this seems a result not of bad research but of a lack of imagination—specifically the paced, structural imagination of a more-or-less linear novel. It may also have something to do with a sense of cultural displacement as a white American liberal in the

'80s. But we'll pick up on that theme a little later (don't you worry).

Erickson is good at getting your juices going over his alternative-world stories; he always leaves me feeling like his books didn't happen to me, I dreamed them. Erickson's novels always come out of the gate like Ben Johnson on steroids. Unfortunately, he usually finishes the race with as much kick as a Dali stopwatch. But if Erickson comes up short on the wind needed to be a long-distance narrative runner, he is, in the clutch, a dogged archaeologist of his characters' secrets:

> One day out on the water, right before the sun fainted into dark, her father picked her up to gaze over the side of the boat. There, for the first time, she saw her own face. She thought that it was a strange and marvelous watercreature, like the roots of trees with pink mouths off the coast of England or the fish that dead men watched in the dirt. Had her father looked over the side of the boat with her, she might have understood it was her face.

My man's last and most critically celebrated novel, *Tours of the Black Clock,* is also his least distinguished. Up until its midpoint, the book seems bent on elevating the horrific moral codes of Jim Thompson pulp to higher literature; then alas, it settles in for an excruciating execution of a premise as hokey as anything ever devised by another Gothic Fabulist, Roger Corman. Set in the '30s and '40s, *Tours of the Black Clock* presents the tale of an adolescent midwestern farmboy turned fratricidal psycho-killer and fugitive. While on the lam he makes a Dantean descent from bouncer (for a New York gangster) to pulp fiction writer to, at last, Hitler's pornographer.

The farm-belt chapters are as engrossing as dime-novel fiction ever gets, so full of language, mystery, and verve that they sustain our interest through the flagging Chicago midsection. The Third Reich windup is a total bust, primarily because Erickson seems to expect the reverberations of Nazi evil to invigorate his flaccid storytelling and his main character's mounting banality. Along the way, some of the most promising material of the early chapters is scrapped—particularly the psychoanalytic breakthrough latent in having Erickson's protagonist murder and maim his family, not for greed, lust, or kicks, but for racial revenge. Having discovered that his family's old half-Native-American servant, whom his two elder brothers had been raping for years, was in fact his mother, and this discovery coming when his brothers try to goad him into having a go at her, he cold loses it. After killing one brother, crippling another, and maiming his father, the narrator burns the house down and hits the road.

Is this Oedipus meets Cochise in search of Neal Cassady, or what? Never mind the turnabout on that American stereotype, the untrustworthy half-breed: Erickson lost a metanovelistic opportunity to expose America's toilet morals by exposing the conventions of two of its toilet genres, the Western and the porn novel. To understand how maddening I found this misfire, imagine what a crock *Mumbo Jumbo* would have been had Ishmael Reed decided midway that Papa La Bas, instead of being the last word on 7000 years of space and time, would live out the rest of the novel as Warren G. Harding's amanuensis. As sad-ass satire such a narrative derailment might have a chance, but Erickson is too somber for such transparent tomfoolery.

In one sense, his books read like brooding boy's-own adventures, the Hardys gone upriver to become lords of the flies. The voice in them is what Muddy Waters once described as Mannish Boy. Its bumbling combination of giddy muscle and emotional immaturity speaks to such a sense of exile in the world of adult responsibilities that you wonder if it isn't the author's own.

Leap Year, Erickson's most recent book, is a New Journalese essay about the 1988 presidential campaign. Here we find Erickson fighting back another form of adolescent regression: he doesn't want to be overwhelmed by cynicism and disillusionment in the face of American electoral politics. For the close-to-the-bone tone alone it is Erickson's most melancholic work, a *Mr. Smith Goes to Washington* for the '90s. *Leap Year* portrays the crumbling idealism of a young intellectual comer who believes in his country more than his country believes in itself.

Erickson finds it hard to admit, during a year of dogging the campaign trail, that he's learned not to trust his homeland. Though the reflexive, reflective, casually moralizing tone of *Leap Year* evokes Norman Mailer's campaign epics, Erickson is both more naive and less optimistic about his nation's regenerative powers than Mailer could ever be. No way he would have written a book so innocently outraged at the quadrennial political spectacle staged by our Big Daddies. Nor would Mailer, who knows how much vitality and resistance runs underground, keep looking for redemption among the most high rather than the most low.

Only after swimming, with much textual pleasure, through Erickson's earnest investigation of the notion that our fate depends on which gringo becomes president did I understand why his fiction so often goes awry. The writer I'd mistaken for a Gothic Fabulist is not, in fact, an anatomist of the nation's nihilistic soul—he's really a Jeffersonian Democrat who believes, against every last grain of American history, that individual liberties and manifest destiny can be reconciled, that somehow populism and capitalism are twains that can meet. Erickson and other liberals realize that the systematic denial of democracy to the government's victims at home and abroad did more damage to the country than anything since the Civil War. Unfortunately, they also believe that assuaging their blood guilt through sensitivity is tantamount to agitating for change.

But the admission of hypocrisy doesn't get it. In *Leap Year*, Erickson breaks up his reportage with italicized sections rendered in the voice of Sally Hemings, the slave whom Jefferson is alleged to have raped when she was 15 and who became his lover later in life. Hemings's voice is symbolic of all those locked out of Jefferson's vision of democracy by his ofay will to power. Hemings's voice is also adoring and power-struck—she wants a chance to get out of the cotton-picking sun and into the big house. But as Erickson circles in on her consciousness, what she's really after is a place somewhere between Jefferson's vision of a nation of yeomen with the wind at their backs and his alienation from their unlettered aspirations to be fruitful and multiply. She wants, in other words, to be not just any slave, but the president's personal slave, a slave of the office and what it represents, in order to secure a future for her children.

This astute observation dovetails nicely with Erickson's reading of Jesse Jackson's humbled and self-aggrandizing performance at the last convention:

The reason many blacks weren't happy with Jackson's speech was that he chose to speak not to his dissatisfactions, and therefore theirs, but rather to his redemption. In that way he spoke over his constituency, to his next constituency, though most of the commentators that night and the next morning told it the other way—a speech by Jesse to make the blacks in the hall happy. . . . Jackson, whose sense of timing had already developed to the transcendent, offered one of the most astonishing mea culpas ever made by a major political figure over national television, the kind of apology that might have saved Nixon had he been shrewd or sincere enough to give it. Jackson didn't just repent, he asked forgiveness, and the masterstroke of the convention was the line "Be patient, God is not finished with me yet." None of us could quite believe what we'd heard. Jackson finessed his dilemma by saying that he was an instrument of God, and that God had been less than hasty in the matter of making Jesse Jackson perfect. If everyone would just give Him a little more time, God would get it right, eventually. . . . Who was going to turn down an appeal to give God a little more time? By begging the crowd to stick with him, Jackson had asked us to stick with God.

Gary Hart was Erickson's man. He liked the fine madness of Hart's vision, which he saw as capable of reconstructing the American character by making it look at uncomfortable aspects of itself. I buy this about as much as I did the argument that a Reagan presidency would produce political clarity, perhaps even inspire revolt among the wretched of the earth. This is where Erickson loses me—he apparently believes that the nation's moral salvation depends on white men overcoming their dark nights of the soul. Burdened by this supremacist folly, Erickson's books wade into deep waters only to wash out with all the weight of a fish gone belly-up.

—1989

White Magic:
Don DeLillo's
Intelligence Networks

> The only thing white people have that black people need,
> or should want, is power—and no one holds power forever.
> White people cannot, in the generality, be taken as models
> of how to live. Rather, the white man is himself in sore need
> of new standards, which will release him from his confusion
> and place him once again in fruitful communion with the
> depths of his own being.
>
> —*James Baldwin*

Off the record (and off the cuff), a white critic once confessed his opinion that white men have nothing else to say in fiction. Before some smart aleck asks why he didn't lop the last two words off and call it a day, suck on this: We hardly need an oracle to know that the fictions of the past 25 years already guaranteed future-classic status have been written by people of color, white feminists, and Latin American men. These writers have become bellwethers of the era's most progressive trends: the deflation of white male supremacy and the decolonization of the imaginations of the oppressed. Because their books move from margin to center the voices of those silenced and stigmatized by centuries of racism, sexism, colonialism, and slavery, they have set the moral, critical and, dare I say, spiritual imperatives for contemporary fiction.

For my book, the white male writers whose tongues needn't be stilled are everybody's favorite French deconstructionists, serious science-fiction novelists, Thomas Pynchon, Milan Kundera, and this essay's white man of the hour, Don DeLillo. Those who wince at the patronizing blurbs found on paperback editions of Wright,

Ellison, and Baldwin books (a backhanded literature of the absurd unto themselves) will share in the perverse pleasure of this next panegyric. To wit: Don DeLillo is the best novelist of the post-modern white male experience writing today because he writes first as a novelist and then as a white man. (If that reads like nonsense to you, think of how boldfaced racist its obverse sounded when slapped on the black novel's Big Three.)

That DeLillo's protagonists often hold positions inside white-male bastions of authority and power—football, rock and roll, the stock market, high technology, academia, government intelli-gence—allows him to deconstruct those domains for all us Others (or insider-underdogs). DeLillo demythifies these strongholds in succinct, descriptive prose that swings with the step-by-step shows of technical competence Ellison loved in Hemingway—minus the faith that such skill made you a member of a master race.

DeLillo books are inward surveys of the white supremacist soul—on the run from mounting evidence that its days are (as the latest in black militant button-wear loves to inform us) numbered. The suspicion that history, the Hegelian version with a capital H, is about to revoke their membership privileges rears up in these protagonists as neuroses, superstitions, and full consciousness that they're strutting around in the emperor's new clothes. DeLillo de-livers portrayals of the white supremacist male as Other, as the savage with the heart of darkness whose civilization has become his jungle. Describing in name-brand detail the degree to which that jungle runs on irrationality has become DeLillo's stock-in-trade. The Lévi-Straussian subtext is that in his bush country, Western man lacks the sort of jungle lore, survival instincts, and wisdom of the ages that sustain so-called primitives in theirs.

White Noise, the inspired novel for which DeLillo won an Amer-ican Book Award, is constructed around the first-person reveries of Jack Gladney, an academic specializing in a field of his own creation, Hitler Studies. Gladney has built a pseudo-fascist (and careerist) persona to match, and lives in fear of being discovered as an intellectual fraud because of his ignorance of German. Since Gladney's work represents the depths to which Americans can take the banality of evil, DeLillo turns his home life into a source for anthropological readings of middle-American consumer culture and the media that service it with tribal lore, superstitions, and a false and lulling sense of security.

Asylum and introspection are more likely to lead DeLillo's characters to delusion and death than to enlightenment. Even if you go stone catatonic, he seems to tell us, you will find no escape from the horrors of Western civilization. The more DeLillo's protagonists attempt to escape their positions of power and privilege—his runaway rock star in *Great Jones Street*, his stock-broker-turned-terrorist in *Players*, his CIA refugee in *Running Dogs*—the more they find themselves in confrontation with the hidden orders of technocratic primates running this monkey show called America.

It seemed inevitable that DeLillo would one day write *Libra*, his new novel about Lee Harvey Oswald and the CIA. Not just because he's fascinated with the conspiratorial bent of the human species, but because in DeLillo's fiction Everyman is as culpable for the state of things as the monstrous secret agencies of power. DeLillo's books don't read like "moral fiction"; he doesn't write moralizing prose. But his fictional worldview has always implied a moral taxonomy unblinking enough to lump the sins of the lowly in with those of the Feds. We assume that big-business government thinks of history as something they've got a lease on, no different from the mortgage they extract from nature, the planet, whatever else gets in the way of master-race schemes.

For DeLillo's small-time operators, history is a wilderness waiting to be conquered by sheer force of personality. The construction of a false persona—which looks like their shot at immortality—instead becomes the arena for a bumrush on insignificance. Hot in pursuit of the neuroses of lost souls, DeLillo subjects their ethical blind sides to the same condemnation he puts down on the powerful. Condemnation, however, is too inelegant a word for the way ethical lessons are handed out in DeLillo's books—mainly in one scintillating sentence after another. The epigrammatic rush of his sentences suggests a prose ménage à trois of Chandler, Sartre, and Barthes. Surgical and shamanistic, a DeLillo sentence mixes existentialism and deconstruction in a style charged with the cool vernacular zing that Crane, Twain, and Hemingway brought into the language and that Chandler made sing like guttertalk.

Like Chandler, DeLillo loves an epiphany as much as he loves a mystery, and in Oswald and the CIA he's latched on to subject matter that allows him to toss some combination lallapaloozas. While other DeLillo novels have read like metafiction whodunits, *Libra* shrewdly involves us more with the mystery of Oswald's being than with why Kennedy was assassinated. On the sly, *Libra* performs a service to popular history by putting to rest the notion of Oswald as a lone gunman who popped out of nowhere.

The weight of facts supporting the argument that Oswald was a pawn or creation of U.S. intelligence—at the very least well known to them long before November 22, 1963—is overwhelming. In Oswald, after all, we have a Marine who defects to Russia after receiving security clearance at a U2 spy-plane base in Japan, goes to the American embassy in Moscow and throws down his passport, belligerently declaring himself a Marxist. He leaves Russia married to the niece of a Russian colonel. Upon his return to the U.S., he's visited by FBI and CIA operatives and pumped for information; soon he's seen passing out pro-Castro literature in Miami.

As DeLillo runs his version, the assassination plot is hatched by the CIA masterminds Kennedy betrayed when he refused air support for their anti-Castro operatives during the Bay of Pigs. In planning an assassination attempt they hope to blame on Castro, these agents concoct an imaginary assassin. The joke is that if Oswald hadn't existed, the CIA would have invented him.

Libra reaches fuguish complexity in floating every possible source for a Kennedy assassination plot you've ever heard—Oswald as lone gunman, Mafia, pro-Castro and anti-Castro operatives, Russians—while clearly settling on a CIA conspiracy. Through narrative legerdemain and a sense of detail bordering on the cartographic, DeLillo doesn't close the door on any of the suspects, even as he's narrowing it down to his chosen ones.

Think of two parallel lines. . . . One is the life of Lee H. Oswald. One is the conspiracy to kill the President. What bridges the space between them? What makes a connection inevitable? There is a third line. It comes out of dreams, visions, intuitions, prayers, out of the deepest levels of the self. It's not generated by

223

cause and effect like the other two lines. It's a line that cuts across causality, cuts across time. It has no history that we can recognize or understand. But it forces a connection. It puts a man on the path of his destiny.

Libra stretches credulity with a string of coincidences that can make even synchronicity diehards beg for relief. Were DeLillo not such a spooky writer, the novel might collapse beneath its parallel narrative shafts and converging plot lines. DeLillo doesn't just invent characters; he possesses them, inhabiting their personas, like a vampire or psychotherapist. His social range, always vast, has never seemed so preternaturally knowledgeable. When he takes you inside the head of Jack Ruby or a Russian intelligence man or Oswald's mama, you feel like a telepathic or unrepentant voyeur—or a gatherer of covert information. Same difference, and another metafictional effect: DeLillo replicates the very thing he's deconstructing.

Geographically and structurally, the novel roams with Oswald all over space and time: Texas, the Bronx, Dallas, Miami, Japan, Russia. It also takes place in the present: Nicholas Branch, a retired CIA historian, has been assigned the fool's task of writing an account of the assassination:

> Branch is stuck all right. He has abandoned his life to understanding that moment in Dallas, the seven seconds that broke the back of the American century. He has his forensic pathology rundown, his neuron activation analysis. There is also the Warren Report, of course, with its twenty-six accompanying volumes of testimony and exhibits, its millions of words. Branch thinks this is the megaton novel James Joyce would have written if he'd moved to Iowa City and lived to be a hundred.
>
> Everything is here. Baptismal records, report cards, postcards, divorce petitions, canceled checks, daily timesheets, tax returns, property lists, postoperative x-rays, photos of knotted string, thousands of pages of testimony, of voices droning in hearing rooms in old courthouse buildings, an incredible haul of human utterance. It lies so flat on the page, hangs so still in

the lazy air, lost to syntax and other arrangement, that it resembles a kind of mind-spatter, a poetry of lives muddied and dripping in language.

Libra is most obsessed with the Spook Mind, the psyche of the secret police set loose upon the world by the powerful. The bulk of the book's characters are spies—Ivy League spooks and aristocratic émigré operatives, anti-Castro spooks and spies who moonlight with the John Birch Society, Russian intelligence men and Japanese double agents, U2 pilot Francis Gary Powers. The cult of secret intelligence is rendered as a faith, the men in it driven less by purpose than by fear of being left out in the cold. Behind the freebooting adventurism is the anxiety of being turned out of the warm womb of the national intelligence apparatus.

While the Kennedy assassination has been seen as the harbinger of things to come in the '60s U.S. of A., prelude to an era of shocking political violence, through DeLillo we come to see the Bay of Pigs and the many failed plots against Castro as the era's true preview—the first inkling that the American imperialist monster might not be such hot shit after all. The CIA cowboys who had to live with the Bay of Pigs disaster had failed the macho credo of the patriarchy. In *Libra*, we come to sense that the defeat embarrassed their culture, and they decided to place the blame on Kennedy's head.

Oswald and the renegade spooks become, in DeLillo's hands, case studies of the white supremacist male as Other, as a species flailing against the reality that history is moving so fast their only hope for survival is going undercover—plotting and scheming against the world because subversion has become the last refuge of their dying doctrine. As with all DeLillo novels, *Libra* is also fiction about the making of fiction, and about those fictionalized versions of the facts that we call history. DeLillo's reconstruction of Oswald from the data that has his CIA historian Branch in a tizzy is a satirical celebration of the freedom of fiction makers to play around with the facts.

The most poignant reward of DeLillo's fiction is being seduced by the pity and compassion he showers on the coldblooded monsters

225
•

among his characters. I'm thinking of a scene involving the most ruthless of DeLillo's CIA cowboys, T-Jay Mackey—though dozens of other close-ups on the domestic lives of spies in *Libra* illustrate the same point: "In stages, through a marriage, a career of sorts as a roving paramilitary, a fall from grace, he had become a man with no fixed address. To a certain way of thinking, this was the stuff of paramount despair. He was getting on to forty, loose in the world, nothing to show for the time and the risk. Yet here he was, starting up his car for the long drive south and . . . feeling charged with advantage. He had Jack Kennedy's picture stuck in his mind and nobody even knew he was out here, a man they used to pay to teach other men the fundamentals of deadly force."

It's DeLillo's portrayal of Oswald, though, that nearly makes you want to cry. Oswald comes on the set star-crossed, fucked from birth. His daddy dies of a heart attack before he's born, and he and his mother spend most of his childhood living at the poorhouse gate. The relationship between Oswald and his mom is claustrophobic, spiteful, and unrooted. In Texas, to which he will one day return on his mission, his Bronx accent gets him figured for a geek. Oswald believes that he's destined for something more than routine white-boydom. In high school he stumbles upon *Das Kapital* and struggles with it like it's a rune whose depths he can only glimpse but whose anti-capitalist surface mirrors his own life. He dreams of joining a communist cell which will send him on "night missions that require intelligence and stealth."

Like several other DeLillo protagonists, Oswald has a problem with language and verbal communication, possibly in the form of dyslexia.

> Always the pain, the chaos of composition. He could not find order in the little field of symbols. . . . [T]he language tricked him with its inconsistencies. He watched sentences deteriorate, powerless to make them right. The nature of things was to be elusive. Things slipped through his perceptions. He could not get a grip on the runaway world. Limits everywhere. In every direction he came up against his own incompleteness. Cramped, fumbling, deficient.

DeLillo might well be alluding to his own tortured creative process—to the burden of needing infinite knowledge to write his kind of books. Not only does he need to know Oswald; he needs to know the Oswald others know. In the metafiction that is *Libra*, every other character seems to be creating a fictitious Oswald, preying on Oswald's impassioned sense of self-destiny and limited self-knowledge—even Oswald, who endlessly invents and reinvents his own myth. But in a sense he remains an enigma to himself. The voice that lays claim to knowing the *real* Oswald belongs to Oswald's mother, who throughout his life is forever negotiating to get him a better deal from fate. She may be the most berserk stage mother ever encountered in literature. As Oswald stumbles toward his destiny, she's always one step behind, attempting to explain the plot that's been in effect against her son's life from birth. And in seeking some plot, any plot, she scrambles and rambles out a first-person history overbaked with irrationality.

Against DeLillo's observation that all plots, and hence all narratives, inevitably end in death, Oswald's mother's narrative is the unhinged and chaotic narrative of life, the force that goes on and on beyond the power of the machinations of men to contain it, control it, silence it, deny it, and ultimately to historicize it. DeLillo makes us remember that even Lee Harvey Oswald had a mother and, therefore, once upon a time, an innocence. Through Marguerite Oswald's arguments, DeLillo demonstrates that the God-novelist not only has the power to peek into his neighbors' skulls and pass judgment, but to listen intimately, to record the fragility and folly of that absolving mechanism figuratively known as the human heart:

> I intend to research this case and present my findings. But I cannot pin it down to a simple statement. I came home to find red welts on his legs at the age of two. . . . I am smiling, judge, as the accused mother who must read the falsehoods they are writing about my boy. Lee was a happy baby. Lee had a dog. This is the boy who spent only one month in attendance at Arlington Heights High School before he entered the Marines when we were living on Collinwood Avenue and there are three

pictures of this boy in the school yearbook. Now, why do you pick out this one boy who is in school so briefly, of all the boys and girls there, and make him the subject of three photographs? People say, "Mrs. Oswald, I don't get the point." You don't get the point? The point is how it goes on and on and on and on. That's the point. The point is how far back have they been using him? He used to climb the tops of roofs with binoculars, looking at the stars, and they sent him to Russia on a mission. Lee Harvey Oswald is more than meets the eye. Already there are documents stolen from me. There are newspaper clippings stolen from my home by one of the branches of secret police. I am all over the world and they are rifling my files.

The point is how it goes on and on and on.

—1988

Dread or Alive: William Gibson

*T*he blood who talked the brother here into checking out William Gibson's *Neuromancer* convinced me by skipping over minor details—like the protagonist's antiheroics—and going straight to the part about the Rastafarian spaceship pilot and his satellite base, Zion Cluster. Needless to say, this pricked enough interest to warrant spending some change. Expecting the Rasta angle to be played for a throwaway bit of exotic color, I was surprised that Gibson was not only genuinely knowledgeable about the religion but empathetic as well: "As they worked, Case gradually became aware of the music that pulsed constantly through the cluster. It was called dub, a sensuous mosaic cooked from vast libraries of digitalized pop; it was worship,

Molly said, and a sense of community. . . . Zion smelled of cooked vegetables, humanity and ganja." Having hooked you, like my friend hooked me, with the most *Irie* passage you'll ever run up on in a science-fiction novel, I'll drop pretenses and admit *Neuromancer* ain't hardly at all about the souls of dread folk.

What it's about is Case, computer interface cowboy cum industrial thief, and Molly, cyborg mercenary whose sunglasses are surgically inset into her sockets and whose burgundy polished nails sheath deadly implants: 10 double-edged, four-centimeter scalpel blades that slide out at whim to lacerate bothersome adversaries. (The Rastas nickname her "Steppin' Razor.") Then again it's not so much about them as about the high-tech, high-sleaze future Gibson has been projecting through his short fictions for the last couple of years. In this respect, *Neuromancer* represents Gibson's first full-blown variation on *Brave New World.* He's created an urban dystopia where multinational racketeering combines, known as zaibatsus, rule; radical cosmetic surgery and cybernetic reconstruction is de rigueur; and decadent subcultures sprout faster than punk accessory shops on St. Mark's. Contemplate the Panther Moderns, who are into terrorism as an expression of personal style, or the Christian Scientists, counter-technological fetishists given to frothing evangelically over young office techs caught wearing "idealized holographic vaginas on their wrists, wet pink glittering under the harsh lighting." By comparison Rastanauts seem mainstream.

Like Samuel Delany, Gibson has a gift for creating elegantly eroticized gems of recombinant exposition out of street argot and techno-jargon; like Philip K. Dick he identifies with the common man and woman lurking inside tomorrow's modish grotesque. (*Neuromancer* is yet another SF novel that asks what it means to be human when you can surgically replace the body of neuroses Nature gave you with one made of perfectly molded assembly-line parts.) Along with Delany and Dick, Gibson suggests that primordial ghosts will haunt the machine-part humans of the future. Yet he eschews Dick's fear of the biotechnological imperative and Delany's shrugging embrace of anatomical hardware. His alternative is a punk-inflected sensibility of semiotic nihilism; rather than moralizing over Big Science, Gibson deconstructs it; rather than being romanced by the modern beat he revels in the probability that the digital revolution, genetic engineering, and the Japanese miracle will hasten the decline and fall of Western civilization.

Indulging a vision of purgatory in the Information Age induces prose as hardboiled as high-tech, but Gibson's proves surprisingly sensitive to rendering the emotional vulnerabilities of cyborgs—their sexual nodes even: "She threw a leg across him and he touched her face. Unexpected hardness of the implanted lenses. 'Don't,' she said, 'fingerprints.' Now she straddled him again, took his hand, and closed it over her, his thumb along the cleft of her buttocks, his fingers spread across the labia. As she began to lower herself, the images came pulsing back, the faces, fragments of neon arriving and receding."

It's not the software porn scenes but Gibson's descriptions of Case's interfacing that make *Neuromancer* a mindbender of a read. When Case is performing his astral hacking routine, what's evoked is every transcendent high available to the human organism, from orgasm to out-of-the-body experience to hallucinogenic visions, not to mention Alfred Bester's paradigmatic SF acid trip, *The Stars My Destination*. The universe of *Neuromancer* is as fully realized in its geopolitical, technological, and psychosexual dimensions as Bester's, and maybe more so than any SF novel since Delany's *Nova*. If contemporary SF has been seeming somewhat reactionary to you, Gibson can read like a one-man revival of the form.

—*1985*

Nobody Loves a Genius Child: Jean Michel Basquiat, Flyboy in the Buttermilk

I did not, when a slave, understand the deep meaning of those rude and apparently incoherent songs. I was myself within the circle; so that I neither saw nor heard as those without might see and hear. They told a tale of woe which was then altogether beyond my feeble comprehension. . . . I have often been utterly astonished, since I came to the north, to find persons who could speak of the singing, among slaves, as evidence of their contentment and happiness. . . . The singing of a man cast away upon a desolate island might be as appropriately considered as evidence of contentment and happiness, as the singing of a slave; the songs of the one and of the other are prompted by the same emotion.

—Narrative of the Life of Frederick Douglass, an American Slave, Written by Himself, *1845*

In these scant lines, Frederick Douglass succinctly describes the ongoing crisis of the Black intellectual, that star-crossed figure on the American scene forever charged with explaining Black folks to white folks and with explaining Black people to themselves—often from the perspectives of a distance refracted by double alienation. *If you want to hide something from a negro put it in a book*. Douglass knew from experience the compound oppression of being poorly fed and poorly read, but also of having to stand Black and proud in isolated situations where nobody else Black was around to have your back.

When the windchill factor plummets that low, all that can steady you is the spine of cultural confidence and personal integrity.

This business of speaking for Black culture and your own Black ass from outside the culture's communal surrounds and the comforting consensus of what critic Lisa Kennedy once described as "the Black familiar" has taken many a brilliant Black mind down to the crossroads and left it quite beside itself, undecided between suicide, sticking it to the man, or selling its soul to the devil. The ones who keep up the good fight with a scintilla of sanity are the ones who know how to beat the devil out of a dollar while maintaining a Black agenda and to keep an ear out for the next dope house party set to go down in Brooklyn, Sugar Hill, or the Boogie-Down Bronx.

> *Dull unwashed windows of eyes*
> *and buildings of industry. What*
> *industry do I practice? A slick*
> *colored boy, 12 miles from his*
> *home. I practice no industry.*
> *I am no longer a credit*
> *to my race. I read a little,*
> *scratch against silence slow spring*
> *afternoons.*
> —LeRoi Jones, "A POEM SOME
> PEOPLE WILL HAVE TO
> UNDERSTAND," from *Sabotage*

To read the tribe astutely you sometimes have to leave the tribe ambitiously, and should you come home again, it's not always to sing hosannas or a song the tribe necessarily has any desire to hear. Among the Senegambian societies of the West Africa savannah, the role of praise singer and historian is given to a person known as the griot. Inscribed in his (always a him) function is the condition of being born a social outcast and pariah. The highest price exacted from the griot for knowing where the bodies are buried is the denial of a burial plot in the communal graveyard. Griots, it is decreed, are to be left to rot in hollow trees way on the outskirts of town. With that wisdom typical of African cosmologies, these messengers are guaranteed freedom of speech in exchange for a marginality that extends to the grave.

The circumscribed avenues for recognition and reward available in the Black community for Black artists and intellectuals working in the avant-garde tradition of the West established the preconditions for a Black bohemia, or a Blackened bohemia, or a white bohemia dotted with Black question marks. Remarkable in the history of these errant Sphinxes is certainly Jean Michel Basquiat, posthumously the benefactor of a loving and roomy retrospective at Vrej Baghoomian gallery. When Basquiat died last year at the age of 27 of a heroin overdose he was the most financially successful Black visual artist in history and, depending on whether you listened to his admirers or detractors, either a genius, an idiot savant, or an overblown, overpriced fraud. Besides affording an opportunity for reappraisal of Basquiat's heady and eye-popping oeuvre, the exhibition invites another consideration of the Black artist as bicultural refugee, spinning betwixt and between worlds. *When the fire starts to burn, where you gonna run to? To a well without water?*

Given the past and present state of race relations in the U.S., the idea that any Black person would choose exile into "the white world" over the company and strength in numbers of the Black community not only seems insane to some of us, but hints at spiritual compromise as well. To be a race-identified race-refugee is to tap-dance on a tightrope, making your precarious existence a question of balance and to whom you concede a mortgage on your mind and body and lien on your soul. Will it be the white, privileged, and learned or the Black, (un)lettered, and disenfranchised?

> *When I die, the consciousness I carry I will to*
> *black people. May they pick me apart and take the*
> *useful parts, the sweet meat of my feelings. And leave*
> *the bitter bullshit rotten white parts*
> *alone.*
>
> —LeRoi Jones, "leroy," from *Black Art*

Spooked, dispossessed, split asunder by his education, his alienation, and his evolving race-politics, Amiri Baraka (formerly LeRoi Jones) sought to perform an exorcism on the learning he'd done at the laps of white men, vaccinate himself against the infectious anxiety of influence that came with investment in that knowledge he'd codified as Western. But we can say that African history and the history of border crossings made by Black artists and intellectuals from this country's earliest founding to the present have blurred, blotted out, and disrupted any proprietary claims the Eurocentrists among us would care to make on the languages of ethics, aesthetics, and logic. In light of the mounting evidence of anthropologists and archaeologists and the revisionist scholarship of peoples of color, there is no province more in danger of dwindling to a vanishing point than that of "white knowledge." Increasing the store of human knowledge has been everybody's project since the beginning of womankind. The idea that the human brain first began functioning in Europe now appears about as bright as Frankenstein's monster.

What remains, however, is the entrenched racism of white-supremacist institutions bent on perpetuating, until their dying breaths, that popular fantasy of slaveholders and imperialists that the white man represents the most intelligent form of life on the planet.

No area of modern intellectual life has been more resistant to recognizing and authorizing people of color than the world of the "serious" visual arts. To this day it remains a bastion of white supremacy, a sconce of the wealthy whose high-walled barricades are matched only by Wall Street and the White House and whose exclusionary practices are enforced 24-7-365. It is easier for a rich white man to enter the kingdom of heaven than for a Black abstract and/or Conceptual artist to get a one-woman show in lower Manhattan, or a feature in the pages of *Artforum*, *Art in America*, or *The Village Voice*. The prospect that such an artist could become a bona fide art-world celebrity (and at the beginning of her career no less) was, until the advent of Jean Michel Basquiat, something of a joke.

My maternal grandfather used to say, Son, no matter where you go in this world and no matter what you find, somewhere up in there you will find a Negro. Experience has yet to prove him wrong, especially where the avant-garde is concerned. In Wilfredo Lam we had our Cubist adventurer. Ted Joans, Bob Kaufman, and LeRoi Jones bopped heads with the Beats. The British Invasion got vamped on by Jimi Hendrix while Arthur Lee and Sly Stone were spear-chucking protopunk and funk into San Francisco's psychedelic Summer of Love. Bad Brains reclaimed Rasta and hardcore rock and roll from the punks. And we won't even get into separating the Black aesthetic inspirations for all these movements, or raising up the counterhegemonic monument that is Black cultural difference.

What's often as exceptional as the artistic talents of the aforementioned Black crossover acts is their genius for cultural politics, the confidence and cunning with which they established supportive bases for themselves in white circles of knowledge, power, and authority. *Nobody loves a genius child?* Basquiat, lonesome flyboy in the buttermilk of the '80s Downtown art boom, was hands down this century's most gifted Black purveyor of art-world politics. He not only knew how the game of securing patronage was played, but played it with ambition, nerve, and delight. Like Jimi Hendrix he had enormously prodigious gifts and sexual charisma on his side. He was also, to boot, another beneficiary of being the right Black man in the right place at the right time. Eric Clapton attributed Hendrix's whirlwind ascendancy in the English rock scene to his arriving just when the scene was in desperate need of some new blood. The blues and soul boom was decaying. Hendrix, Black and from the birthplace of blues, soul, and rock, was extraordinarily fluent in all three styles, could whip up a frenzy from the stage like Dionysus on a tear, and was a preternatural innovator besides. The question with Hendrix is never why him, but how could the British rockers resist?

There is a sickness to the black man
living in white town. Either he is white
or he hates white, but even in hating, he
reflects, the dead image of his surrounding. . . .
There is a sickness to the black man in white town, because
he begins to believe he can beat everybody's ass, and he can,
down there, where each man is an island, and the heaviest bomber,
throwing down tnt can establish some conditional manhood in the
    land
of the dead, in the country of the blind.
        —Amiri Baraka, "Poem for Religious Fanatics"

235
•

The period of ferment that produced Basquiat began on British soil and was then transplanted stateside. *1981 the number, another summer, sound of the harmolodic drummer!* Let's go back to post-punk lower Manhattan, no-wave New York, where loft jazz, white noise, and Black funk commune to momentarily desegregate the Downtown rock scene, and hiphop's train-writing graffiti cults pull into the station carrying the return of representation, figuration, expressionism, Pop-artism, the investment in canvas painting, and the idea of the masterpiece. Whether the writers presaged or inspired the market forces to all this art-commodity fetishism and anti-Conceptualist material is a question still up for grabs. But just as the classic blues, rock, and soul cats were the romanticized figures who made the very idea of a Hendrix seductive to the Mods, it was the invigorating folk culture of the graffiti writers—operating at a subterranean remove from the art world that made them all the more mysterious, manageable, and ultimately dismissable— that set the salon stages and sex parlors of the postmods up to be bedazzled by Basquiat. Phase II, Daze, Crash, Lee, Blade, Futura 2000, Lady Pink, Fab Five Freddy, and Ramm-El-Zee. These writers and others might have tunneled their style wars out of "Afrerica" (© Vernon Reid) and into the gallery affairs of the snooty, the elite, and *la bohème*, but it would be the Haitian boy-aristocrat with the properly French name who'd get to set their monkey-ass world on fire.

236
•

Jean-Michel is the one they told you must draw it this way and call it black man folk art, when it was really white man folk art that he was doing. That's what he draw . . . white man folk art. He does not draw black man folk art because they told him what to draw. . . . They called us graffiti but they wouldn't call him graffiti. And he gets as close to it as the word means scribble-scrabble. Unreadable. Crosses out words, doesn't spell them right, doesn't even write the damn thing right. He doesn't even paint well. You don't draw a building so that it will fall down and that's what he draws, broken-down imagery.

—Ramm-El-Zee, *B. Culture*, No. 1

I just love the houses in the South, the way they built them. That Negritude architecture. I really love to watch the way Black people make things, houses or magazine stands in Harlem, for instance. Just the way we use carpentry. Nothing fits, but every-thing works. The door closes, it keeps things from coming through. But it doesn't have that neatness about it, the way white people put things together; everything is a 32nd of an inch off.
    —David Hammons to Kellie Jones in *Real Life*, No. 16

Negative gesture can be just as important as positive thrust. Indeed I got a richer sense of this characteristic of his work when I showed Basquiat a quick sketch I made of one of his works, *Unrevised Undiscovered Genius of the Mississippi Delta*, a painting of Southern Images, and all he would say was, "You forgot to cross out CATFISH."
    —Robert Farris Thompson, catalogue essay for Basquiat's
    1985 Mary Boone exhibition

Clearly Basquiat's conception of making it in the Western art world transcended those of the train-writers. To Basquiat, making it did not just mean getting a gallery exhibition, a dealer, or even collecting big bank off his work. Making it to him meant going down in history, ranked beside the Great White Fathers of Western painting in the eyes of the major critics, museum curators, and art historians who ultimately determine such things. What he got for his grasping for immortality from the gaping mouths of these god-heads was a shitload of rejection, (mis)apprehension, and arcane or inconclusive interpretations. That he refused to let the issue of his genius die on the spent pyre of his accumulated earnings re-minds me of some cautionary advice I was given by filmmaker Haile Gerima: "Whenever white people praise you, never let it be enough. Never become satisfied with their praise, because the same power you give them to build you up is the same power they can use to tear you down."

By all accounts Basquiat certainly tried to give as much as he got from the American art dealers, critics, and doyens, most effec-tively in the end by his sustained levels of production, excellence, and irreducible complexity. Though we can certainly point to rac-ism for the refusal in certain quarters to consider Basquiat a serious painter, we shouldn't overlook the fact that Basquiat, like Rausch-enberg and Warhol, his brothers in canvas-bound iconoclasm, made paintings that were unrepentantly about American culture. There is a strain of Europhilia among our art historians and critics that is as uncomfortable with American artists looking to this culture for subject matter and vernacular as they are with artists holding the celebrity of household names. Looking to the uncertainty and reticence that abounded—and still abounds—in so much writing about Stuart Davis on down through Robert Rausch-enberg, Bob Thompson, Roy Lichtenstein, Andy Warhol, Romare Bearden, Red Grooms, Betye Saar, David Hammons, Alison Saar, and Jeff Koons, it seems that the surest way to be consigned dilettante-hick status, ruining your chances for fawning art-historical hagiography, is to act as if you thought the United States was spilling over with the stuff of Art.

That Basquiat, like Bearden, made work that was unmistakably and vehemently about being a Black American male did not help matters any. Basquiat was as visually fascinated as anybody in our culture by cartoons, coon art, high-tech, and the idea of private ownership. References to these elements are constants in his work, sometimes framed critically and other times as a stream-of-conscious shopping list, pointing up our daily overdose of mass culture's effluvia. But he also gave equal attention to exhuming, exposing, and cutting up the nation's deep-sixed racial history, in all its nightmarish, Neo-Expressionist gory. If you're Black and historically informed there's no way you can look at Basquiat's work and not get beat up by his obsession with the Black male body's history as property, pulverized meat, and popular entertainment. No way not to be reminded that lynchings and minstrelsy still vie in the white supremacist imagination for the Black male body's proper place. (Anyone doubting the currency of this opinion need only look to the hero's welcome Spike Lee got in see-a-nigger-shoot-his-ass Bensonhurst or to Robert Hughes's *New Republic* "review" of Basquiat's death in which he defames the brother by calling him the art world's answer to Eddie Murphy.)

In the rush to reduce the word games found in Basquiat works to mere mimicry of Cy Twombly's cursive scrawls, we're expected

238
•

to forget that Basquiat comes from a people once forbidden literacy by law on the grounds that it would make for rebellious slaves. Expected to overlook as well that among those same people words are considered a crucial means to magical powers, and virtuosic wordplay pulls rank as a measure of one's personal prowess. From the perspective of this split-screen worldview, where learning carries the weight of a revolutionary act and linguistic skills are as prized as having a knockout punch, there are no such things as empty signifiers, only misapprehended ones.

Basquiat's exhausting lists of weights, measures, numbers, anatomical parts, cuisine, and pop icons function as autopsies on forms of knowledge, reading the historical entrails of literacy and numeracy for traces of their culpability in the subjugation and degradation of Black people. In so many paintings it seems Basquiat is on a mission of retribution against the Anglos' precious and allegedly value-free banks of information, here gutting the store of numbers for racking up the surplus-labor of human chattel, there looting the warehouse of words for legislating the difference between slaveholder and savage. Similar abstract historicizing can be found in the work of Basquiat contemporaries, playwright Suzan-Lori Parks, Conceptualist photographer Lorna Simpson, and performance art collaborators Alva Rogers and Lisa Jones.

All of which is one way of reading Basquiat's wordiness. But remember that this is also an artist who began his public career, roughly around 1978, as SAMO©, a street-level graffiti writer of non sequiturs. The tag, spoken twice, is Black slang for "the same old shit" but also invites the cruel and punning to identify the writer as Sambo. Poised there at the historical moment when Conceptualism is about to fall before the rise of the neoprimitive upsurge, Basquiat gets the last word and the last laugh during '70s conceptualism's last gasp, pronouncing the brute shape of things to come by way of the ironic, sardonic slur he'd chosen for a name. Having a voice, giving a name to new things, multiplying and refracting meaning were always a part of Basquiat's survival game and image-making procedures.

So Basquiat enters the field as a poet. Truly, many of his paintings not only aspire to the condition of poetry, but invite us to

239
·

experience them as brokendown bluesy and neo-hoodoofied Symbolist poems. Often the cerebral pleasures of his work are derived from sussing out the exquisite corpses he's conjured up through provocative conjunctions of words and images. One painting entitled *Catharsis* is a triptych whose left panel abounds with symbols of power drawn on what appears to be the inside of a subway door: a crown, a clenched Black fist, a circus strongman's barbells, a model of an atom, and the word *Radium*. On this last we find the vowels scratched out to produce the Jamaican patois term *Ridim* or rhythm, another radio-active source of energy. The middle panel lumps the words *liver* and *spleen* with *throat* and positions the term *il mano*, Italian for "the hand," between the thumb and forefinger of a limp and possibly blood-drained hand.

Things get more active again in the right panel. The top left half is dominated by a leg with a dotted line cutting across the base of the foot, over which reads *Suicide Attempt*, an inscription that invokes race memories of the risks undertaken by runaway slaves as well as the tragedy of urban dance-floor guerrillas without feet to fly their escapist maneuvers. (Much has been made of Basquiat's ruder street-connections, but his links with hiphop are high-handed deployments of scratchnoise, sampling, freestyle coloring, and bombing the canvas.) Named and labeled throughout the rest of the panel is a plethora of other detached or phantom limbs, four left paws, two thumbs—a dissection chart whose mix-matched labels for animal and human body parts speak to the fate of the captive Black body as much as the energy sources surging through the first panel allude to the Black body in motion, bionic and liberated.

Just as diagrammatic and zig-zag with meanings is *Wicker*, where the scratched-up name of Black boxer Henry Armstrong is boxed into a rectangle crowned by the words *buzzer* and *bell*. Nearby hovers a Romanesque figure with exposed intestines and a tag indicating its bladder. The boxing anecdote forms a parenthesis around a text all about the bestial body work done to the image of Black men. On one side of the painting a speared elephant is being levitated, his (he has tusks) physique branded with a black band like that used on TV reports to keep the interviewee's identity protected and disguised. Implanted into the elephant's hide is a tacky Instamatic camera. Floating around the right side is one of Basquiat's patented Black-ghost figures, this one materializing out of the urbanized jungle of a willowy potted plant in a wicker basket.

In juxtaposition these images hit us as loaded symbols: of Western man haunting the wild with his voyeuristic technology, and of Black spooks haunting the living spaces of the privileged with their irrescindable presences.

The one thing Vladimir Nabokov said that left a lasting impression on me was that the only thing a writer has to leave behind is her style. When people ask Miles Davis what he wants from a musician, he usually croaks, "Somebody who can play a style," by which I've always thought he meant a musician with a unique sound and a personal way of turning a phrase. The best contemporary musicians to come through the academy of Miles have developed styles that enfold emotion and intellect into a captivating species of lyricism. Like any of those musicians, or like Baraka's poetry in his *Dead Lecturer,* what's finally so compelling about the Basquiat corpus is the indivisible meshing of style and statement in his sui generis tones and attacks.

Initially lumped with the graffiti artists, then the Neo-Expressionists, then the Neo-Popsters, in the end Basquiat's work evades the grasp of every camp because his originality can't be reduced to the sum of his inspirations, his associations, or his generation. For all his references to pop America and the gestural vocabulary of the late-modern American Abstract Expressionists, Basquiat's signature strokes dispossess themselves of any value but that of being in a Basquiat painting. He has consumed his influences and overwhelmed them with his intentions, leaving everything in his work a map of his imagination and intellect. In the same way that the music made by Miles's bands always sounds like orchestrations of Miles's trumpet-persona, Basquiat's paintings read as hieroglyphic ensembles that glow with the touch of his hands and the unmistakable sign language that evolved out of his free-floating psyche.

But can't you understand that nothing is free! Even the floating strangeness of the poet's head? The crafted visions of intellect, named, controlled, beat and erected to struggle under the heavy fingers of Art.

—LeRoi Jones, "Green Lantern's Solo"

You are the only very successful black artist. . . .

I don't know if the fact that I'm black has something to do with my success. I don't believe that I should be compared to black artists but rather to all artists.

—Basquiat to interviewer Isabelle Graw

In the November issue of *Elle* there's a Peter Schjeldahl essay about Basquiat and the Baghoomian retrospective in which the critic attributes Basquiat's significance to his difference from other Black artists: "Most work by non-whites in the New York mainstream has been marked by a tendency, mordantly popularized by Spike Lee in *School Daze* as 'wannabe': a diffident emulation of established modes, whether already academic or supposedly avant-garde. So I would not have expected from a black artist Basquiat's vastly self-assured grasp of New York's big-painting esthetics—generally, the presentation of mark-making activities as images of themselves in an enveloping field. . . . I would have anticipated a well-schooled, very original white hipster behind the tantalizing pictures."

In a recent Sunday *Times* essay about African-American artist Martin Puryear's first-place award in the São Paulo Bienal, Michael Brenson asks, "Why is he [Puryear] the first black American artist to be singled out for international attention?" To Brenson's mind the answer boils down to Puryear's difference from other Black artists: "Part of what distinguishes Puryear from many other minority artists is his lack of defensiveness about mainstream American art. He remains something of an outsider, with one foot outside the mainstream, but he has one foot comfortably within it as well. Many blacks feel too alienated from the mainstream, or too angry at it because of its continuing failure to make room for black artists."

Taken together these two opinions present us with quite a conundrum. Whom can we trust? Schjeldahl, who believes that Black artists can't make the grade because they're trying too hard to be white, or Brenson, who thinks they're too busy being Black, mad, and marginalized to take notes during art history class or keep up with the "mainstream" (read white, male, upper-middle-class) art world? But of course I'm being much too coy and polite.

What's wrong with these patronizing and patriarchal pictures is their arrogance and presumptions. Most of the serious Black artists I am familiar with know as much about art as any of their white contemporaries but would certainly have no interest in proving their Blackness to satisfy Schjeldahl or in taking a quiz from Brenson. In trying to help other white men figure out by what freakish woogie magic Basquiat and Puryear made it out of Coontown and into Cracker Heaven, Brenson and Schjeldahl regurgitate two very old and very tired ploys. Divide-and-Conquer is what we call one, One-Nigger-at-a-Time-Puh-Leeze names the other.

The cold fax is this: the reason that Puryear's work came before the judges in São Paulo, and thereby under Brenson's scrutiny, is because of Kellie Jones, the first Black female curator with the unprecedented clout to nominate a Puryear and have it mean something to the art world's powers that be. Before we can even begin to appraise Puryear's exceptional talents we need to recognize the political struggles that positioned Jones in her exceptional historical position.

In every arena where we can point to Black underdevelopment or an absence of Black competitiveness there can logically be only two explanations: either Black folks aren't as smart as white boys or, racism. If the past 20 years of affirmative action have proven anything it's that whatever some white boy can do, any number of Black persons can do as good, or, given the hoops a Black person has to jump to get in the game, any number of times better. Sorry, Mr. Charlie, but the visual arts are no different. Black visual culture suffers less from a lack of developed artists than a need for popular criticism, academically supported scholarship, and more adventurous collecting and exhibiting.

During the furor that arose around Donald Newman's "Nigger Drawings," I recall hearing talk in the art world demanding to know why Black people should expect to be exceptional at anything else just because they were so good at music. If the Eurocentric wing of the art world wants to remain a stronghold of straight-up white-

243

boyism, one has to suspect it's because the white-boyists want something they can call their own. This might be understandable if they didn't already own every fucking thing under the sun and made no bones of dehumanizing the rest of us to maintain hegemony.

The bottom line for people of color is that we don't need any more Basquiats becoming human sacrifices in order to succeed. We don't need any more heroic Black painters making hara-kiri drip canvases of their lives to prove that a Black man or woman can do more with a tar brush than be tainted by it. What we need is a Black MOMA, or, Barr-ing that, a bumrushing Black MOMA-fucker.

—1989

Fear of a Mutt Palette: Art and Ancestry in the Colored Museum

244
.

As a coffee-table survey of African-American visual art, *Black Art, Ancestral Legacy* surpasses any existing tome for its pan-Africanist perspective and the range, quantity, and quality of its color reproductions (320 illustrations, 170 in color). Like Paula Giddings's *When and Where I Enter* or *The Autobiography of Malcolm X*, it deserves a place in every home where a premium is placed on Afrocentric sources of knowledge, recognition, and inspiration.

Black Art, Ancestral Legacy is based on a Dallas Museum of Art exhibition scheduled to travel to Milwaukee and Virginia between now and the spring of 1991. The exhibition includes everything from anonymous African walking sticks to the paramodernist paintings of the Chicago-bred Africobra schools. In between there's room for Southern Black visionary artists, Haitian contemporaries, and Kongo ancestors. As its title suggests, the book emphasizes artists and works that improvise on motifs from traditional African art. Of the several essays included in *Black Art,* the best are Robert Farris Thompson's *The Song That Named the Land* (an investigative tour of the ties that bind Black artists to Central Africa) and the close readings given the color plates by Black scholar and curator Alvia Wardlaw.

All this should make me a happy nappy, but it doesn't. As much as I enjoy eyeballing the plates, aspects of Wardlaw's polemics rub me the wrong way. The reasons have everything to do with her brand of cultural nationalism.

In her interpretations of the plates, Wardlaw offers a narrative of African-American art that reads as if Western art history never happened. While I can appreciate this conceit as a form of invective—the white boy wrote us out of his-story so we're gonna write him out of ours—it makes me wonder whether such an exhibition of outrage doesn't exacerbate the ghettoization of Black art.

Thompson's essay shows that you don't have to ignore white history in order to honor our own. He marks differences with white practice where appropriate, highlights Black cultures as aesthetic sources, and emphasizes the way African value systems have inspired both images and ethics. Read him on the work of Houston Conwill and you can immediately locate the artist in the crossfire of the world's complexity.

Conwill was not recording, like Robert Smithson, "a sense of the earth as a map undergoing disruption." He was developing a genealogical impetus, tracing ties from Africa to the U.S.A. Consider a sample latex scroll of the late seventies . . . a fish of Jesus over three arrows, perhaps alluding to the Trinity; a woman in a triangle; a Dogonizing figure with helmet-like head standing beside a fish, like an African deity in tandem with the Saviour; three further Dogonizing spirits, translating, perhaps, The Trinity into African terms.

Both Thompson and Wardlaw recognize in Black work bedrock concepts derived from African and African-American religious beliefs. It's a testament to their knowledge of those beliefs that, even when the work being described appears, for example, abstract and expressionistic, they find the transcendentally African behind the formal. The polylingual Thompson usually goes with specifics, while Wardlaw tends to speak in mystical pan-African generalities. Of a painting by Rip Woods (*It Seems That I've Been Here Before*), Wardlaw writes:

> Dogs barking behind a fence might not readily be recognized as having particular significance. However, the power of animals, forest, water and fire spirits are all conveyed in African folk tales, narratives, music and visual imagery. The suggestion in the title that the spirit of the animal may have existed before indicates the artist's attempt to interpret the connectedness of time through the physical properties and spiritual presence of this subtle subject matter.

246
•

In the artists' statements in the back of the book, Woods says that generally his art is about "the mystique [of Africa]. . . . I've had an opportunity to respond to a form of magic and, in my response, recreate my own form of magic." Woods's own explanation of Africa's influence on his work is quite a bit more modest that Wardlaw's. I get the impression Wardlaw is uncomfortable with Black work that doesn't overtly proclaim its African roots, or whose debts to the continent are more Conceptual than devotional. And just as Wardlaw rigidifies the vision of Africa she finds among Black artists, she reduces African philosophy to a mythology of nature. This pens in discussion of Black art in the same way that Clement Greenberg's formalist diatribes did. It also raises the question of how different Black criticism should be from the European model.

. . .

Over the past 80 years or so, the near-religious investment by white critics in the idea of art for art's sake has generated an infinite vocabulary of schools, styles, gambits, and gestures. Placing a premium on signs that are ambiguous and free-floating, modernism's critical language came to prize the rendering of indeterminacy and the erasure of all signification that had designs on Art's autonomy: visual sophistication became the equivalent of whipping up a hermeneutic sound and fury that signified *nada*. Post-Greenberg critical talent applied itself to leveling formalist values and arguments with retro-Dadaism. Who would defend mere formal play when the play of anarchic ideas is the thing? Postmodernism has simply taken this over the top. In the most political, post-Foucault, white art criticism today, the kind that looks at the big picture, fear of reifying the aesthetic may outrank fear of meaninglessness as the major postmodern crisis; visual sophistication has come to mean critiquing the idea that art could even signify anything more than its relationship to power.

So what does this have to do with being Black in America today, or with ancestral legacies? It comes down to the question of how wide a circle you draw around your intellectual world, and how much you want to engage with what a critic might call "white influences." We all know Black people made great art long before white people got here—*Black Art, Ancestral Legacy* proves it in living color—and will continue to make it long after they're gone. (This isn't some racist millennial prophecy, by the way. I'm just pointing to the fact that artificial melanin injections are the only known protection white people will have from the ultraviolet rays that'll be pouring through the atmosphere once the ozone layer dissipates. Everybody's gonna wannabe Black in a minute.) In the wide, wide world of philosophical discourses, however, Black intellectuals must labor under the burden of reading, rejecting, transfiguring, and contesting white folks. Such are the dialectical and existential realities of Black and white in the realm of power relations. There is no exit.

The late literary scholar and writer Larry Neal once said that to be Black in this culture is to *always affirm something*; everything we do is against the odds waged on our insignificance and inferi-

ority. Black cultural nationalism of the '60s variety has proved to
be, by far, the most revolutionary and militant affirmation of self
that Black people have devised to counter racism—*in theory*.
Though there are certainly political theories that propose more
radical or sensible liberation strategies for Black people, none of
these can be said to make such inspirational and rallying use of
Black cultural differences, desires, and communal practices.

In the Blackness discourse, as defined first by the theorists of
the '60s and later by ivory tower cult-nat reformists like my man
Skip Gates, *signifyin'* and *self-determination* are indispensable key-
words. Black folk can no more afford to embrace meaninglessness,
aesthetically or otherwise, than we can to just lie down and take
it. Unlike for Mallarmé, the whiteness of whiteness doesn't cut it
with our crowd. Nor are such notions as scientific progress and the
Study of Man out of vogue with us. Enlightenment ideas (humanism,
rationalism) considered anathema to the projects of white modernism and postmodernism are cornerstones of the Blackness discourse.

What this all points to is an investment in Western philosophical
language, for purposes of contestation, that laughs all over any
notion that this implies slavish devotion to white superiority. Black
practice distinguishes the racist application of analytical tools from
scientific analysis as a tool of struggle. Once we overcome the
anxiety of influence, the question becomes how to bend, warp, and
woof those tools to satisfy Black cultural biases—much in the same
way that mastery of the saxophone in the European tradition would
merely mark the beginning of one's training to become a virtuoso
in the Black tradition.

The problem with cultural nationalism as it has been theorized
over the past three decades—discussing how it's been *practiced*
requires another therapy session altogether—is its propensity to
circumscribe the definition of Blackness, that is, to traffic in what
has been disparagingly referred to as Black essentialism.

In critical practice, essentialism sometimes is the best handle
we have on the specific forms of Black cultural resistance. For
example, Black essentialism works fine with writing on Black
music, and in no way diminishes the complexity of the discourse,
primarily because Black musical culture has so aggressively dis-

ciplined, domesticated, and subsumed its European influences into the funk that they mama wouldn't recognize 'em. The differences between European classical music and African-American music are so pronounced a dog could dance around them.

This is far from true in the visual arts. While Europe's major 20th century composers sought to erect a new classicism, their visual-arts contemporaries set out to destroy European classicism by embracing Freud and African aesthetics. Because of European visual culture's history of tanking up at Africa's filling station, one more often experiences déjà vu than shock-of-the-new when confronted with the uses academically trained African-American artists make of African visual materials. By the time Black artists returned to Africa, its most common forms and processes had virtually become art-world clichés; Picasso had already been both blue and "black." Unlike the moneyed defenders of the Euro-American classical-music tradition, the institutions backing the Euro-American visual arts have long supported the plundering of Black culture (and Asian and Native American and Aborigine . . .). For this reason Black art historians shouldn't just talk about how the massive mandalas of a painter like the Africobra school's James Phillips draw on Coltrane's modal solos and African textile patterns, but how he proposes fresh uses for African-inspired geometry in painting when Cubism and Constructivism were thought to have exhausted them.

249
•

Writing on Ben Jones's wall sculpture *Black Face and Arm Unit*, Wardlaw points up how cultural nationalism, with its psychologically corrective Black Is Beautiful campaign, provided a Black value system capable of aestheticizing Blackness:

> The work celebrates the recognition of the black body as a temple of creativity. Like jazz musicians improvising on the same theme, each face and arm has distinctive patterns which make them visually unique. The ensemble has its greatest impact, however, as a visual chorus, each element contributing a slight variation within the grand and rhythmical repetitions.

Cultural nationalism has taught Black people to bask in the pleasures of Black collective difference, and to look beyond them for definitions of humanity among Africans that predate the slave trade and colonialism. Where classic cultural nationalism fucks up is when it becomes another supremacist manifesto, positing Africans as the master race or reducing us to ideal stereotypes, and denying the exchanges that inform identity and ethnicity in the 20th century. Ultimately what I fear from Black thinkers like Wardlaw is what I fear most for my own Black critical self: a refusal to end my love affair with a romanticized Black culture. Black isn't always beautiful, nor does it exist outside of art-historical space and time. Ferrying us off to our own realm of the aesthetic will not set us free.

Ancestral Legacy's head essentialist and I aren't the only ones who'd like to keep Africans pure and simple. Kim Levin, in a *Voice* review, described Zairean painter Chéri Samba as "a sophisticated artist whose work has nothing to do with our history. That's rare." I could spend hours on how wrongheaded this is: the 20 paintings in the "Magiciens de la Terre" exhibition that brought Samba international recognition were done *in Paris;* the artist's origins were as a Western-derivative sign painter; and I seriously wonder how any person from a former European colony could have nothing to do with "our history." Just which history is Levin referring to—Western art history, the history of Soho, or the history of imperialism and white supremacy? And how rare is it, really, for visual sophistication to arise from outside any of these histories?

Both Wardlaw and Levin seem to desire a modernism of pure African stock—no mulatto mixtures, but the real megillah. The search for the ultimate exotic, the ultimate Other, continues: in Wardlaw's case out of our struggle for justice and power, and in Levin's out of . . . what, boredom? Or the dreaded good-liberal intentions? Fundamentally, Wardlaw's and Levin's positions further dehumanize African people by denying us a history in the world. No people are more ill-served by ahistorical analysis than Africans, who are still considered to belong to the prehistory of the human race on more American campuses than you'd care to know about. As much as Black intellectual work must generate new histories, it also has to examine the old stories that have passed for human history. Art history included.

Ancestral Legacy shows, through some telling lapses, that an essentialist curatorial approach to Black art is bound to exclude some major work. Conceptual and Abstract work by Black artists is scant; no mention here of Jean Michel Basquiat or Bob Thompson, and only one brief reference to David Hammons. These omissions are peculiar, not just because Basquiat, Thompson, and Hammons are recognized throughout the art world—Black, white, and Otherwise—but because all three have ceaselessly engaged in recoding the semiotics of "Blackness," manipulating signs of ethnic derogation and deliverance alike into works of high-handed playfulness and elegance. Maybe that's why they're not in this book. Basquiat, Thompson, and Hammons have produced work as enigmatic and private as that of any European modernist, and as transparently emblematic of Black culture as any of the work in *Ancestral Legacy*. But their open and avowed embrace of both African and European models, their ambiguity and complexity, deny them a place in Wardlaw's effort to circumscribe and collapse all Black art into an ethnically pure African reclamation project.

—1990

251

•

Cinematic Sisterhood

t came from *Elle:* "Rage Comes of Age: A wave of films directed by black filmmakers chronicles the perils of manhood in the city." Gag me with a spoonful of testosterone. Can't even open a women's magazine these days without getting a dick-whipping in the process. Don't get me wrong. Spike Lee, the Hudlin Brothers, Keenen Ivory Wayans, Bill Duke, Mario Van Peebles, John Singleton, Matty Rich, Robert Townsend—I'm proud of all my brothers fighting the Black film fight. I just wish the next time one of these muhfukuhs turns up on *Donahue*, or *Oprah*, that they'd acknowledge their sista filmmakers out here without that information having to be flushed out by high colonic.

Let me be straight up: The intention of this article is to move perception of Black women filmmakers from margin to center stage.

Fuck who got a feature clocking dollars on the deuce or fortydoowop and who don't. We need to take stock of those Black filmmakers, male, female, and indifferent, who serve up visions of Black life beyond homeys slangin' and gangbangin'. I'm as down with the hiphop aesthetic making it to the big screen as any muhfukuhs around, but I know that's not the be-all and end-all of an oppositional and potentially liberating Black cinema. As much as we need stone-cold, crass commercialist, crossover-mentality mugs coming back with multimillion-dollar box offices to keep the studio dollars flowing, we also need to promote the development of a Black film culture—an appreciation for achievement that doesn't stop at directorial budgets or bank accounts.

Black film can be a political, spiritual, and historicizing power base for us as well as an aesthetic and economic one. Quiet as it's kept, if you want to find a group of Black filmmakers kicking that kind of science, you got to go to the sisters. Matter of fact, after interviewing sisters for this piece, I stepped back feeling like a lot of the young brothers out here on the Black film mission ain't about nothing but some self-serving, self-aggrandizing, macho-posturing-ass bullshit. Yo, what do a brother know? If we're talking about visionary narratives and subject matter, and filmmakers grounded in daily struggles against sexism, white supremacy, and professional marginalization, the sisters are the ones I hear taking no shorts and talking no sellout.

They're more about solidarity. There's not one woman I talked to who didn't take the opportunity to pump up three or four of her sister filmmakers. My sister of all-inclusive Libra-ninity, Julie Dash, let me know how upset she would be if there wasn't mention of Neema Barnett, who is making a transition now from episodic television, and will be shooting her first feature in New York this summer, or writer/director Demetria Royals, whose script *Weeping in the Playtime of Others* ("One of the best I've ever read," says Dash) Whoopi Goldberg and Joe Morton have committed to do.

Camille Billops isn't here because I'm planning a feature on her oeuvre of confessional exposés, *Older Women in Love; Suzanne, Suzanne;* and *Finding Christa.* We also need to send shout-outs to Harlem's Jessie Maples, Australia's Tracey Moffatt, Black British filmmakers Maureen Blackwood, Martina Attille, Ngozi Onwurah, and Karen Alexander, the whole next wave NYU posse blasé blasé, Denise Bird, Lisa Jones, Desiree Ortiz, Michelle Patton, Stephany Minor, and dream hampton, curator of the recent Cinema by the Sistas festival, experimental videographer Yvette Mattern and music video directors Darnell Martin and Millicent Shelton. Whew! Finally, any project of this nature would be revealed for its total bogus-ity if it did not acknowledge the life achievements of the late Kathleen Collins, especially her *Losing Ground.* And we're outta here like Aunt M'dea'.

253

Michelle Parkerson

Me and Michelle Parkerson go back a ways. Parkerson holds the dubious honor of being both the first Black woman filmmaker I ever met and the first Black lesbian as well. That initial meeting takes us back to 1977 and Washington, D.C., where she was born and raised, and where I was reared and used to run tame in the streets. Besides being a filmmaker and sexual suspect, Parkerson, a '53 Capricorn, is also a poet and fiction writer of severe wit, insight, and colloquial lyricism, and our paths often crossed on the stand-up Black poetry circuit. Her requiem for Dorothy Dandridge still resonates in my memory.

Among Black independent cinema's cognoscenti, Parkerson is known for three stirring documentaries on Black woman artists, *But Then She's Betty Carter*, *Sweet Honey in the Rock*, and *Storme: Lady of the Jewel Box*. Less well known is her short, *Sojourn*, a Temple University graduation project made with cinematographer Jimi Lyons, that won a Junior Academy Award. Presently Parkerson and producer Ada Gay Griffin of Third World Newsreel are gearing up to edit her new project, an epic documentary on Black lesbian writer and activist Audre Lorde. From the fundraising trailer I saw, the film encompasses not only Lorde's life, but the lives of folk Lorde has affected.

Parkerson's passion for film was inculcated by the first Black woman she ever loved—her mother. "My mother was the first person who turned me on to really scrutinizing film. She knew all the directors' names, knew the names and importance of the costume designers, actors, actresses. I learned a lot about the awesome power of film over the spectator from her and to associate names with what I was looking at in terms of craft. My mother made a big effort to point out Dorothy Dandridge to me. That made a big difference in my life, recognizing that this Black woman was doing something that hadn't been done, was a Black first. Watching the March on Washington and the killing of Lee Harvey Oswald over Cheerios one morning were two tele-events that left a lasting impression. The way media embosses imagery, i.e., history, on our minds was stamped on me at those two points."

Parkerson credits the '60s news show *Black Journal* with instilling the belief that she could become a filmmaker, not least because of producer/director Madeline Anderson (according to Parkerson's research, the first Black woman to work behind the camera since '30s evangelist Eloise Gist and Zora Neale Hurston). She remembers being especially impressed with the work of St. Claire Bourne's program on her father's church, the United Church of Christ, *Let the Church Say Amen*. Having spent umpteen years as a documentarian, Parkerson now finds herself compelled to deploy the powers of imagination present in her fiction and poetry.

"The documentaries have served as a way for me to put issues forward without it being my voice, allowing these Black women to speak for themselves. Now I have a need to put words in people's mouths. I turned toward narrative when I realized that I wanted *Storme* to make a more radical statement to a post-Stonewall audience about being gay. But what I wanted her to say was not Storme's language, nor the way she would express her experience as a pre-Stonewall pioneer."

I relate to Parkerson a critique of African-American women's cinema. Some question the way it exalts superheroic Black women. "I think there's some truth in that criticism. I think for so long we've been trying to combat images of us as underclass, as Other, as invisible, that we go for celebratory portrayals of people who have led epic lives, who have visibility because they are artists. I think I'm moving into narrative film because I want to illuminate some of these so-called ordinary lives. Sidewalk stories, to borrow Charles Lane's phrase, people you'd bump into on the street. The focus for me will continue to be African women. I don't think I'll ever run out of stories."

Jackie Shearer

Like Parkerson, Jackie Shearer is a professional documentarian readying herself to do the narrative film thing. You saw her work on *Eyes on the Prize*—the Dr. Martin Luther King and desegregation of schools in Boston episodes. She recently completed a

project for PBS's *The American Experience* on the 54th Regiment, the Black soldiers whose story was told in *Glory*, or so we thought. Shearer's segment reveals that the real men of the 54th were more educated and assured of their manhood than *Glory* portrayed them to be. A historian by training, Shearer came to media work "through the political door" in Boston in the '70s, where she was involved in housing and educational organizing. "I knew I didn't have the temperament for organizing, but I liked the idea of media as a political tool since it had been an effective tool for socialization against me. I wanted to master an enslaving technology for empowering uses."

Largely self-taught, she worked for the Boston ABC affiliate and did industrials with *Eyes on the Prize* executive producer Henry Hampton. The narrative feature project she's developing, *Addie and the Pink Carnations*, is the story of a Southern woman who goes North in 1936 and is taken in by an organization of domestic workers. Counter to cinematic stereotyping, domestics in this period were "autonomous, strong, kickass women who did not sacrifice their own mothering responsibilities to raise white women's children."

Does this Sagittarian believe Black women can be cinematic innovators?

"One of the things I'd like to do in *Addie* is break up the narrative with little documentary nuggets. It might be jarring to some people, but I like being jarred myself. I don't know whether to ascribe that to being Black and female and growing up in the projects with the TV going on all the time or to the fact that I'm such a self-taught film barbarian."

Ayoka Chenzira

If you've ever attended a Black film festival, you've seen Ayoka Chenzira's *Hair Piece: A Film for Nappyheaded People* (1984), a hilarious animated short about the hair question. Not one for idling, Chenzira has since completed another animated work, *Zajota and the Boogie Spirit,* and a video on sexual abuse, *Secret Sounds Screening: The Sexual Abuse of Children. Ya So Dey So (Here to There),* her full-length feature, is nearing completion. Ostensibly a coming of age story, it parallels the sexual awakening of a teen-ager and the sexual reawakening of her mother. Shot in luminous color by Ronald K. Gray, veteran cinematographer for Kathleen Collins, it's a film Chenzira hopes to have ready for distribution by August. Scorpion Chenzira, winner of the 1991 Sony Innovator's Award in Media, has no problems identifying herself as an artist with a capital A.

"In this society everyone is looked at in the context of who is successful. So in this case if it's Spike, you're not taken seriously until you've crossed that line. And people will have the nerve to come up to you and say things like, Oh, you're like a female Spike Lee.

"A lot of the Black men directors who are popular now I've known for years. Back when they were lobbying for Black film like I was, before they decided to go to Hollywood and said fuck it. I've seen articles written by men and women about the 'new Black cinema' and no one seems to ask, where are the women? Because it's so obviously missing you just tend to go, Hello, hello? Obviously, and I underline obviously, the women are missing from the arena and the men tend to act as if the women don't exist.

"I really don't intend to sound either overly romantic or cosmic or ethereal, but to me it's real simple: I'm a person here on the planet who's here working out some stuff. I come to film thinking of it as an art form. My work comes from a very private place. It doesn't come from marketing statistics. People who come to film to play the stock market can talk about it within that context."

Daresha Kyi

When Ada Gay Griffin, who knows more about what's happening with filmmaking women of color than anyone in the known universe, tells me I need to check out the work of Daresha Kyi, it's EF Hutton time, end of story. Kyi's dramatic short, *Land Where My*

257

•

Fathers Died, now in rough cut form, is a closely observed slice of Black cultural naturalism highlighted by the filmmaker's soulful and riveting performance as the protagonist (though she's nearly upstaged by Lee Dobson's crazed performance as her bone-freaky uncle). A dreadlocked New York professional woman and her nouveau-nationalist photographer boyfriend spend the last day of her return home (to "*Anywhere*, USA," says Kyi) visiting the father she hasn't seen in years. The reunion, a tragicomic farce, provokes an epiphanic moment between the lovers when it's revealed that they're both the wounded children of alcoholics. "Being the child of an alcoholic, I had a lot of reservations about doing this film because I didn't want to present a negative image of a Black man as an alcoholic in a vacuum. Every time I talked to someone and told them about it, every single person was the child of an alcoholic without exception. I'm talking Black, white, rich, poor, across race, class, sex, everything. I thought if it's this pervasive, then we need to confront it."

Kyi, "Capricorn with an Aries moon and Sagittarius rising, and my destiny number is 22," and native of Dayton, Ohio, received her training in NYU's undergraduate program. "I was at NYU at a good time. I got a lot of scholarship money to go there. The hardest part was watching all these rich white kids squander money to make bad films when I didn't have no money. They were renting cranes, shooting 50 rolls of film on one five-minute project. I learned how to cut corners, beg favors, and be nice to people. I learned the true value of friends in the business.

Currently Kyi is developing treatments for other shorts and a feature-length script about a "Black woman who escapes from slavery in 1835 and goes to Florida where Blacks and Seminoles are at war with the government."

Ellen Sumter

Ellen Sumter makes films about working-class women suffering from socioeconomic and existential inertia. Poignant long-take dry-longsos spilling over with the drudgery-filled days and claustrophobic nights of women on the edge of emotional oblivion. Her *Rags and Old Love* portrays the stillness so effectively that even jazz rhythms seem like acts of terrorism. The film ranks with Charles Burnett's *Killer of Sheep* as a depiction of how dead-end jobs ritually flog the soul. A native of Gadsben, South Carolina, Sumter, a Pisces, attended Howard University along with emergent auteurs Arthur Jafa and William Hudson. Presently she is fund-raising for her first feature, *Savannah*, about a Black woman whose yearning and complacency seduce and then sedate an unsuspecting jazz drummer captivated by her mystery.

"The people I want to make films about aren't movers or shakers. They're people who are too slow to move. I see myself in them. I feel like I'm a little bit behind everybody else. I feel like I'm just coming out of the '70s. I've never had the pulse of my generation. I am amazed at people who can do things about rap like Spike. I'd like to do a film about my mother, who was a bus driver in the '50s, or an adaptation of Paule Marshall's *Praisesong to the Widow*, which is very similar to my mother's story. I've also got a series of short scripts about psychic detectives who are really healers, people who appear in different guises to help people make it through troubled times."

259

•

Dawn Suggs

"You're going to talk to Dawn Suggs right? As soon as I saw her short, I got excited—I recognized she had a voice, which is the rarest thing of all in cinema. There's big-name Hollywood directors who don't have their own voice." This is my brother Arthur Jafa talking, prizewinning cinematographer on Julie Dash's *Daughters of the Dust*. Jafa's encouragement converged with my reevaluation of Suggs's *Chasing the Moon*. The film is a breakthrough among breakthroughs. The postpunk dress and manner of the restless protagonist, coupled with her sexual inscrutability, injects an East Village contemporaneity absent from other films. Unlike other films by Black women, where the protagonists function as alter egos, Suggs's has a Borgesian quality, evocative of filmmaker and protagonist dreaming of each other. Though she credits Camille Bil-lops's film *Suzanne, Suzanne* with inspiring her to become a filmmaker, film as medium connects up with her desire to heal other lesbians.

"I felt it would be cathartic to put feelings of alienation and desire-anxiety on film. It was a response to so many women I'd met who'd had devastating, traumatic experiences in their lives, a lot of times from sexual abuse, and were seeking to escape in every way imaginable—drugs, strange relationships. It's not a literal film, I just wanted to speak to that pain.

"We need to see more work about Black lesbians and their world. I'm editing a film about a lesbian couple where one woman wants to have a baby, doesn't want artificial insemination, but through having sex with an old male friend, so that's the conflict. Another script plays with this idea of lesbians as wild sexual freaks."

Does Suggs believe Black women invoke silence as a signifier in their work?

"Silence is one of our languages too. Silence can be used in a very empowering way. Through your marginality you find different types of tools. In time our silence can be used very effectively."

260

•

Zeinabu Irene Davis

Of all the women here, Zeinabu Davis's how-she-became-a-film-maker story is my favorite because it sounds so Hollywood.

"I wanted a break from Brown University, so I went to study in Kenya. The government shut the university down because of student participation in political action, so that was the end of my formal education in Kenya. By the time that happened, though, I had met the celebrated Kenyan writer Ngugi wa Thiong'o. He was putting on a play called *I Will Marry When I Want*.

"What made filmmaking crystallize for me was being at the bars and verandas of Nairobi and seeing all these European film and television crews doing *Mutual of Omaha*–type documentaries on Kenyan wildlife. I thought, This is kind of bogus, because there are 17 ethnic groups in Kenya. You hardly ever see anything on the people unless it's the Maasai. Ngugi said, Zeinabu, one day you should come back here and we should make a film about Kenya. That planted the seed."

The Aries did her training at UCLA, has completed three films and four short video projects to date, and hopes to finish a short, just-under-an-hour-length feature, *A Powerful Thang*, by the end of this year. Her *Cycles* is a popular rental for Davis's distributor, Women Make Movies, often paired with Daresha Kyi's *The Thinnest Line*. *Cycles* is a playful interrogation of a woman whose period is late. "My concerns are with women and issues that are specific to women like menstruation, pregnancy, menopause, intimacy in relationships, be they relationships with men or with women. People enduring abusive relationships just because they want a man. If you want to label me a feminist, that's fine, I don't care.

"Julie Dash and Michelle Parkerson were and are big influences on me. I look to them to see how to continue to develop Black women in film. We don't even know each other that well, but it's important for us to know that we're all out here, because people will make you crazy thinking you're the only one. Being able to chant everybody's name all the time keeps me sane."

—1991

Soapboxing for the City

Leadership Follies

*T*he Central Park rape and assault case is now being played out in two major theaters—that of the city's white-owned tabloid press and that thrown up by the black community's nationalist mouthpieces, our activist lawyers, advocacy journalists, and de facto televangelists. Lost in the purple haze of pitched battle between these polemical Janus masks are the real issues, which make it impossible to reduce this brutal eruption to a matter of either rape or race. What we're confronted with in large measure from both sides are transparent attempts to deny the virulence of racism and sexism in this social order.

When we come upon, for example, the front pages of last week's *Amsterdam News* and find a lead article disclosing the victim's identity, and space given to defense attorney Colin Moore's theories comparing routine police interrogation to Nazi atrocities, we're seeing knee-jerk nationalism at its most atrocious. When we read Jerry Nachman in the *Post* tacitly defending police racism on the grounds that "cops . . . cannot remember the last time one of their number was killed by a white man," we're seeing knee-jerk racism at its most Klannish.

When a woman as courageous and committed as *City Sun* editor Utrice Leid blazons the headline IT'S AN OUTRAGE! above a front page editorial that reads like a pathetic whine of sour grapes over Tawana Brawley, we witness how skewed political priorities can overcome the capacity for compassion. When Pete Hamill devotes an entire column to clearing the good name of wolves from guilt by wolfpack association, we know the only theater we're in now is that of the absurd. When I was told this same column had driven some of the city's leading black professionals to distraction at a meeting ostensibly called to discuss the school system with Chancellor Green, I was hysterical. Almost as hysterical as I'd been left by Alton Maddox's eruption into Holocaust-denial mode on WLIB, where he stomped more Brawley grapes, demanding proof that there had been a rape in the Central Park case. Does he want semen samples for his personal delectation?

The folly of our grandstanding lawyer-activists is that they refuse to realize their moment in the phosphor-dot sun is up. They lack the judgment to see that in many black homes they just come off like a pack of jackasses with law degrees. They are able slapstick performers whose constituency is as witless as they are. If these are watchdog race-men then I'm a foot-dragging Uncle Tom.

The extent to which this case of gang-rape is an expression of sexism run amok in the black community remains ignored by the black press. The degree to which malign neglect allows crime to be all but legalized in the black community remains a nonissue in the white press. I know from the responses of friends that racism has left some of them, men and women alike, so numb, even to the point of indifference, to an assaulted white woman that I sometimes feel as if their minds have been momentarily possessed by the perpetrators. They want to play Dostoevski, understand these deformed brothers' psyches. I was much less forgiving. Like my homeboy in Atlanta whose response to their remorseless confessions was "Castrate 'em," I had no stock of pity for them or their actions. Nor do I lose sleep worrying what this will make white people think of my people. A headline in the *Times* like HARLEM RESIDENTS FEAR BACKLASH FROM PARK RAPE has to be a joke. I mean, when in 400 years has the lash let up? Has the crack of the whip become so anesthetic that only the accusatory glare of massa's media shames us into recognition of our powerlessness and victimization? Black people need to stop acting as if the worst of us represent the rest of us. White supremacists have never needed a few bad eggs to justify dehumanizing people of color.

Rape is a universal crime. No one has to wander around bewildered that these youngbloods did this without being under the influence of crack, or that some were choirboys, went to good schools, had two parents in the home, and even a little spending change in the pocket. Boys from good homes commit rape all over this planet every day and there ain't no mystery why. Male aggression and violence against women are accepted practices in nearly every culture known to man.

What's worth isolating and studying in this case is: Where did these young black men learn to commit sexual violence as casually as Calley and company committed the My Lai massacre? By the same token, we need to dissect the disregard for black life that allows City Hall to pretend class and race don't matter when 30 new cops are assigned to Central Park and none to the East Harlem neighborhood these same sociopaths had been terrorizing for months with nary a peep from the police or the press.

Where do we go from here? If the question is squarely answered at City Hall and in the black community, we need a society that doesn't consider the lives of the disadvantaged as no more than cannon or crack-pipe fodder. If black people want institutional power then we're going to have to fight for it the hard way, through the corrupt system in place. Leadership cannot be handed by default to loudmouths with law degrees. It's time for those of us in positions of privilege, power, and authority to stop playing our cards so close to our chests. Start speaking from the heart and stop holding civil tongues out of gutless gratitude for honorary white status and fear of catching flak from the mau maus and mr. charlie. The time for piecemeal measures and mealymouthed apologias is over. Either we're about long-term organizational and political strategies that embrace the destinies of all of us regardless of pedigree, or we ain't about shit.

And as long as we use simplistic sociological cliches to excuse rape, bludgeoning, and attempted murder, we have no ethical mandate and surrender our claim to the moral high ground.

—1989

267

•

New York 8+, Feds 0

Your enemies have run into a brick wall
—*Chinese fortune cookie served to the New York 8+,*
Monday, August 5, 1985

At the beginning of the trial of the New York 8+, Judge Robert Carter declared, the only hope these nine radical defendants could have of beating the government's case would be to have a lot of luck, get the best lawyers in the world, and become beneficiaries of serious blunders on the part of the government. After their acquittals on August 5 of seven charges of conspiracy to commit prison breaks, armed robberies, and racketeering, 14 counts of carrying weapons in commission of federal crimes, and eight counts of possessing illegal weapons and explosives, Judge Carter told defense counsel he thought it was a good verdict, one that showed the government shouldn't try to overreach, then added he hoped the acquittals had taught the defendants a lesson about how it was still possible to get a fair trial under the American judicial system. Guess it's like they say: Everybody loves a winner. *Now* here comes the judge.

Because the New York 8+ were battling a 51-count conspiracy indictment nobody dared dream they'd win, let alone wind up mopping the floor with the opposing team. Albeit not without suffering a few scrapes in the process: Convictions were brought in on four illegal weapons charges, a mail fraud count, and four uses of false identification. Sentencing for these will take place on October 1. U.S. Attorney Rudolph Giuliani's office is pushing for maximum penalties for these heinous crimes against humanity, but there's a fair chance Judge Carter, reputedly a liberal sentencer, will take the government's major losses into consideration and won't throw the book at them.

Before the verdict, what defendants and defense counsel hoped
for at best was a hung jury. Or at least partial acquittals on the
more ludicrous schemes they'd been accused of by the government
and government informant Howard Bonds: namely, a penny-ante
plot to rob a Nathan's hot dog restaurant in Yonkers; a plan to
hijack a helicopter, hover over the Brooklyn House of Detention,
and, using bolt cutters, free Brink's convict Sekou Odinga; another
Odinga escape scheme that involved defendant Coltrane Chimurenga waltzing into Metropolitan Correctional Center with a 50-
foot rope and 7 pounds of dynamite strapped around him, blowing
out the wall of the attorney counsel room, scampering down a rope
into the alley behind Federal Court at One Police Plaza, and making
a clean getaway to Brooklyn on the BMT. At the very least folk
figured that nonsense wouldn't wash with the jury, given how as-
inine Bonds's *Mission: Impossible* scenarios were rendered by wise-
cracking attorney Bill Mogelescu.

It's now known that the jury stopped believing the government
not long after finding itself downwind from star snitch Bonds. But
then the man who said the New York 8+ were plotting to rob
Nathan's, blast Odinga out of MCC, and hijack a helicopter is the
same man government surveillance had observed making daily
visits to a known drug dealer, spending nights at Plato's Retreat,
and, according to his arrest report, probably staking out a God-
father's Pizza joint the night he was picked up on a gun charge in
Brooklyn back in March '84. Would you buy a used terrorist plot
from this man?

Apparently the prosecution figured coupling Bonds's tall tales
with circumstantial surveillance evidence and weapons seizures
would make the jury put 2 and 2 together and, as the saying goes,
come up with 5, if not 150 years. Seems they also figured that the
hodgepodge of guns, conspiracies, surveillance, and home recordings of inflammatory radical rhetoric would so traumatize the jurors
they wouldn't even bother to sift fact from fancy. What the prosecution didn't bank on was how offensive the jury would find the
government's bag of dirty tricks. (After the trial some jurors told
the 8+ they were expecting surveillance and phone taps of their
very own soon.)

For five days before the final verdict came in, the jury (four of whom were black, six white, and two Hispanic) had been dead-locked 10–2 in favor of the defendants. Signs that they had sided with the 8+ came when José Rios was acquitted of the single charge the government had stuck on him (complicity in the hot-dog stand stickup) when he'd refused to corroborate Bonds's stories. Another indication came when Chimurenga and Wareham were absolved of all weapons and explosives charges connected with an alleged Brooklyn "safehouse." Only after the jury met with the New York 8+ was the full extent of their sympathy and support for the accused known.

The degree to which the jury had taken the side of the defendants is perhaps best summed up by an anecdote I got from Chimurenga: One of the white jurors, a fiftyish woman, told him that on many occasions when he came in court and gave his comrades the black power salute, she wanted to respond in kind. Five of the jurors also turned up to celebrate at the New York 8+'s victory party a week later.

When defense counsel Michelle Jacobs mentioned to one juror that everybody was on pins and needles before the verdict, the juror wondered why Jacobs was worried, given how shaky the government's case was.

Judging from the derisive miscoverage the New York 8+'s re-sounding vindication received in the local tabloids (*New York Post*: 7 FREED IN BRINK'S CONSPIRACY) you'd think the New York 8+ had somehow beat the rap on the sly and not royally kicked the government's ass.

Understand that this is the case where the government tried to destroy the lives of nine black activists with everything at its dis-posal short of gunning them down in the street: the combined investigative powers of the FBI, Joint Terrorist Task Force, NYPD, and U.S. Attorney Rudolph Giuliani's office; 22 months of sur-veillance, including eavesdropping, video, and wiretap recordings; and an arrest involving 500 JTTF men armed with machine guns and bazookas. And if that ain't enough, throw in "preventive de-tention" under the new No-Bail Law signed into effect a week before their arrests, grand jury inquisitions that resulted in the incarceration of five of the defendants' friends and three of their spouses for periods ranging from three-and-a-half to eight months;

a 51-count indictment carrying maximum penalties of 150 years led off by a RICO (Racketeer-Influenced and Corrupt Organizations) charge; and last but hardly least, brother Bonds.

Yet, totaling up all those tactics doesn't begin to figure in the disruption and destruction done to the professional and family lives of the New York 8+ : the terrorizing of their children by the military overkill operation that brought their parents into custody, the loss of jobs and homes, combined with the harassment of family and friends nationwide that occurred in the course of the government's investigation. Nor does it expose the complicity of the major media with respect to practically allowing the government to conduct the trial of the New York 8+ in secret. (Who knows, even now some people may be hearing about it for the first time.) The fight of the New York 8+ to prove their innocence was uphill all the way. When you see how much bullshit that battle entailed wading through, it's not hard to understand why nobody expected them to end up at the top of the heap.

Review but a sampling of the testimony provided by agents of the Joint Terrorist Task Force and you get the feeling this case was headed towards frame-up from jumpstreet.

- Special Agent Robert Cordier, director of the JTTF, testified that Coltrane Chimurenga became a target for investigation when he was seen in the company of a fugitive in the Brink's case, Sheri Dalton. The problem with this supposition, as defense brought out in court, is that Chimurenga was seen with Dalton weeks before she'd even been issued an arrest warrant. If this can be called evidence of anything, it would have to be the JTTF's presumed powers of precognition.
- Detective Richard Bushrod saw Chimurenga writing in the vicinity of a Manufacturers Hanover Trust. Chimurenga was observed "planning a crime," according to Bushrod. Add telepathy to the psychic talents of the JTTF.
- Agent David Sanchez testified that Roger Wareham became targeted for investigation when Chimurenga was seen showing Wareham a map outside a restaurant. Anyone, in fact, seen with Chimurenga became subject to JTTF suspicion,

271

said Sanchez. Maybe Chimurenga was suspected of carrying the Black Plague.

- Among the acts the accused were charged with is rehearsing a robbery at Randall's Island. Yet when the agent who purportedly made that observation took the stand, he admitted the defendants had spotted him hiding in the bushes and that all he really observed was sprinting and karate exercises.

- Another charge in the indictment has Chimurenga and Viola Plummer allegedly observed standing outside the Brooklyn House of Detention pointing at the roof, purportedly in furtherance of the plan to spring Odinga with a helicopter. But the agent who took the stand to corroborate that gem of inductive reasoning said under cross-examination he at best saw the defendants pointing *towards* the prison from their car across five lanes of rush-hour traffic with one lane moving between himself and them.

With charges like these, you wonder why the prosecution even bothered bringing in agents who couldn't possibly corroborate them without risking perjury. Sound wacko? Ah, but it gets better.

In two instances, the prosecution was ordered to correct its transcripts of surveillance recordings. In one case, Judge Carter determined that the statement "We are materialists" had been transcribed by the prosecution as "We are terrorists." In another, the statement "That would be a put-down" had oddly been transcribed as "That would be a stickup." In a case where defendants were accused of using coded language it would appear the deciphering got to be equally arcane.

On June 27, *The New York Times* carried its first coverage of the trial. The front-page Metropolitan section headline read: A REHEARSAL FOR A "STICKUP": TAPE LINKED TO BRINK'S CASE. Never mind that this wasn't the Brink's case or that the *Times* had carried no coverage whatsoever of Bonds's testimony, the foundation of the government's case. What made the New York 8+ news fit enough to print was a transcript of a weapons-training session led by Chimurenga that was provided to the *Times* by prosecutor Kenneth Roth. The funny thing is that while that version of the transcript quotes Chimurenga saying "Freeze. This is an armed stickup," no such statement appeared in the version the government filed during the defendants' bail hearings. In his summation, prosecutor Roth would concede that though the "armed stickup" line was the government's contention, it couldn't clearly be made out on the tape. (More than likely, Roth made this admission because the jury could've asked to hear the tape again.)

No one can deny that the weapons and fraud convictions fly in the face of the notion that the New York 8 + are as pure as the driven snow, as the white folks say. On the other hand, you'd have to stretch those convictions a mite far to justify the government's conduct and charges in this case.

In his summation, defense lawyer Mogelescu compared the government's idea of justice in this case to the Queen of Hearts's in *Alice in Wonderland*. There, if you'll recall, the Queen held the belief that first came the sentence, then the trial. Were the New York 8 + sentenced first and then tried? Taking into consideration how the fertile imagination of Howard Bonds was used to get an indictment, you be the judge. Then answer why if they weren't terrorists was the government so hot on seeing them carted off to jail by hook or by crook for well into the 22nd century?

The simplest answer is that after two years of coming up with zip the government decided it would fiscally justify the matter by turning to the vague theory of conspiracy. (Estimates of how much the government spent on this big zero run into the millions. The defendants know from the bill the government tried to stick on their court-appointed lawyers' tab that reproducing cassette versions of the countless hours of surveillance recordings alone cost U.S. taxpayers $160,000.) If you can't buy the theory that the maximum-profit motive urged on the government's conspiracy to get the New York 8 +, they offer additional explanations as well. The 8 + believe they were targeted because they are principled black Marxist-Leninists who promote black people's right to bear arms and right to self-defense. Black revolutionaries, they believe, are considered by the U.S. government to be the most dangerous threat to its rule within these borders. They also sense that the government found them particularly threatening because their Ivy League educations and formidable intellects were put as much to the service of radicalism as to maintaining middle-class stability.

(Coltrane Chimurenga was finishing up an educational doctorate at Harvard prior to his arrest; Roger Wareham is a Harvard graduate with a Columbia law degree and was a practicing attorney before the busts; Omowale Clay went *pro se* and represented himself in a trial where the judge held the opinion that the defendants didn't have a prayer without being represented by the best lawyers in the world; I know from experience that Viola Plummer can make fundamental Marxist economic theory as easy to grasp as See Spot Run.)

Without trying to convince anybody whether the big to-do about being principled revolutionaries is just party line, I can say, after three months observing the 8+ in and out of the courtroom, that they are committed to propagation of their politics. Because the same people who were on trial for being radicals were the same folk who held weekly sessions on revolutionary theory at Harlem Fightback and spent their lunch hour marching in front of federal court with placards brandishing such messages as "B.L.A. ALL THE WAT," "FREE THE OHIO 7," and chanting, "FBI, you better start shaking because today's pig is tomorrow's bacon," and "Freedom or death." A couple of weeks before the verdict, Viola Plummer was enthusiastically mapping out plans for publishing the next issue of their newspaper *Arm the Masses* from behind bars, no matter if they were scattered in prisons from here to Lompoc. The 8+ would also idle away hours waiting for the verdict explicating stuff for the masses like the difference between modern finance monopoly capitalism and the beast in its primitive accumulative stages of development, or reading Engel's *Anti-Duhring* for their ongoing study group. Less dogmatically they'd swap prison stories. (Funniest I heard was also the saddest—had to do with a brother called Exit Stage Left who tried to get Muslim Chimurenga to sign his Vanessa Williams poster like all the other cats on the floor had. As it turns out, this blood also was given to banging his head into the wall to get solitary confinement.)

Given time off for a little R&R, the New York 8+ are basically just regular black folk like you and me (and okay y'all, maybe Amilcar Cabral too). At the victory party they demonstrated black radicals like to shake a tail feather too. And Chimurenga, I found out, not only digs 'Trane but Frankie Beverly and Maze as well and is a fanatic devotee of Rolling Rock beer. He remains so even after it was brought to his attention that the brand is a well-known Yuppie beverage. Even dialectical materialists, it seems, are subject to bouts of commodity-fetishism. Plummer, by the way, holds the contention that much JTTF surveillance of Chimurenga roving all over Manhattan only trailed him hunting down the cheapest places to cop his beloved brew. Dub this The Rolling Rock Defense.

I hold immeasurable admiration for the integrity, tenacity and courage of New York 8 + and for the eight brave grand jury resisters who went behind bars rather than aid the government in crushing their camaraderie and canceling their constitutional rights. If nothing else, this ordeal has shown the degree to which any of these 17 black people would sacrifice all personal considerations to uphold their common principles. No one can say the option of choosing otherwise wasn't there. Howard Bonds certainly took advantage of it—the "prisoner witness" protection program, open to all prospective agent provocateurs and snitches. José Rios opted for jail before the Judas bit, but he got a chance to look over the menu: new home, new identity, and the prison and sentencing judge of his choice.

Whether Bonds serves a day's time or not you can bet he ain't out looking for new jobs like his ex-comrades are, or rooming with friends and in-laws, or on public assistance, or struggling to bring a modicum of security and stability back into the lives of the children. Don't think I bring all this up to make a martyrdom case for the New York 8 +, because I figure any folk strong enough to resist being totally decimated by what Bonds unleashed upon them will probably survive the rat race. But no sense in sidestepping the aftermath here.

Though your initial response to this people's victory against government repression may be to perceive it as one small ray of hope for America's future, you may also be given to wonder what schemes are already being hatched to crush the next band of dissidents who fall into government disfavor. (Or even *this* band since Chimurenga reports he was tailed out of town by JTTF cars a week after the verdict, and grand jury resister Olive Armstrong tells of friends in Canada being visited by the FBI only a few weeks ago.)

In response to such flights of fancy the 8 + make a couple of predictions. First off—and no big surprise—the 8 + expect to be

275

•

government targets for the rest of their lives. Secondly, they predict the attempt will soon be made to do away with the jury system altogether in cases involving political dissent.

Attorney Mogelescu took a less alarmist view, emphatically pointing to the acquittals as a major affirmation of the American jury system. He also noted that no Irish Republican activists have been given jury trials in Britain for years.

With regard to what we can expect next from the JTTF, which the 8+ see as no more than a national secret police force, Clay put forward the cheery thought that there is no reason to think a government that trains, finances, and protects right-wing death squads from Johannesburg to El Salvador won't eventually move to crush dissent in this country, using the same fascistic tactics. The 8+ believe that what happened to them was but a dress rehearsal for the coming institutionalization of fascism in America, for the domination by the extreme right of every sector of society. In part they see that process beginning with the erosion of the constitution through the legal system.

Some people I know hold the notion that, given their politics, the New York 8+ were just asking to get vamped on by the feds. And will hold it even more so knowing how extensively the activists had researched both COINTELPRO and the government program that superseded it: Key Black Extremists (KBE), whose objective was revealed in court to be "neutralizing" black leadership. (An aside here: In reading his charge to the jury Judge Carter told them that though they'd heard a lot in the trial about government programs to target black activists, such programs would, if they existed, far exceed the scope of our current laws and constitution. Right on, judge, right on.)

Depending on how deeply you hold the belief that U.S. citizens have the right to dissent, you may not be willing to confuse the 8+'s politics with government's decision to launch an assault upon them. Should you figure those rights are de facto forfeit for loudmouth (or even undercover) black radicals in light of recent American history, I say in light of history and the present there's no such thing as a political safety zone for black people who engage in progressive politics. Check it out: Black activists in several Alabama counties were recently charged by the Justice Department with, get this, voter-registration fraud. (Some were acquitted a few weeks back; another trial ended in a hung jury last week.) Grand jury and police intimidation was used recently against members of the Harlem Reclamation Project, a housing rights group, for trying to exercise squatters rights. And not only don't black people get to decide when we've become "dangerous" in our dissent, we don't even decide when our right to life is perceived as a threat. Remember Michael Stewart, remember Eleanor Bumpurs, remember—hey, you, fill in the blanks.

With their families, homes, Harvard doctoral pursuits and city payroll jobs, the New York 8+ obviously weren't people who believed the revolution was right around the corner, or even folk who thought all reform measures were pointless until America's appointment with Red October rolled around. Look, for example, to the work of their Black Unemployed Youth Movement, which successfully boycotted neighborhood businesses in Flatbush to get 40 black teens jobs. If that's urban guerrilla warfare then so was the struggle for black voting rights of two decades ago.

The New York 8+ say the 1980 Klan/Nazi murders of Communist activists in Greensboro, North Carolina (an attack the FBI knew about in advance—thanks to its undercover agent in the Greensboro Klan—and did nothing to prevent), motivated them to begin armed self-defense and weapons training. Meaning that their gun purchases and defacements may not have been the result of some suicidal urge to rip off a Brink's truck or free the BLA all the way.

There needs to be another chapter written about the real *realpolitik* of the New York 8+. Now that they're free (though "not free, just *loose*" is how grand jury resister Milton Parrish would describe their condition after the acquittals), maybe they can write it. If you're so inclined, you can join them October 5 at 23rd and Madison for a rally being organized around building a broadbased coalition against government terrorism.

I'm told certain segments of the New York black activist community aren't as enamored of the New York 8+ as your reporter and the 60 or so other supporters who came to court daily during the final days of the trial. Bad blood over past political contradictions with the 8+ and so forth. Supposedly there's even some folk

277

whose differences with them go so deep they're sorry the 8+ didn't go to jail. Talk about sour grapes. Maybe that dirty laundry is best kept behind closed doors. Maybe not. In any event, having spent the summer listening to the New York 8+ run their line, I'm ready to bet *their* bottom dollars they'd be willing to square off with anybody, anytime, anywhere on radical strategy for the '80s, '90s, or the 21st century for that matter. After bearing the brunt of lightweights like the Joint Terrorist Task Force, I'm sure they'd welcome the challenge.

—1985

Now We Come by Thousands

278

My gut reaction to the lynching of Michael Griffith wasn't anger, shock, or empathy, but cynicism—cynicism born of the suspicion that the black community would prove too impotent to respond in the form of symbolic protest, let alone retaliation. I've grown so used to thinking of black people as inevitable victims that the fact of Griffith's murder registered more as an ideological abstraction— another act of white racist violence crying out for our collective uproar or avenging even—than as the killing of an individual black man. The ideologue in me didn't wonder, for instance, about the suffering of Griffith's family—the ideologue wondered how Griffith's death might serve the cause of neo-nationalist organizing in the '80s. If that sounds exploitative and unfeeling, well, I know of more hard-bitten souls now declaring without a trace of shock intent that black-on-black crime outrages them considerably more than this incident of white mob violence—and wishing blacks could get as mad over that as they have over Howard Beach. While I'm not so cavalier about prioritizing what needs remedy in the black community, I do wish that the mass furor Griffith's murder is generating could be directed toward institutional racism and our internal problems before this moment's catalyst exhausts itself.

To be black and conscious is not just, as James Baldwin once quipped, to be in a constant state of rage, but to rage constantly against those who would deny how America's past racism sets the stage for present injustices. The anger and pain that Griffith's lynching arouses is no more immediate than what I feel when I see illustrations of slave ship holds, or read about the black war heroes slaughtered in the Red Summer of 1919, or wish I could raise an army to keep black elders from being terrorized out of slumlord properties. Everywhere we turn, whether back through history or around the corner, we see black people being laid low and driven to their deaths. My heart goes out to Griffith's friends and family, but I was mad about the America that killed him long before he was beaten and chased into the path of a car whose driver now claims he thought the body that collided with his windshield was an "animal" or a "tire."

As black church leadership comes front and center to organize mass demonstrations and race relationship conferences (and thanks to the right Reverend Al Sharpton, even pizzeria munch-ins), the black community's response to the violence done Griffith becomes a fait accompli. Each morning's newspapers tack a new and more surreal sideshow onto the case. A young white student is attacked by black teens chanting "Howard Beach, Howard Beach" like a Schoolly D refrain. The fireman allegedly beaten by Griffith's alleged attackers for pissing on a truck turns out to have been in a crack bust a month ago. Attack victim Timothy Grimes is arrested for stabbing the woman he lived with in the back. Ernestine Washington, the black ex-girlfriend of the reputedly South African suspect, Jon J. Lester, joins other black friends of those initially arrested in defending them from charges of racism—apparently more stunned by the slander on their white chums than by the

279
•

attack on Griffith, who could have been any one of them. (On evidence of Ms. Washington's sentimental feelings toward him, it appears Lester must have made interracial romance an exception to his apartheid philosophy—certainly no new kink in American race relations.)

And so we digress: The Griffith lynching turns for some into a race&sex&crime melodrama, soon surely to be a TV movie. Why don't we spare Swifty Lazar some work? Let's option Malcolm-Jamal Warner to play Griffith, cast Michael J. Fox as Lester and Kim Fields as Ernestine Washington; Ed This-is-the-most-horren-dous-incident-in-the-history-of-my-administration-like-Eleanor-Bumpurs-never-happened Koch and Reverend Al Take-a-bite-out-of-crime Sharpton can appear as themselves.

The inevitable result of Howard Beach's inevitable subjection to press scrutiny has been the burying of the real issue—racism American style—down among those skeletons always skulking around waiting for newshounds whenever a story this juicy breaks. But conveniently enough, Howard Beach provides us ideologues license to adduce our own context. We get to point up racist assaults like those *Newsday* reported are occurring with increasing regu-larity not in "insular," "isolated," "tight-knit, white-ethnic work-ing-class communities," but on the campuses of Smith, U. Mass., and MIT. Griffith's lynching has made racism American style a public issue again, and if we're smart we won't let it die before we form a coherent and collectivist black political praxis for the '80s and '90s. I consider it a tragedy of another kind that black community response to the Howard Beach lynching played like a mystery in my head even overnight. That we were all left in the dark on that one until three or four thousand brothers and sisters made Saturday's demonstration is evidence of how little the black community knows of its political vision and strength in these times. By dint of crisis-management thinking, black folks in New York have now renewed a sense of kinship in struggle. Would that those of us fired up about Howard Beach could maintain that unity and march on Harlem, Brownsville, the Bronx, and City Hall as the times come to demand us to.

If Michael Griffith's death induces the black people of New York

280
•

City to maintain that sense of kinship, it could mean more than just extra publicity for the protest-professionals: It could mean we'll never again have to wonder if anything is going to be shaking when the next Howard Beach goes down.

—1987

Love and the Enemy

he question: Black identity. The problem: Who names it, claims it, and decides who profanes it. Here at the crossroads, whose Black Consciousness movement is it anyway? Like the man said, Van Glorius's. In other words, it's every man for himself on that one, G. When I was younger and very much the aesthetician, I believed that Black cultural difference was gonna set us free—that our salvation and liberation would come in realizing how great Black art set us apart from the illin' white boy and his creations. If we could make Black political parties function like Parliament-Funkadelic, we'd be kicking much ass. Having witnessed participatory democracy at work in our Black Power renascence of the past five years, that delusion has gone the way of P-Funk's fabled Mothership. (Park it in the dustbin of history, boys, and don't stop for fading spotlights.) The resurgence of Gotham's Black Power movement has been both a welcome and a woeful affair. Welcome because of the bridge it has formed between today's young rebels and the long-toothed tigers of yon; woeful because fatuous male posturing, demagoguery, and generational envy have also made a sorry comeback.

281
•

Spike Lee and Amiri Baraka at each other's throats over who owns the legacy of Malcolm X is one more pathetic episode in our movement farce. For the record, I think Baraka has about as much business telling Spike how to make a politically correct movie about Malcolm X as Spike would trying to instruct Baraka on verse structure. I'll be stunned if Spike overcomes his immaturity as a storyteller and makes a film with anything approaching the complexity of Malcolm's world and worldview, but c'est la vie. Ain't nothing but a movie y'all, and after those two hours in the dark are over we'll all still have to get up the next morning and deal with being Black men and women in America. Which at the end of the day is about what? Learning to love and struggle with one another, end of story.

Three weeks ago, at the funeral services for a flame of a life named E. Tamu Ellington Bess, I realized that the meaning of being Black is summed up in who comes to bury you, who gathers together in your name after you've gone, what they have to say about how you loved, and how you were loved in return. Offering such testimony at Tamu's services was a cross section of our community's Afristocracy, politicos, artists, activists, bereaved friends, and family. People presented songs, dances, poems, and soliloquies in her honor. By the end, without knowing any more than the sketchy details of Tamu's life, you knew she'd made everyone she'd touched more aware of the sacrifice, service, and devotion Black Consciousness demands.

282
•

Though I didn't know her that well, Tamu was revealed to me as one of those exceptional Black folk who are at home wherever African people are, regardless of geography, class, custom cuisine, or creature comforts. If there's any legacy of '60s Black Nationalism I find ennobling and empowering, it's that movement's Pan-Afrikanist embrace of Black folk everywhere as *brother* and *sister*. Recognizing a loss to our community like Tamu Bess's, you realize that any liberation or empowerment strategy that doesn't grow out of love, in its most constructive, critical, and compassionate senses, is useless.

What makes the oratory of Malcolm endure as a source of enlightenment isn't just his clarity about how white supremacy works, but also his desire to see us love our African selves more than we love the world of the oppressor. We still listen to Malcolm because we hear the voice of a lover, sometimes asking what Bob Marley asked—*could we be loved*—other times asking us why do we love white America, or at least its status symbols, more than we love ourselves. I find the essence of Malcolm's critical ardor for Black people lacking in most of our grandstanding spokespersons of the present. The Black love you find manifested today is mostly a love for Black Male Posturing. Now, BMP is truly a marvelous thing. Yet do I marvel at it every day. Where would hiphop or jazz be without it? Basketball is defined by it, and the streets of downtown New York would be looking mighty shabby for its absence. But the impotence of current Black nationalist politics comes from its being phallocentric to the core, so caught up in stroking its own hard-on that it makes no space for the balance offered by feminine wisdom. We have never in our history had a movement that wasn't well populated with female leadership. These days, part of the reason issues of daily violence and oppression never get discussed is because the people on the frontlines, women and the children in their care, have no voice where legal-eagle activists prevail. So even when the victimization of a Black woman is at the heart of our rallying, it becomes reduced to what dream hampton refers to as a "nut-grabbing contest."

The tragedy of this isn't the gesture itself, but how misguided the movement is in terms of targets and objectives. When I look up to see hundreds rally behind Professor Leonard Jeffries when he's predictably attacked for Jew-baiting, I got to wonder what's the goal beyond reactive rage. (And on the "Jew-baiting" charge, let's be real. When you put bait on your line, expect fish to bite, especially if the bait is live and in living color. Jews may be disingenuous about holding economic, cultural, and political power and privilege and abusing it, but some Black folks can be just as disingenuous about admitting they despise Jews more than they despise the average cracker who isn't a cop.)

Large numbers of Black folk in this town get more upset over being disrespected than they do over being disempowered. Why look for respect from a power structure so greedy it would destroy the planet on which its grandchildren will have to live? I expect neither justice nor respect from white power and certainly not love.

283

What I expect from Black folks is for us to organize in such a way that we make the white power structure understand that it would be in its own best interest not to fuck with us. But no. We're more concerned with scoring intellectual brownie points than we are with that kind of unifying. (Or, for that matter, with raising the level of reading and writing skills of Black kids in this city or even with improving the rude physical plant of their learning environment. Far as I know, there are currently no plans afoot for mass, fire-breathing demonstrations to protest toilet-bowl classrooms.)

Favoring issues of disrespect over strategies of empowerment will keep us chasing after love from a muhfuh that don't love nobody. Such folly leaves us with a politics of reactive rage and race-baiting that my friend Melvin Gibbs astutely defines as "just another form of Tomming and minstrelsy because the audience is always the white man." My suggestion is we give up the white man as the problem per se and start thinking of him as a natural disaster, a catastrophe we may be unable to prevent but whose destructive effects can be overcome and reversed. I also think we need to let go of the idea that some real natural disaster like the dissolving of the ozone layer is going to wipe the white plague off the face of the earth. You know by the time that day comes, these muhfuhs will be living in bubble cities and have your ass in the cold paying for air sandwiches faster than you can say Jackie Robinson. Later for Black to the futurism. Your mind may be in Khmet, bro, but yo . . .

When reactive rage is the dominant form of our politics, when it takes police or mob violence to galvanize us into reaction, it means that there is an acceptable level of suffering and misery. When quality of life issues are not given the same attention as our antilynching activities, it means we have a low level of life expectations. It also means, as Dr. Frances Welsing has pointed out, that there is a general state of depression operative in the Black community that provokes other problems, such as drug abuse. The warriors we need to step forward now aren't the confrontational kind, but healers. Folk who know how to reach into where we really hurt, to the wounds we can't see and that nobody likes to talk about. Outside of Joan Morgan, no one has spoken on the traumatic impact John Singleton's *Boyz N the Hood* had on many young Black ghetto escapees for whom it screened more as a nightmarish flash-back than as escapist entertainment. If Black male leadership doesn't move in the direction of recognizing the pain and trauma beneath the rage, as the work of Toni Morrison, Ntozake Shange, Alice Walker, bell hooks, and other women writers have done, if we don't exercise our capacity to love and heal each other by digging deep into our mutual woundedness, then what we're struggling for is merely the end of white supremacy—and not the salvaging of its victims.

—1991